Management and Leadership Development

'This is the first really thought-provoking book that I have read on management development. It will stretch those who read it and challenge them to adopt a broader perspective on the topic than current practitioners are inclined to do, one that acknowledges the values and beliefs – individual, organizational, and societal – that management development implicitly embraces. The multi-discourse approach is highly illuminating, and, of itself, developmental.

'This is a book primarily addressed to students, but in this field, we are all students. Hopefully, the book will contribute to a more reflective management development practice. It merits a wide readership both among practising managers as well as among those responsible for developing them.'

Max Boisot, ESADE

'Mabey and Finch-Lees inject a breath of fresh air into the management development field by expanding upon its heretofore functionalist base sustaining managerial prerogative and organizational performativity. They offer an informative critique of mainstream views, featuring alternative discourses to examine such hard questions as why management development hasn't quite delivered on management's considerable investment in it. As a veritable tour de force in its absorbing integration and review of a large tract of literature, the book informs both management scholars and practitioners what might be expected from management development's intended but also unanticipated outcomes.'

Joe Raelin, Northeastern University

'In a well-written, accessible and yet sophisticated text, Mabey and Finch-Lees show themselves to be as familiar with the latest in management development practice as they are with the sometimes arcane theoretical literature that surrounds it. Its great strength is to recognize the plurality of discourses – some overlapping and complementary, others distinct and oppositional – about the subject. This book can be recommended as a unique resource for students and scholars of management development.'

Chris Grey, University of Warwick

'This book represents a significant step forward in the theory of management and leadership development. It offers an international perspective in this era of globalization and a new and questioning perspective on the common belief that leadership is something completely different to, and more important than, management.

'This book will be of great help to the serious theorist and researcher of management and leadership development. It is an invaluable point of reference for a broad range of theory and research in this area, which it summarizes with admirable brevity and clarity.'

John G. Burgoyne, Lancaster University Management School and Henley Management College

Management and Leadership Development

Christopher Mabey and
Tim Finch-Lees

SAGE Publications
Los Angeles • London • New Delhi • Singapore

SAGE Publications Ltd
1 Oliver's Yard
55 City Road
London EC1Y 1SP

SAGE Publications Inc.
2455 Teller Road
Thousand Oaks, California 91320

SAGE Publications India Pvt Ltd
B 1/I 1 Mohan Cooperative Industrial Area
Mathura Road
New Delhi 110 044

SAGE Publications Asia-Pacific Pte Ltd
33 Pekin Street #02-01
Far East Square
Singapore 048763

Library of Congress Control Number: 2007927621

British Library Cataloguing in Publication data

A catalogue record for this book is available from the British Library

ISBN 978-1-4129-2901-1
ISBN 978-1-4129-2902-8 (pbk)

Typeset by C&M Digitals (P) Ltd, Chennai, India
Printed in Great Britain by The Cromwell Press Ltd, Trowbridge, Wiltshire
Printed on paper from sustainable resources

Contents

Acknowledgements

Although authored by the two of us – and we take responsibility for the final outcome – we are indebted to a number of colleagues who took the time to read and comment on earlier versions, notably Scott Taylor, Tess Finch-Lees, Jo Duberley, Roger Bell and Vanda Morgan. The genesis of this book has also been informed by many conversations and discussions with academic partners of the European Management Development network (a research team of scholars in nine countries), with associates and staff at ASK Europe plc (with whom the first author has gained significant experience over the years as leadership development consultant) and with Diageo plc (where the second author held a number of director-level roles over a 14-year period). We are also grateful to the SAGE team for their encouragement during this project, particularly Kiren Shoman who has guided wisely from the outset and Rachel Burrows who has helped us see it through to completion.

Part I

Understanding the significance of management development

Despite the intense interest in the development of managers and leaders and a good deal of research over recent decades, the field remains ripe for enquiry with many vexing questions still unresolved. How can managerial capability be benchmarked and to what extent can productivity at a national or organizational level be linked to the calibre of managers and leaders? Cultivating leadership talent is expensive and time-consuming for employers; the opportunity costs can also be high, design lead-times can be lengthy and the time-lagged effects difficult to determine. Given this, how confident are we that such resource allocation is worthwhile? Individual investment can be considerable too; participants frequently make personal sacrifices to update their expertise and develop their professional capability and training activities often involve high stretch and risk. Do the rewards outweigh the costs? Management development programmes are often used as a device to reduce discriminatory attitudes and improve diversity in organizations; yet it is not unusual to find such development actually exacerbating inequality in the workplace.

All this begins to suggest that at least some of the significance attached to management and leadership development may lie elsewhere than in its performance impact or personal utility. Perhaps, for example, the potency of such activities is more to do with the way precious resources are being allocated, the way corporate messages are being disseminated, the way ideologies and ethical stances are receiving reinforcement or being undermined, the way managerial identities are being forged and so on. In the first chapter we attempt to create some reflexive space in order to explore these differing conceptions of management development. We argue that *discourse* is peculiarly suited for this kind of analysis, and the rest of the book dips into a range of discourses to illuminate some of the fascinating facets of management and leadership development interventions. Each reveals something different, surprising and occasionally disturbing about such programmes and events. Furthermore some of the discourses sit very uncomfortably alongside each other; it is perhaps for this reason that they are rarely compared or considered in the same piece of writing. Yet for us, the real challenge and excitement in writing this book has been to wrestle with the contradictions and conundrums that arise when trying, both systematically and faithfully, to inhabit these contrasting views of the world. Before we embark on this, given that the title of the book refers to the development of both managers and leaders, we need to explore what is implied by these labels. This we address in chapter two, as well as sketching in the shifting borders between management development and its neighbouring fields of management education, management training and management learning.

1

Management development: paradox, reflexivity and discourse

The university stands for things that are forgotten in the heat of battle, for values that get pushed aside in the rough and tumble of everyday living, for the goals we ought to be thinking about and never do, for the facts we don't like to face, and the questions we lack the courage to ask. (Gardner, 1968: 90)

After reading this chapter you will be able to:

- **Explain a number of reasons why the study of management development is important**
- **Describe the related notions of reflexivity and discourse in relation to the study of management development**
- **Use these twin notions to critically appraise the reasons for studying management development**
- **Explain the virtue of discourses for analysing and understanding management development, compared to that of frames or paradigms**
- **Distinguish the key features of four Grand Discourses of management development**
- **Understand the structure and rationale for the book**

Introduction

This first chapter may not be quite what you expect. We firmly believe that a fresh analysis of the concept and practice of management development is overdue and we give some reasons as to why this is the case. However, in doing so it becomes apparent that there is more to management development than initially meets the eye. Certainly it is a potent and high-profile human resource (HR) activity, involving some of the organization's key players and attracting high investment both in terms of corporate budgets and expectations. For this reason alone, management development deserves sustained scrutiny. But as a 'project', management development also attracts a wide range of reaction from those touched by its programmes, activities and associated techniques and trappings. And such experiential accounts often reveal much that is unanticipated, paradoxical and contentious about development interventions, well intentioned or otherwise. It is also evident that, far from being a value-neutral instrument for upgrading skills or changing attitudes, few if any management development activities are devoid of moral assumptions and ethical consequences. Taking this a step further, it is not difficult to see how such activities can be used as a tool to emancipate and release talent on the one hand, but also as a means to control and suppress difference on the other. If we acknowledge the possibility that these different 'readings' of management development exist and matter, then we also require a means of analysis that allows these contrasting interpretations to be explored. It is for this reason that in this chapter we propose a multi-discourse approach. The advantage of this approach is that it allows us, in the spirit of the Gardner quote at the start of the chapter, to examine management development in all its intriguing facets. Among the questions which we seek to answer in this book are:

- Why do some management development activities lead to the opposite of what was intended (e.g. conformity rather than creativity, discrimination rather than diversity, scepticism rather than inspiration, individualism rather than team-working)?
- Why is management development often obsessed with 'getting it right' as against learning from getting it wrong? Who defines what is 'right' and what is 'wrong' in the first place, on what basis and with what motives?
- What does the language associated with management development achieve and what does it frequently omit, obscure, conceal and distort?
- Why is management development typically preoccupied with programmes and events rather than the developmental space between them?
- Why do efforts to improve workplace performance often remove the manager from his/her everyday context?
- Why does so much management development stress the importance of collective collaboration, yet employ methods that focus uniquely on the individual?
- Despite the presence of overt or stated objectives, why does management development sometimes feel like a game with unwritten rules?
- Why is there so little in the way of serious attempts to evaluate management development?
- Why does there continue to be so much investment in management development when its promise remains so often unfulfilled?
- When the dust has settled who are the real winners/losers from a given management development intervention?

We assume that in reading this book you have some interest in such issues. This may be as a researcher seeking to identify the value and significance of management development activities; you may be an HR specialist desiring to improve and/or assess the impact of a new development programme; you may run your own organization and be weighing up the value of developing your managers; or you may simply be curious about the development process as a participant. Whatever your particular stance, our aim is to deepen your understanding by helping you become more reflexive about the intentions, practices and consequences of management development activities.

Why is the study of management development important?

There are a number of compelling reasons to engage in the study of management development and we set out a few here in no particular order of importance. Perhaps the two most obvious reasons are economic and financial.

Economic

From the macro-economic perspective there has been a long-standing belief that national productivity can be attributed to three types of investment: in firm-specific production, in distribution and in managerial capabilities. The last is widely recognized as the most important (Chandler and Hikino, 1997; Cassis, 1997; Kay, 2003). Although the logic and plausibility of this skills–performance link is open to question (e.g. Grugulis and Stoyanova, 2006), this does little to diminish the concern of governments, both national and international, about the calibre of managers. This is often accompanied by the notion that lessons can be learnt from competitor countries. So in Europe for instance, the globalization of business and the emergence of a new knowledge-based economy are seen to be challenging the adaptability of European education and training systems (European Commission, 2000). And the EU's poor productivity relative to the USA and other industrialized countries has been linked, in particular, to the inferior quality of management in small and medium-sized enterprises (SMEs), especially in the use of information and communication technologies (O'Mahoney and Van Ark, 2004). This is also reflected in the developing economies of Europe, where in some cases the needs are more fundamental (see Box 1.1).

Box 1.1   Developing managers in Central Europe

In 1998 and 2000 a cross-country analysis of management training was conducted in nine Central and Eastern European (CEE) countries, including several preparing to join the EU (Gudic, 2001). Based on interviews in over 1,000 companies, the following findings were highlighted:

- The existence of a passive, even negative, attitude towards change, culturally embedded from a long experience of living in a static environment – this is limiting the managerial capabilities desperately needed to conceive, develop and implement appropriate strategic responses.
- The HR function is primarily focused on staffing activities while neglecting those dealing with human resources development (HRD) and management development.
- According to general managers, the greatest capabilities are concentrated at the highest levels of management. This reflects an attitude that the hierarchy remains untouchable or that managers are assessed according to their experience rather than against criteria of innovative behaviour, social and cultural competence, etc.
- Managers have difficulty articulating their training needs and tend to follow what's on offer from training providers, who market their current product/service portfolio rather than investigate what their customers' needs really are.

Financial

From the financial perspective at firm-level (our second reason), management development is often expected to lead to bottom-line gains. Such expectations have led to management development generating an industry of its own throughout the world. Government departments, professional institutes, training agencies, consultancies, business schools, corporate universities are just some of the groups who stand to gain from the continued and increasing preoccupation with creating a new generation of business leaders and managers. The global investment in management development activity, estimated to be $37 billion some years ago (Boyatzis et al., 1996), has increased markedly since then. In developed economies like the UK, some 20 million days per year are spent on programmed management training, a figure that could well be doubled if less formal development is taken into consideration (Burgoyne et al., 2004). This is quite apart from the indirect aspects of investment such as time spent on design and delivery, opportunity costs, the setting up of training systems and evaluation activities. In France, there is a legal requirement for employers to allocate 1.5 per cent of total annual payroll to vocational training, although it is the employer who decides how, and on whom, this is spent. Turning to emerging economies, there is a rapid game of 'catch-up' taking place, as governments and enterprises across all sectors seek to address their management and leadership deficiencies (e.g. Osman-Gani and Tan, 2000; Wang and Wang, 2006). In Central Europe the investment in training managers for individual companies ranges from several thousand US dollars up to $135,000 in Romania and up to $625,000 in Slovenia (Gudic, 2001). Naturally, given the number of days devoted to manager training and the amount of investment in these activities, there is keen interest in knowing whether these are resources well spent. Training days and development budgets are only input measures. There is consistent clamour for some measure of the outcomes, but such evidence about the quality and benefits arising from management development is difficult to come by.

All this prompts us to pose a perplexing paradox central to the book: would so much management development take place in the absence of the kind of economic and financial imperatives set out above? Intuitively, we may answer in the negative. But the picture becomes less clear when we consider that there are actually very few studies that unequivocally support the economic and financial case for management development. This raises a number of questions as to what other interests or purposes are being served by, and/or what other levels of meaning are invested in, this activity, leading us in turn towards a number of alternative, non-financial reasons for studying it.

Diverse meanings

Accordingly, a third reason for the study of management development relates to the array of meanings the activity can take on. Each of the various players involved in management development is likely to ascribe a different rationale to such activities, depending on their respective roles (Lees, 1992). For example, the ultimate sponsors of a management development initiative (e.g. senior executives) may well make sense of it at least partially in terms of the company image they wish to project. Participants in the programme may read other meanings into it. For example, they may see their selection for the programme as a symbol of their value to the organization, a reward for a job well done or conversely a remedial form of punishment. By the same token, non-participants may share yet other understandings of the programme, perhaps seeing it as a means to exclude them from fast-track career development. Meanwhile, HRD specialists may regard the design of management development as a means to boost their flagging corporate influence and professional status among peers. Because management development is invariably a high-profile activity, encumbered with high expectations by different parties and conducted close to the power nexus of the organization, it offers a superb opportunity to observe at close quarters the alternative accounts and political machinations of those involved.

Moral

A fourth reason for the study of management development relates to an examination of its moral or ethical currency. Training and development processes can be demanding. In terms of extra-mural effort and personal time, much is asked of the participant. In some cases this discretionary effort can extend to their line manager, their colleagues and even their family and non-work relationships. Furthermore, the emotional and psychological demands of certain development activities can place managers in a position of vulnerability (see Box 1.2).

Box 1.2   Challenging the ethics of 'self-revelatory' management development

Management development often transcends a rationalist concern with skills training, drawing on emotional experience in an attempt to remould the attitudes, character and even the personalities of practising managers. By challenging the individual as a person as well as a manager, Ackers and Preston (1997) claim that certain development initiatives have entered an existential terrain that was previously the province of the religious conversion process. Since career progression is typically linked to the observed adherence to values, beliefs and behaviours typically communicated via management development, participation in such programmes often signals vulnerability not power. The further such programmes penetrate into the manager's private psychological or emotional space, the more acute resulting anxieties may become. As such, Ackers and Preston believe that there are good grounds for questioning both the ethics and efficacy of programmes that cross the border between skills enhancement and psycho-therapeutic character (re)formation.

(Continued)

(Continued)

The authors illustrate this with reference to a management development programme at a UK footwear retailer. The programme required each participant to reveal in front of others their personal history (from childhood onwards) in a bid to tease out self-perceptions of strengths and weaknesses. This formed the basis for much subsequent group discussion and the elaboration of personal developmental action plans. Such plans were intended to deal with the 'whole person' rather than specific work-related issues. Almost all managers seemed enthusiastic about the process, reporting enhanced self-awareness and understanding. A few, however, questioned the intensity of the programme and the self-disclosure it required, speaking of the fears and anxieties it provoked. One manager professed to feeling almost driven to tears at times. The authors conclude by suggesting that there is something disturbing and inauthentic about this type of programme, with its attempt to provoke a search for deep personal meaning within the walls of a modern business organization.

Such accounts raise a number of questions: In what kinds of activities are managers being asked to participate under the guise of development? How are such activities being 'sold' to managers? Using what kind of language? Who gets either included or excluded and on what grounds? And notwithstanding the stated objectives of the programme, whose or what interests are ultimately being served by it? Most HR practices incorporate an ethical dimension, but in many ways it is management development that brings such issues into sharpest relief.

Identity-creation

A fifth and somewhat related reason for considering the study of management development to be important is that the activity plays a significant part in defining what it is to actually be a manager. Here we are not talking just in terms of the formal transfer of knowledge and skills that takes place during development programmes. We are also referring to the informal processes, including those of socialization that surround the activity. Such processes might be considered as being beside the point when it comes to management development. However, as we shall see repeatedly throughout this book, the label 'manager' is by no means self-evident. When does an individual start to be, or cease to be, a manager? What differentiates a manager from a leader? What does the ascription 'manager' imply? And how are the answers to such questions communicated, sustained and/or contested? Management development as a project is central to such concerns (see Box 1.3).

> ## Box 1.3   The gendered construction of managerial identity
>
> A study was made of both formal and informal socialization processes among a group of graduate trainees in a Swedish corporation (Eriksson-Zetterquist, 2002). The author's particular focus was the ways in which such processes contributed to the gendered constructions of managerial identity. She distinguished the messages being sent out by the company via management training as to whether they were overt or covert on the one hand and whether they contested or confirmed stereotypical portrayals of gender on the other hand. She found that, despite the company sending out overt messages that it valued women and wanted more of them among its more senior ranks, the upper echelons of management remained stubbornly male. She put this down to the dogged persistence of a more covert or implicit image of the manager as stereotypically masculine. 'Real managers' in this company remained people who were able to rely on a dutiful spouse in the home who could take care of domestic responsibilities. Those aspiring to be managers who did not fit the masculine/heterosexual model were subtly constructed as deviant, not real managers at all. Such findings were echoed in a study of graduate trainees in a UK audit firm, wherein one respondent cited the importance to managerial success of having a 'well packaged wife' (Grey, 1994).

These are processes where language and the use of metaphor play a key role in shaping our view of the organizational world and also of our own managerial selves. This then underlines why the analysis of management development is so topical and compelling. It provides a window on to the identity formation of managers themselves.

A manifesto for the study of management development

So if these are some indications as to why much is yet to be learnt about management development, what is the current knowledge in the field and which are the most promising lines of further enquiry?

Existing research: the 'state of play'

The study of management development has indeed produced a rich seam of research over recent years. Leaving aside a good deal of writing which is under-theorized and conceptually lacking, what might be termed naïve empiricism (Johnson and Duberley, 2000), authors have tended to invoke a wide range of theories in their studies (economic, sociological, psychological, institutional, to name just a few) and an array of methodologies (positivist, ethnographic, interpretivist, among others). Perhaps the majority of research, however, seeks to explain management development in instrumental terms and is concerned with representing the benefits in the language of accounting and economics professionals (e.g. Swanson, 2001). Much of this goes unquestioned, but some deem this to be an unhealthy preoccupation with performance, because it tends to subjugate developmental activities to an over-simplified means–end calculation (Kamoche, 1994). It is also criticized for underestimating the processual, unfolding nature of management development decision-making (Martocchio and Baldwin, 1997).

Another school of thought draws upon grand narratives to point out the socially divisive nature of management practice, noting that unequal power relations are frequently reinforced rather than remedied by training interventions (Reed and Anthony, 1992). It could be argued that such a critique rules out the possibility that carefully constructed management development has the potential to empower individuals (Bowen and Lawler, 1995) and lead to productive outcomes for the employer organization (Willmott, 1997). Indeed, some go so far as to claim that this critical approach can result in replacing one type of absolutism, that of performativity, with another, namely the elevation of partisan rights (Fournier and Grey, 2000). A further strand of theory explores the conditions which facilitate individual learning and development. This approach has been variously criticized as disinterested in the politics of training (Ezzamel et al., 1996), uninformed about the effects of learning as discourse (Fairclough and Hardy, 1997) and preoccupied with the benefits to individuals at the expense of furthering organizational performance, although this last criticism has been staunchly countered by Holton (2002), who argues that to separate individual and corporate value is a false and unhelpful dichotomy.

So there is no shortage of analysis (although it should be noted that critical theory in particular lacks extended empirical studies). The problem is that such disparate attempts to conceptualize management development frequently fail to cross-fertilize and inform practice. At worst, researchers remain so committed to their favoured paradigms that they are dismissive of findings of work from other traditions. To onlookers, this may appear like esoteric in-fighting between academics. However, management development is a field particularly prone to anecdotal advice, to fashion (Bell et al., 2002a) and to 'genre training' (Mole, 1996). Using appropriate methods and research tools to sift the claims, the rhetoric and the truth statements concerning management development may actually prove to be a timely contribution to those responsible for researching, designing, commissioning and assessing such activities.

How can this be done in a way that does justice to the full range of potential explanations? What is required is a means to magnify the different facets of management development. Metaphors provide a useful start.

Metaphors and management development

We only have to reflect on the language invoked by organizations to appreciate that there is no single, definitive interpretation of management development activities.

By providing highly vivid, mental pictures, metaphors in particular can play an important part in determining how we construe actors and events. Why is this? They can make abstract ideas accessible. They can communicate more powerfully than literal descriptions. They often convey emotions in a way that more cerebral communication does not. They can throw new light and meaning on familiar concepts. And they can do all of this succinctly. Consider these statements taken from the management development literature of British Plaster Board (BPB), part of the Saint Gobain business headquartered in France (Box 1.4).

Box 1.4   Management development in Saint Gobain

BPB is a big business – a global family of more than 13,000 people with different backgrounds, cultures and approaches. We are also very successful – each one of our businesses is strong in its own right, even though they are operating in an environment that continues to be competitive, demanding and constantly changing. In order to create our management and leadership capability, we have introduced a number of leadership development programmes.

Being big and successful brings many things. It brings challenge, excitement and diversity. It brings opportunities. It also brings a need for uncompromisingly high standards and responsibilities, to our customers, our people, our shareholders and to the environment in which we live. We need strong leaders to deliver these. Being a leader at BPB is about entering into a partnership. BPB leaders continually push the boundaries towards achieving our vision, and in return gain a breadth and depth of expertise, skills and qualities that they take with them for life.

Reflection point

What are the key metaphors in this brief excerpt and what do they communicate? How do they engage your emotions and what do they imply for those participating in management development for this organization?

The first metaphor is one of family. This simultaneously conveys a sense of belonging and obligation. One is led to think of being looked after and cared for. This could imply dependence on parents, who 'know best'. Unlike more transactional ties, familial relationships are for life and cannot be revoked. Given the harshness of the competitive environment that is also alluded to, one wonders what might happen to family members if the organization performed poorly. Likewise, how might the family react if an individual announced his/her departure? Another metaphor is one of partnership. This communicates a relationship of equals, with give and take. In return for supreme effort, the leader receives skills for life. This is quite a different perspective from the first, though the subject matter is the same. Here one's attention is drawn away from the security of family bonds to the expectations of leaders. The language implies an organizational promise to the individual of special treatment and accelerated career progress, presuming, of course, that they are able to maintain the 'uncompromisingly high standards and responsibilities'.

At this point we are not arguing for the rights or wrongs of St Gobain's conception of leadership; simply that metaphors have the ability to quickly 'hook' the emotions and allegiances of the hearers, and that the judicious use of analogy can extract from the same or similar events very different meanings. Metaphors imply that a certain solution is inevitable and we can be seduced by the persuasiveness and potency of the image without realizing there is another view. They call for action rather than argument, as in the example above: '*We need strong leaders*', people who will '*continually push the boundaries towards achieving our vision*'.

Because metaphors are a kind of 'short-hand' they will not tell the whole story; they will probably give only one version of events and omit certain details. Nevertheless, they paint a picture of 'reality' and the meanings we attribute to what is going on around us influence the actions we take. The relevance of all this to the training and development of managers is unmistakable. Metaphorical language plays an important part in the way different players construe the organization (a global family? a headless chicken? a sinking ship?); in the way the imperative for management development is articulated (the need to extend boundaries? the need to delight the customer?); and in the way the impact of changes are subsequently assessed (a change in hearts and minds? a leaner, meaner way of working? deckchairs rearranged on the decks of the *Titanic*?).

If, as seems clear, there are multiple readings of management development, this leads us to a further quandary. How can management development be theorized in a way which does justice to these contrasting perspectives?

Reframing management development

In this section we consider three possible approaches: the use of frames, the use of paradigms and the use of discourses. While each has its value, we conclude that the last of these is best suited for exploring the multifaceted nature of management development.

Frames
The way we think about organizations and the way we evaluate organizational practice is typically myopic and ingrained. In their book *Reframing Organizations*, Bolman and Deal (1997) offer four different frames for making sense of the value-dilemmas, factional pressures and multiple constituencies of modern corporate existence: the structural, the human resource, the political and the symbolic. Their central thesis is that managers habitually adopt one, or at best two of these frames. However, armed with the insights gained from viewing events and incidents

through the other frames or lenses, the authors argue that managers are better equipped to understand and influence their part of the organization. The primary focus of their book is leadership and the manager as agent of change; it is therefore highly pertinent to management development. Others have applied four-frame thinking to leadership in academic institutions (Bergquist, 1992; Birnbaum, 1992), to identify strategies for informal learning during periods of organizational instability (Marsick et al., 1999) and to the conceptualization of human resource development (Mabey, 2003).

Despite the intuitive appeal of Bolman and Deal's four frames, a number of questions remain about their utility (Palmer and Dunford, 1996). First, further research is needed as to whether the improved cognition afforded by reframing actually enhances the day-to-day skills of the manager. Second, are the four proposed frames in some way superior to others that might be invoked, and if so, on what basis? The value of metaphor as discussed above is that it encourages lateral and creative thinking, without limiting the analyst to a predetermined set of lenses. Third, and more fundamentally, although the device helpfully prompts deliberate reframing, all four of the frames are essentially positivist in their orientation: 'The reframing perspective retains a sense of there being an underlying reality which the aggregation of frames is able to more accurately portray' (Palmer and Dunford, 1996: 147).

Naturally, there is a place for functionalist studies and positivist methods. A good deal of this book will consider such work. The difficulty arises when this is assumed to be the only way to analyse and understand organizational activities like management development. In fact, the focus of our study (site, subjects, context, and so on), the tools and methods we use for analysis, the way we report what we find and the conclusions we draw are not 'givens' but choices (Box 1.5).

Box 1.5   Researcher choices: ontology and epistemology

Ontology concerns the status of social and natural reality and epistemology is the study of the criteria by which we can know what does and what does not constitute warranted, or scientific, knowledge. A positivist ontology assumes that an objective reality exists, independent of the researcher, and a positivist epistemology proposes that, given the appropriate tools and techniques, this reality can be faithfully ascertained and reported as scientific knowledge. Although dominant in management journals, this is just one of several ontologies/epistemologies adopted by management research. For example, a subjectivist ontology asserts that researchers, like everyone else, creatively construct their own culturally derived paradigms, which will determine the object of study, how it is studied, the criteria for choosing problems, and so on. Therefore reality has no independent, verifiable status; rather it is the creation of our consciousness and cognitions. A subjectivist epistemology is interpretative and concerned to understand the multiple versions of reality with particular reference to the role of language in social construction.

The tendency to rely upon a functionalist stance has been well explored in the related fields of organization behaviour and human resource management (HRM). Indeed, it leads one commentator to characterize HRM as largely a modernist project: 'Positivism, with its realist ontology, seeks to explain and predict what happens in the social world by searching for regularities and causal relationships between its constituent elements. ... To a greater or lesser extent this is the logic which reigns in much of the research on HRM, even when it is case-study based...' (Legge, 1996: 308). Similarly, in the arena of work and organizational psychology, Symon and Cassell (2006: 310) note that most researchers fail to make a 'conscious (political) choice to adopt positivism but that it is more of a default option'. The authors attribute this to conventional research training, which is steeped in the precepts of positivism and neglects other perspectives.

To a wide extent, this is also the case in the field of management development. Functionalist objectives are often taken for granted and research is often restricted to evaluating the extent to which these are met. Such an approach has been criticized for failing to deal adequately with causality (Kamoche, 2000) and for taking a unitarist perspective, where organizational members are assumed to share a single set of motives and interests (Burgoyne and Jackson, 1997). Some would go further, casting management development as a largely one-sided attempt by senior management to impose control or advance ideological power interests rather than as a means to 'develop' employees in any kind of holistic or benevolent sense (Ackers and Preston, 1997). Management development has also been portrayed as a bureaucratic and potentially harmful irrelevance, where standardized portrayals of management bear little resemblance to the diverse worlds of 'real' managers (e.g. Grugulis, 2002). In contrast to these broadly negative critiques, other authors have suggested that deeper insight might be gained by trying to look beyond questions of good or evil (Townley, 1998), success or failure (du Gay et al., 1996) and by searching for more multifaceted ways in which management development might simultaneously work for and against the interests of any particular agent. It is in this regard that paradigms and discourses come to the rescue.

Paradigms

Probably the most influential attempt to delineate contrasting paradigms (and liberate researchers from the confines of functionalist assumptions) in the field of social theory and organizational analysis is that of Burrell and Morgan (1979). They propose two axes. One axis concerns the nature of the social world and how it might best be investigated, ranging from subjectivist to objectivist assumptions about ontology, epistemology, human nature and methodology. The other axis refers to the nature of society, ranging from regulation at one extreme to radical change at the other. This leads to four paradigms: functionalism, interpretivism, radical humanism and radical structuralism. These appear to offer fruitful avenues for researching aspects of organizational behaviour (e.g. Hassard, 1991; Schultz and Hatch, 1996), including management development and organizational learning (e.g. Ortenblad, 2002). Burrell and Morgan (1979) emphasize that these four paradigms are mutually exclusive, and by accepting one set of meta-theoretical assumptions the researcher denies the alternative. 'Because the meta-theoretical norms of one paradigm are not translatable into those of an alternative, there cannot be any *a priori*, independent, neutral or rational grounds for debate or for deciding upon which paradigm has the better problem-solving capacity' (Johnson and Duberley, 2000: 80). Reducing such analysis to a choice between discrete alternatives has, however, been challenged. For example, it has been argued that regarding the four paradigms as polarized sets of assumptions is probably not sustainable in practice (Willmott, 1993b), and it is proposed that by blurring the 'transition zones between paradigms it is possible to construct bridges that link the apparently disparate concepts in these zones' (Gioia and Pitre, 1990: 599). Another way out of the cul-de-sac of incommensurability is to derive some kind of meta-theory (Alvesson and Deetz, 2000; Johnson and Duberley, 2000). This presents the possibility of 'rising above' commitment to any single ontological stance in order to assess the comparative contribution of the conflicting theories in any given research domain (noting that any such meta-theoretical stance inevitably involves partiality!). Probably the most promising means for achieving this is that of discourse.

Discourse

The notion of discourse has been defined and used in many different ways (Alvesson and Kärreman, 2000).

Reflection point

Consider, for example the various definitions set out in Box 1.6. What similarities do you see between them? Do you also see any contrasts between them? If so, what might be the practical effects of these?

Box 1.6   Defining discourse(s)

[A discourse is] a connected set of statements, concepts, terms and expressions which constitutes a way of talking and writing about a particular issue, thus framing the way people understand and act with respect to that issue. (Watson, 1994: 113)

A discourse is a particular way of representing some part of the (physical, social, psychological) world – there are alternative and often competing discourses associated with different groups of people in different social positions. ... Discourses differ in how social events are represented, what is excluded or included, how abstractly or concretely events are represented, and how more specifically the processes and relations, social actors, time and place of events are represented ... (Fairclough, 2003: 17)

(Continued)

(Continued)

> Discourses are sets of ideas and practices which condition our ways of relating to and acting upon particular phenomena: a discourse will be expressed in all that can be thought, written or said about a particular topic, which by constituting the phenomenon in a particular way influences behaviour. In these respects, discourses constrain and stabilize the free-play of signifiers into a particular gaze. ... Discourses are social constructions and the existence of a reality independent of their knowledge constitution is at best precarious ... we can never attain any knowledge save that constructed in and by some discourse. (Johnson and Duberley, 2000: 102)

> Discourse refers to the language used for talking about a topic and for producing a particular kind of knowledge about that topic (du Gay 1996). Far from reflecting an already given social reality, language which is taken for granted constitutes reality as it appears to us ... meaning is not constant across discourses (for example between feminist and management discourses) and is subject to historical change. (Rees and Garnsey, 2003: 556)

As authors we find all of the above definitions both useful and relevant to the project we embark upon in this book. They are all similar in describing discourses as the means by which the world comes to be represented in particular and often competing ways, each of which is subject to change and evolution through time. They also all allude to the implications of this for our own relationship to the world, that is we are likely to speak, think, behave, act and react differently depending on the discourse(s) to which we subscribe (implicitly or otherwise) at any one point in time. The differences between the various definitions are also worth pondering for a moment. Some of them equate discourse fairly narrowly to the use of language. Others, notably Johnson and Duberley, embrace a much broader definition, linking it to non-linguistic practices as well as mere speech acts. These might include, for example, the physical segregation of high potential managers from lower performing ones in a fast-track programme. Another example comes from Fournier (1998), who noted how 'entrepreneurial' finance trainees in a UK public utility were physically located in plush city-centre offices in contrast to IT trainees located in drab offices located in a run-down part of town. For Fournier, this is a discursive (if extra-linguistic) means of constituting social relations in a particular way (i.e. hierarchically) and of conveying meaning. In both instances, distinctly different career paths are signposted in ways that transcend the linguistic.

A further difference between the definitions relates to ontology or, in other words, the ultimate reality of our world (see Box 1.5). Note, for example, how Watson's and Fairclough's definitions speak of how discourses can differentially 'frame' or 'represent' a phenomenon (e.g. an issue, a social event) but without calling into question the ultimate (or ontological) status of such phenomenon.

Contrast this with the latter two definitions that imply that discourses are also the means by which the very reality of a phenomenon is actually constructed (which also implies the notion of multiple and competing realities). We would claim that each of the above definitions of discourse also constitutes a mini–discourse in and of itself in as much as it seeks to ontologically represent the world of which it speaks and thus create knowledge about that world. Equally, any attempt by us as authors to choose between such definitions must also be seen as an example of discourse in action. And this leads us into a fundamental tenet of this book, which is to consciously (and as reflexively as possible) invoke different discourses in order to scrutinize management development (see Box 1.7). In so doing, we trust that our book will encourage you to analyse management development in a more reflexive manner. Whether you are conducting a research project, planning a new management development initiative or reviewing a consultant's proposal, the aim is to equip you to test assumptions, critically weigh any data, assess the way it is presented and linguistically portrayed, and draw more informed judgements about how to proceed. We will outline our chosen discourses in a moment. Before doing so, however, we would like to say a few words about the thorny issue of how to identify discourses and delineate their boundaries.

Box 1.7   Being reflexive as a researcher and practitioner

Johnson and Duberley (2000: 66) are admirably succinct in describing reflexivity as 'thinking about our own thinking' in explicit acknowledgement that the search for knowledge will take different avenues depending on the paradigms and metaphors we choose to engage.

Willig (2001: 10) is more expansive in her treatment of the concept, distinguishing between two types of reflexivity: personal and epistemological:

'Personal reflexivity' involves reflecting upon the ways in which our own values, experiences, interests, beliefs, political commitments, wider aims in life and social identities have shaped the research. It also involves thinking about how the research may have affected and possibly changed us, as people and as researchers. 'Epistemological reflexivity' requires us to engage with questions such as: How has the research question defined and limited what can be 'found?' How has the design of the study and the method of analysis 'constructed' the data and the findings? How could the research question have been investigated differently? To what extent would this have given rise to a different understanding of the phenomenon under investigation? Thus, epistemological reflexivity encourages us to reflect upon the assumptions (about the world, about knowledge) that we have made in the course of the research, and it helps us to think about the implications of such assumptions for the research and its findings.

(Continued)

(Continued)

Finally, Cunliffe (2003: 985) expounds what she calls a 'radical' form of reflexivity that goes further than questioning the truth claims of others:

> to question how we as researchers (and practitioners) also make truth claims and construct meaning. This assumes that all research, positivist and anti-positivist, is constructed between research participants (researcher, 'subjects', colleagues, texts) and that we need to take responsibility 'for [our] own theorizing, as well as whatever it is [we] theorize about' (Hardy and Clegg, 1997: S13). In other words, we need to recognize our philosophical commitments and enact their internal logic, while opening them to critical questioning so that we expose their situated nature.

Recalling Watson's definition, a discourse can be thought of as a connected set of statements, concepts, terms and expressions which constitutes a way of talking and writing about a particular issue. But as others point out, discourses are social constructions that are subject to constant evolution. As such, there are no hard-and-fast rules as to what constitutes a discourse nor as to where the boundaries of any such discourse might lie. In this sense, the identification of individual discourses is more an art than a science. Having said this, Fairclough (2003: 129) makes two recommendations for the identification and delineation of discourses within a text:

1   Identify the main aspects of social life which are represented in the text or, in other words, the main 'themes'.
2   Identify the particular perspective, angle or viewpoint from which these aspects are being represented.

See if you can use the above to suggest any latent discourses within the following extracts taken from different participants in a recent qualitative study of management development (Finch-Lees et al., 2005b):

> Just from my personal point of view, I would feel that the company is not going to invest money in you or send you on a course for no reason.

> I think if the company is prepared to invest in an individual and the individual can see that, the company can see the individual grow and actually takes probably more notice of that individual.

> My pay since I've joined has gone up 70% in four and a half years. ... Now that is partly because of, I suppose, the work that's been done here. It's also partly I guess because the company feels confident in the individual that they're investing in. Now that has got to be because I'm also taking part in growing myself as an individual.

Our own assessment is that the main aspects of social life being represented in the above are those of *development* and its *impact*. But notice how the company, in all three extracts, is represented as 'investing' in the individual, who is then expected to 'grow' as a result of such investment. This might easily be dismissed as unremarkable and simply the way 'normal people' speak. Indeed, we can imagine similar representations being uttered within most, if not all, contemporary organizations. However, this does not detract from the fact that the notion of development 'as investment' is a metaphorical rather than a literal interpretation of the activity. As such, we would characterize the above as examples of an individualist, accounting discourse of development. Here the perspective being taken is that of the entrepreneur or stockholder who makes financial investments in the expectation of maximizing her/his financial returns. In this case it is the organization which is being discursively constructed as the stockholder with the individual being constructed as the entity (e.g. stock or asset) that is being invested in. Banal or not, this is not the only way in which development can be represented and evaluated. Participants might equally have chosen (and may in other contexts choose) to speak of the more collectivist and perhaps less quantifiable impacts of development, such as those relating to social responsibility, sustainability, diversity, community or general quality of life. Our last point here is that the discourses with which we engage are not inconsequential details of speech but have the capacity to enable as well as to either broaden or restrict our thoughts, actions, beliefs and behaviours.

Following on from this, Johnson and Duberley (2000: 101–2) have observed that:

> any management discipline would be seen as a particular historical and social mode of engagement that restricts what is thinkable, knowable and doable in its disciplinary domain. Through their education and training, managers learn to speak this discourse and the discourse speaks to them by structuring their experiences and definitions of who they are.

Using discourse to understand management development therefore seems highly apt. If this is the case, which particular discourses have most relevance?

Discourses of management development

Given the noted shortcomings of reframing on the one hand, and paradigms on the other, we choose to use discourse (which includes attention to metaphor) as the primary vehicle for examining management development in this book. We do this in two ways. First, by referring to four overarching theoretical perspectives (or 'Grand Discourses', see Box 1.8), namely functionalism, constructivism, dialogic and critical. In the middle part of the book we look at each of these in some detail. Second, we examine management development through the lens of three emblematic practitioner lenses (or 'meso-discourses'), namely best-practice, institutional and diversity. These constitute Part 3 of the book.

Box 1.8   Levels of discourse

Alvesson and Kärreman (2000) distinguish between four different levels of discourse: micro-discourse, meso-discourse, Grand Discourse, and finally Mega-Discourse:

- Grand Discourses (purposely written with a capital 'D') are described by the authors as 'an assembly of discourses [note the little 'd'], ordered and presented as an integrated frame. A Grand Discourse may refer to/constitute organizational reality, for example dominating language use about corporate culture or ideology' (2000: 1133). It is at this 'Grand' level that we situate our four theoretical discourses, with functionalism being the dominant one when it comes to the everyday workings of the typical organization.
- Meso-discourse (purposely written with a small 'd') can be thought of as language and social practice whose meaning is more context-specific than Grand Discourse, but which nevertheless transcends the particular text in question, thus forming broader patterns of meaning that can be generalized to similar local contexts. It is at this 'meso' level that we situate our three practitioner discourses. Note, however, that there is no neat fit between levels. For example, any discourse at the meso-level could conceivably straddle two or more at the Grand level and vice versa.

We do not concern ourselves particularly with either a Mega-Discourse or a micro-discourse approach in this book. However, for the sake of completeness, each can respectively be understood as follows:

- Mega-Discourse: the idea of a universally standardized connection of discourse and meaning.
- Micro-discourse: the idea of discourse forming purely localized forms of meaning that are unique to the context in question and cannot be reliably generalized to other contexts, locations or situations.

Four theoretical or 'Grand' management development Discourses

In order to map out the theoretical assumptions (and indeed Discourses) underlying different avenues of management development research, we adopt a framework devised by Schultze and Stabell (2004). In exploring their chosen arena of research, that of knowledge management, these authors draw upon previous paradigms of social and organizational enquiry (Burrell and Morgan, 1979; Deetz, 1996). The basis of their approach is the derivation of two dimensions or sets of assumptions: those concerning social order and those concerning epistemology (see Box 1.9).

Box 1.9   Two dimensions of discourse

Social order: consensus versus dissensus

Research in the social sciences can be differentiated according to the stance it takes towards existing social orders, or, in other words, the extent to which it either serves to support or disrupt prevailing discourses within its respective field of study. In the words of Alvesson and Deetz (2000: 26), the consensus pole of this dimension 'draws attention to the way some research programmes both seek order and treat order production as the dominant feature of natural and social systems ... through the highlighting of ordering principles, such existing orders are perpetuated'. In contrast, research located at the dissensus pole considers conflict, tension, dilemma and struggle to be natural facets of the social world. As such, any semblance of order is to be treated with suspicion and as an indication that the full variety of human interests is in some way being suppressed. Research located towards this end of the dimension generally seeks to reclaim conflict with a view to somehow altering the balance of power within a particular field or, indeed, within society more generally.

Epistemology: dualism versus duality

Here the interest is in the nature of knowledge and how it is captured. Schultze and Stabell (2004) characterize this epistemological dimension as dualism versus duality. Dualism seeks to answer the question 'what is the phenomenon' or focus of our study and implies 'either/or' thinking which prompts the researcher to look for theoretically driven classifications and tax-onomies. It is assumed that the phenomenon under investigation is frozen in time, has an identity that is separate/separable from the rest of the social world and can be fully understood. Causal relationships are uni-directional and, with appropriate research tools, can be faithfully determined. In contrast, dual-ity is more concerned with the question 'when is the phenomenon?'; although grammatically awkward, the idea is to highlight the unfolding nature of social phenomena rather than treating them as objectively analysable and frozen-in-time. This perspective also resists the construction of false dichotomies and mutually exclusive opposites, preferring to apply 'both/and' thinking. Researchers acknowledge that the object of their study is continuously shap-ing and being shaped by situated practice; as a consequence, theorizing is associated with emergence and cyclical causality. 'Theories based on duality are particularly useful for studying contradictions and paradoxes because they consider opposing forces that act simultaneously on the same phenom-enon' (Schultze and Stabell, 2004: 554).

From these two dimensions they derive four distinct research perspectives, or Discourses, which they claim to be particularly apposite for exploring the contradiction of managing tacit knowledge in organizations. They label these four Discourses: the neo-functionalist, the constructivist, the critical and the dialogic.

We choose to adopt these Discourses to analyse management development in this book for a number of reasons. In their account, Schultse and Stabell trace more carefully than most the theoretical assumptions underlying extant research. This helps to cue us in to contrasting, and on occasions conflicting, literatures pertaining to management development. Also, their subject matter, the way tacit knowledge is managed, is closely aligned to the paradoxical issues associated with developing managers and leaders in organizations. Furthermore, as has become clear, the advantage of Discourses over paradigms, is that they are not intended to be theoretically watertight boxes and their permeability allows us to be more imaginative about the way they might flow into each other. The term 'Discourse' is preferable because it 'highlights that each is plagued by internal debates, that the edges between worldviews are not well demarcated, and that debates in one worldview influence debates in the others' (Schultze and Stabell, 2004: 555). This presents the interesting possibility of employing, for example, functionalist or indeed critical Discourses from an ultimate standpoint of the dialogic, which is something that the more static notion of paradigm would preclude. However, we replace the term 'neo-functionalist' with 'functionalist' because it is not clear to us (and not explained by Schultze and Stabell) why this Discourse is distinctively new or 'neo'. Table 1.1 begins to characterize how each Discourse treats the field of management development.

In Chapters 3–6 we examine each of these Discourses in turn. Each provides valuable insight and explanation, in part complementary and in part contradictory, as to what the management development 'project' signifies.

We do not intend to promote any one of the Discourses referred to above as being necessarily superior to the others. Having said this, we do acknowledge that the very notions of Discourse, and indeed reflexivity, sit least comfortably in the positivist world of functionalism (Cunliffe, 2003) and most comfortably within the three epistemologically subjectivist Discourses (i.e. the dialogic, the critical, and the constructivist). As Alvesson and Deetz (2000) point out, the idea of text (spoken or written) creating or constituting 'reality' is a central tenet of a subjectivist epistemology. They go on to point out that discourses can be viewed as 'systems of thought which are contingent upon as well as inform material practices, which not only linguistically but also practically – through particular power techniques [...] produce particular forms of subjectivity' (Alvesson and Deetz, 2000: 97). However, the fact that functionalism does not readily embrace the notion of discourse does not prevent it from being analysed *as a Discourse* in and of itself. This we attempt to do throughout the book, especially since (as already noted) it typically forms the dominant Discourse within everyday organizational life. However, and especially in Chapters 3, 7 and 8, we also engage (to an extent at least) with functionalism on its own terms. In other words, we will often write as if we accept its realist/objectivist ontology and epistemology, rather than merely dismissing these, as is the tendency of many critical and/or dialogic texts. While this kind of 'ontological oscillation' is polemical to say the least (Cunliffe, 2003), we do it here in the spirit of a reflexive multi-discourse approach to organizational

TABLE 1.1   *Four Discourses of management development (MD) research*

	Duality	**Dualism**
Dissensus	**Dialogic Discourse**	**Critical Discourse**
	Metaphors of MD: discipline, carnival, reproduction, dressage.	*Metaphors of MD*: political struggle, religious conversion, cultural doping.
	Role of MD in organization: a vehicle for the active construction of identities which are themselves inherently multiple, shifting and negotiated.	*Role of MD in organization*: to produce and resist order, predictability, control, domination, subordination.
	Theories: post-structuralism, feminist post-structuralism, postmodernism, deconstruction, Foucauldian social theory.	*Theories*: critical theory, labour process theory, some forms of feminism.
	Research domains: MD as discourse, identity construction within MD, deconstructing the language of MD.	*Research domains*: MD as a means to either change or preserve the balance of power within organizations. MD's role in perpetuating capitalist ideology.
Consensus	**Constructivist Discourse**	**Functionalist Discourse**
	Metaphor of MD: drama.	*Metaphor of MD*: a tool-kit.
	Role of MD in organization: enabling collective learning and self-development, conferring meaning/status.	*Role of MD in organization*: building skills and knowledge to address performance gaps and optimize resources.
	Theories: agency, role behaviour, learning, resource-based, theories of practice, sense-making.	*Theories*: intellectual capital, open systems, HRM, institutional, contingency, resource-based.
	Research domains: modes of MD and their outcomes, cultural significance of MD.	*Research domains*: performance impact of formal MD activities, evaluation studies.

analysis. It is also in this spirit of reflexivity that we encourage the reader to engage with it.

Up until now we have used words such as 'explore', 'examine' and 'adopt' to describe what we plan to do with these Discourses in Chapters 3–6. To an extent such terms are appropriate. But they do risk creating an impression of exaggerated solidity around the whole notion of discourse. They do this by making the four Grand Discourses sound as if they 'exist' in the sense that something like, say, a book exists. However, Discourses are not something that can be plucked from a shelf and simply 'read off' before being subjected to analysis. As such, it needs to be acknowledged that we, as authors, will not just be 'exploring', 'examining' or 'adopting' these Discourses. We will also be contributing to their maintenance and transformation. But as we explained earlier, the delineation of any Discourse is a problematic enterprise with no hard-and-fast rules. Our very acts of characterizing and commenting upon other works as functionalist, constructivist, etc., must themselves be seen as discursive acts. In other words, *each chapter in this book can be considered to be a discourse in itself* and we would encourage readers to regard the assertions we make as modest and localized 'truth claims' as opposed to 'the truth'. For us to make any pretensions towards the latter would be to strive towards a grand 'theory of everything' in relation to management development. Had we considered this to be a realistic or worthwhile endeavour, we would not have embarked upon it by invoking the notion of discourse. Finally, a key aim in this book is to demonstrate that the practical implications of a subjectivist, multi-discourse approach are no less 'real' than those of an exclusively objectivist approach. As an aside, our comments in this paragraph apply just as equally to the meso-discourses we 'explore' in Chapters 7–9.

Before closing this section, we briefly reflect back on the five reasons for studying management development set out earlier in this chapter in order to say a few words about which of our four Grand Discourses might be best placed to tackle each.

Reasons 1 and 2: Economic and financial

The functionalist Discourse, with its objectivist and quantitative methodologies, is best positioned to address economic and financial concerns. Indeed, the major-ity of the management development literature is preoccupied with identifying the variables which enhance outcomes and with tracking, as precisely as is possible, the performance impact of such activities whether this be productivity at enter-prise or national level. However, as already stated, for all the functionalist research that has taken place in this area over the years, there is actually very little hard evi-dence that management development can systematically lead to improved eco-nomic and financial outcomes. The three other Discourses help to problematize economic and financial imperatives while providing alternative explanations for the continuing popularity of management development.

Reason 3: Diverse meanings of management development

It is here that the constructivist Discourse comes into its own. This is a Discourse which privileges the multiple interpretations of a given phenomenon (in our case, management development) as seen through the eyes of different stakeholders. As such, management development is considered meaningful only to the extent that different stakeholders create meaning around it or read meaning into it. Although excellently placed to explore the less visible, subjective significance of manage-ment development, the constructivist researcher tends, however, to simply report the experience of participants, thus taking their accounts as face-value evidence of what is really going on in their heads. This is partly what differentiates the con-structivist Discourse from the dialogic and the critical, both of which tend to overlay their own interpretations of stakeholder accounts.

Reason 4: Moral/ethical issues

It is in this realm that the critical Discourse provides penetrating insight. It does this by drawing on a large and complex body of critical theory to expose what it sees as dynamics of power and domination within seemingly benign activities.

Reason 5: The construction of managerial identity

It is in relation to this question that the dialogic Discourse comes into its own. Management development within this Discourse is to be considered as an important means among many by which organizational, managerial and non-managerial identities are created, adopted, resisted and negotiated.

Three practitioner discourses

So far, we have concentrated upon Grand Discourse, but meso–discourses, as described in Box 1.8, are also influential in the way management development is construed and practised. Of the many that we could have chosen, we single out three such discourses which appear to have considerable resonance in the field at this time. The notion of *best-practice* has been applied to many aspects of organizational life and management development is no exception. This discourse includes the ways in which policies, techniques and methods for developing managers come into vogue, gain credibility and come to govern activities in an almost sacred manner. This is not far removed from the *institutional* discourse, whereby the need to gain legitimacy with significant others (perhaps competitors, government, professional bodies, shareholders, one's own employees) is a prime driver for an organization to pursue certain management development activities and eschew others. This lens of analysis naturally requires a good understanding of the cultural and socio-economic context of the organization concerned. A last discourse to which we turn our attention is that of *diversity*. The issue of diversity in organizations has generated a vast literature, but it is the interface between the concern for a more diverse workforce and management development (frequently heralded as the best means to achieve such a goal) that is of particular interest here. We devote a chapter to each of these three discourses later in the book, although you will observe traces of each washing through earlier chapters also.

Conclusion

A cursory look at the field of management development leads to a reasonably encouraging picture. In most countries and firms, a good deal more prominence is being given to management development than in the past. This is matched by a steady stream of research reporting its extent, effectiveness and/or significance. Yet the 'state of play' remains somewhat unsatisfactory and baffling. We note, for example, that despite the difficulties associated with tracking the direct and measurable benefits of management development, there continues to be high investment in this activity. This is perplexing and suggests that there are ways of understanding management development other than in terms of its utility, performance and impact alone. We might also note the systemic and political complexity of conducting management development: conventional wisdom would have us believe in a linear, rational and controllable process, but our experience tells us that unintended consequences occur, good development ideas are drowned out by more pressing organizational demands and excellently conceived programmes often fail to live up to their promise. And at a more personal level, many individual managers sometimes struggle with the relevance and meaninglessness of the training and development activities in which they are involved. Understandably they baulk at the compromises and, in some cases, sacrifices they have to make as participants. Others wonder why such development opportunities do not come their way at all. All this leads to a central conundrum of the book. Given that, at several levels, the high expectations invested in management development often remain unfulfilled, why is it a subject/activity that continues to command such intense interest from scholars and practitioners alike?

In this chapter we have begun to identify why management development is such a hot topic and briefly reviewed what current academic research tells us about management development policies and practices. To deepen our understanding of this arena and to address the above conundrum, we have proposed a multiple discourse approach. This is not without contention. For example, are such ways of viewing management development intended to be contingent whereby one perspective is particularly suited to a given set of circumstances, to be replaced with another as circumstances shift? Or do all discourses apply simultaneously as intriguingly discordant, multiple meanings of the same event or process? We take the latter view, acknowledging, however, that the dominance of any one discourse is as much a product of the inclinations and predispositions of the analyst as it is a reflection of the situation being researched. Second, and linked, is the question of whether competing discourses are commensurable. In their original discussion, Burrell and Morgan (1979) maintain that sociological paradigms are mutually exclusive constructions which, by definition, generate distinctive analyses of social life. Later, however, Morgan (1990) advocates the use of a range of perspectives to build up a composite picture of organizational issues and this is the approach we take in this section. We concur that a fundamental/theoretical synthesis of perspectives (or, in our case, Discourses) cannot be attained. Yet we believe our understanding of management development, which is the purpose of this book, can be significantly enriched by first identifying different Discourses and then finding stepping stones, or at least room for dialogue, between them.

Adopting a multi-discourse approach may be welcomed by many, especially those of a postmodernist and/or critical persuasion. But such authors would argue (rightly in our view) that any drive towards synthesis or ultimate consensus is misguided, partly because it is a fruitless mission epistemologically and partly because any such 'consensus' will inevitably favour dominant coalitions. This does, however, present a risk of increasing fragmentation of knowledge which undermines the significance of the management development 'project'. This echoes what may be taking place in the broader fields of Organization Behaviour and HRM. In his review of a number of such texts, Morgan (2000) refers to the development of research and theory on organization culture, for instance, and notes that intellectual differences are typically handled by silence: 'That is, writers simply ignore any opposing viewpoints. ... [M]odernists, with a few exceptions, have ignored the postmodernists. However, postmodernists have been severely critical of the modernists. The concern here, therefore, is that further "conversations" will not degenerate into more "war games" ' (2000: 863), resulting in a loss of ideas and disillusioned people. To this we might add a further loss: that of confused or alienated practitioners! An alternative route, and one we propose to take in this book, is to encourage the interplay of multiple discourses, seeking dialogue between them but without any search for ultimate synthesis or consensus. This will create tensions and contradictory data, but it is only as such complexities are confronted (without necessarily being resolved) that some of the more hidden meanings and significance of management development activities will become apparent.

One purpose of this book is to provide a text for those studying management development, leadership, HRD or related topics as part of a higher education course. For this reason, the ten chapters are designed to allow students to follow the material over a typical ten-week semester. Broadly speaking, the first part of the book (this and the next chapter) introduces the subject, defines some key terms and assembles a set of analytic approaches to guide a reflexive examination of the subject matter. The second part (Chapters 3–6) encourages us to step back and review the (largely implicit) theoretical perspectives which motivate and shape the study of management development. Here we explore four Grand Discourses (the functionalist, constructivist, dialogic and critical Discourses) in turn, assessing how each reveals different facets and offers unique explanations. This multi-discourse approach is extended in the third part of the book (Chapters 7–9) with reference to three further meso-discourses: those of best-practice, institutionalism and diversity. Again, we argue that each is highly influential in its own way, in shaping our understanding of management development.

The overall intention of the book is to encourage reflexivity in the study and practice of management development. In the final chapter we offer some principles to guide those designing, those implementing, those participating in and those researching management development in the hope that your endeavours will be more constructively critical, more illuminating and, ultimately, more satisfying.

Summary

- Management development has attracted a good deal of research, most of it from a functionalist perspective.
- Despite persistent attempts to attribute enhanced performance to management development, the evidence-base for this relationship is equivocal at best.
- It is highly probable that reliance upon positivist methods means that much of the significance of the management development project is routinely missed.
- Of the various proposed ways to understand the management development project more deeply and more reflexively, a multi-discourse approach holds most promise.
- The Grand Discourses (dialogic, functionalist, constructivist and critical) each provide the possibility of unique illumination of what is happening in the name of management development.
- In addition, the three meso-level discourses of best-practice, institutionalism and diversity offer further opportunities to be reflexive about the management development project.

2

Meanings of management development

We educate children. We train monkeys, dentists and doctors. But we develop managers and there are important differences between these three verbs. (Paauwe and Williams, 2001: 91)

After reading this chapter you will be able to:

- **Problematize the distinction between managers and leaders**
- **Define what is meant by management development and how it relates to the fields of management training, education and management learning**
- **Identify some contrasting historical/cultural conceptions of managers and leaders and the implications of these for management development**
- **Explain why the development of leaders and managers is so important**
- **Describe a number of guiding principles that are needed to deepen our understanding of management development**

Introduction

In the first chapter we established that due to the fascinating confluence of several historical debates and current trends, management and leadership development has become a centre-stage activity or project for those working in and researching organizations. We went on to propose an analytical strategy for examining this project in more depth, a strategy that does justice to the subtle and shifting nature of how, why and to what effect managers are developed. Before we get started on this quest in earnest, we need to define terms. Many make a point of differentiating between the development of leaders and managers. This supposed distinction deserves explanation and we deal with this issue first. Next, given the burgeoning fields of learning, education and training, we need to be clear how we are using the concept 'management development'. The term 'manager' also requires some scrutiny as this too means different things to different audiences. Assisted by these reference points we can begin to examine management development more precisely. In addition to the value gained by taking a multi-discourse approach, the third section in this chapter outlines four further principles which we believe should guide such analysis.

Management and leadership: a dubious dichotomy?

Where does the science of management stop and the art of leadership begin? For every article or book on management development there are probably 20 devoted to identifying and developing leaders. The idea of separating the qualities of leaders and managers can be traced back to an influential paper by Zaleznick (1977), in which he depicts the manager 'as a rational, bureaucratic, dutiful, practical and unimaginative dullard but the leader as a visionary, restless, experimental, even twice-born dynamo' (quoted in Raelin, 2004: 132). Kotter (1990) is one of many writers who have reinforced this distinction, extolling good management as necessary to bring order, consistency and quality to otherwise chaotic organizations and contrasting this with leadership which is about preparing the enterprise for change and helping employees cope as they struggle through it. While such ideas were still felt to have currency a decade later when the same paper was reprinted in *Harvard Business Review* in 2001, the basis of this dichotomy has to be questioned on several grounds.

Delayering of organizations

First, these characterizations were predicated upon large, hierarchically structured and bureaucratized organizations where managers had responsibility for well-defined roles such as planning, budgeting, controlling, staffing and problem-solving. Far fewer organizations fit this description of predictability now. The decreasing numbers employed in workplaces, and the decline in the number covered by systems of consultation and negotiation, has shifted the manager's power base from positional to personal. The increasing fragmentation of the workforce, with differing patterns of working, contractual forms, outsourcing and homeworking, calls for a more flexible management style, as does the need to manage their own and others' work–life balance. All of this is happening in a human resources management (HRM) context which is increasingly moving towards individualized employment contracts. The capacity to scan boundaries, to establish strategic direction and to inspire others to follow are no longer the exclusive preserve of those at the top of organizations. Most staff with responsibility in organizations, whether they be entrepreneurs in a small or medium-sized enterprise (SME), project managers in a matrix structure, supervisors with remote working staff or those part of a virtual, international team, will be called upon to lead – and follow – at different times in their working week, irrespective of their job title.

Eclipsing of leadership theories

Second, studies of leadership have moved on. Trait theory pointed to a set of intrinsic qualities possessed by some individuals and not others. Although largely discredited for failing to account for social, historical or situational variables, the idea that leaders are born not made and possess an indefinable X-factor persists (Kirkpatrick and Locke, 1991). Contingency theories and leader–member exchange theory finesse this idea by elevating the importance of considering the relationship between the leader, and their environment (Fiedler, 1996) and their followers (Graen and Uhl-Bien, 1995) respectively. However, these theories remain fairly prescriptive and individualistic in their focus. More recent leadership development approaches have emphasized the relational element of leadership residing in the networks, commitments, trust and mutual exchange between members of a community, which collectively create social capital (Day, 2001). Here leadership is emergent rather than prescribed, self-evident rather than appointed. As Paauwe and Williams (2001: 94) point out: 'Management in the sense of controlling what people do is hardly useful when dealing with knowledge workers. They have to be rather supported and defended. They cannot really be managed. They can only be led.' So again, the distinction of leader and manager becomes immaterial, where everyone is potentially a leader (or indeed a manager (Grey, 1999)) and leadership is seen as an effect not a cause. While this concept of dispersed leadership is appealing, it can underestimate the power dynamic in organizations. Those in privileged positions as a result of historical antecedents will rarely relinquish their differential status. And even if they do, followers may react by swiftly replacing them with traditionally oriented alternative leaders, such is the natural superiority of the leader in the collective psyche (Ray et al., 2004)!

Culture-bound concepts of leadership

A third reason for caution is that much of the theorizing about leadership has taken place either in a Western context (e.g. Trompenaars, 1993; Yukl, 1998) or from a masculine perspective (Olsson, 2002; Vinnicombe and Singh, 2002) or indeed both (van der Boon, 2003). An in-depth analysis of leadership across 62 different countries called Project Globe is seeking to understand if and how leadership varies across different cultures (House et al., 2002). Certain attributes associated with charismatic leadership, for example, may be important for successful leaders worldwide, but the expression and meanings of such attributes may depend on cultural context (Von Glinow et al., 1999). So, although concepts such as transactional and transformational leadership may be universally valid, specific behaviours representing these styles may vary profoundly. Indonesian inspirational leaders need to persuade their followers about the leaders' own competence, a behaviour that would appear unseemly in Japan. Vietnam, like its Chinese neighbour, is a society based on Confucian values, such as harmony, hierarchy, collectivism and personal relations. Thus, developing long-term relationships is seen as critical for management success in Vietnam (Berrell et al., 1999). In such contexts, hierarchy means the complete acceptance of the authority of leaders by subordinates in order to maintain harmony; in other cultures, individuals have to earn their right to lead.

Corporate convenience

A fourth reason to be suspicious of the leader–manager split is the convenient way it elevates the self-importance of corporate leaders. Popular management theory, and again this originates primarily in the West but is readily available at the book shops of international airports, is redolent with values that appeal fundamentally to managers aspiring to be leaders. Clark and Salaman (1998) argue that there is a very good reason for the enormous success and impact of this literature. This is the fact that it appeals to managers, not simply because it displays qualities managers themselves value and use, but because it enhances their confidence in performing their role as corporate leaders through their mythic story-telling. Whether self-help business handbooks, case accounts of successful turn-arounds or cult biographies of successful CEOs, such literature 'defines' the qualities necessary for effective leadership in the contemporary organization. The cumulative effect is to characterize and ultimately legitimize the 'otherness' of leaders. Alvesson (1990) argues that part of the corporate attraction of these texts is that 'the questions formulated and answered, the perspective taken, the sectional interests supported etc. are grounded in a worldview, a set of beliefs and values, which indicate that the top managers of corporations and other organisations are a highly important group' (1990: 27). The danger of course, is that such leaders come to be seen, and come to see themselves as above criticism, immune to dissent. The mystique becomes a defensive device. But leadership is not an inherently moral concept. As Kellerman (2004) points out, some leaders are trustworthy, courageous, generous; many are not. And even 'successful' leaders are not necessarily good people, as reports of corporate scandals and exploitation of privilege constantly remind us. In Box 2.1, Mangham reflects on the changing face of business leadership in the the City of London.

Box 2.1   The changing face of leadership

The ethos of managerial or gentlemanly capitalism has been replaced by an emerging individualistic, less community-centred set of explanations and values, and a brasher, harsher, more exploitative variety of interaction. This ethos demands a new type of leadership. In the brave new Darwinian world of shareholder capitalism there is a greater focus on the individual leader. He or she is no longer a professional manager. His/her role is to set the direction for the company, to motivate and energize the employees, but primarily to deal with the analysts, the accountants, the banks, the government authorities, the media, the public and – above all – to deliver ever richer dividends to the shareholders. Becoming a leader in this day and age is seen to be a matter of 'communicating an essential optimism, confidence and can-do attitude' (Khurana, 2002: 71). Leaders have become much more visible, subject to much more comment from analysts, the business media and the gossip sheets; some, for example Richard Branson in the UK and Bill Gates in the US, have become celebrities. Some have become important players whose advice is sought by governments, and some pontificate at international

(Continued)

(Continued)

economic forums. A specialized market has arisen for such people. They are induced to take on the responsibilities by very large salaries, substantial bonuses and extensive stock options, as well as guaranteed redundancy/pension rights. Personality, image, dynamism and charisma are now the attributes that are seen to be the key criteria in selecting a leader. (Mangham, 2004: 49–51)

However, although the cult of the individual, flamboyant leader is still alive, Mangham predicts that interest in the long-term growth of companies will become fashionable once more, and consequently, there will be a return to a measured style of business leadership at the top of our organizations. There may well be, he proposes, a return to 'managers' rather than 'leaders'!

So in the context of management development, what are the implications of saying that managers are one thing and leaders another? It is true that managers are often bureaucratically appointed and thus have a mandate to get things done in their part of the organization. It is equally evident that in some cultures, inviolable respect is invested in leaders. But as Raelin (2004) reminds us, managers:

…don't have to be 'hired hands' … who are condemned to a life of unimaginatively carrying out corporate goals or endorsing the status quo. Managers [or indeed, we might add, non-managers] are hardly excluded from leadership. They need to work with their peers, bosses, subordinates, and others, and in this constant interaction, there is opportunity for leadership to emerge from anyone. What might be most impressive about the manager is not taking the reins but supporting others to take them as the situation warrants. … Might our leadership development efforts be better directed toward the role of leadership as a mutual social phenomenon rather than as a position of authority? (Raelin, 2004: 132)

Another perspective from which to challenge the management/leadership divide follows from our introduction of the notion of 'discourse' in Chapter 1. This directs our attention away from ontological debates concerning what management 'is' or 'is not' in relation to leadership (and vice versa). Instead, it directs us towards an examination as to how both terms might serve as discursive or linguistic resources in the construction of social reality, including the social negotiation of identity (see Box 2.2).

Box 2.2   Management competencies or leadership capabilities?

A study by Finch-Lees et al. (2005a) sought to evaluate a programme of management development based around a framework of leadership capability statements within CapCo, a UK multinational. The study included a tracing of the processes by which the capability statements were originated within

(Continued)

(Continued)

the company. It was explained that they came into being as a result of the need to forge a common identity, subsequent to a series of mergers and a major business reorganization. The 'leadership capability' statements themselves were originated and developed using, among other sources, the various 'management competency' profiles existing within the disparate parts of the business prior to the reorganization. No employee was able to offer any convincing explanation as to the difference between a management competency and a leadership capability. Indeed, the two terms were often used interchangeably in their talk. Alvesson and Willmott (2002: 629) point out that 'defining the person directly' (a form of control through the regulation of identity) serves to 'suggest expectations for people who occupy the social space that is thereby defined for them'. In this sense, the very label of leadership capabilities for something that could equally have been called a set of management competencies serves to redefine the person and set correspondingly aspirational expectations. No longer is 'competent management' sufficient. From henceforth, what the company expects is 'capable leadership'. This also serves to differentiate CapCo employees identity-wise from those of other organizations (who might typically employ the vocabulary of management competency) and also by differentiating the 'new' CapCo from previous incarnations of itself (which certainly did employ the vocabulary of management competency).

To conclude, in this book we choose to use the term 'management development' but for the reasons given and unless otherwise stated, we take this to include the development of leaders in an organizational context also.

What do we mean by management development?

From a functionalist perspective, it is generally agreed that management development refers to the process by which individuals improve their capabilities and learn to perform effectively in managerial roles (Baldwin and Padgett, 1993; Mumford, 1997; Thomson et al., 2001). The enduring simplicity of this definition is deceptive, however. Each element attracts controversy. For instance, what exactly is included in the term *development* and how is this to be distinguished from management training, education and learning? Why should we focus exclusively on *managers* and managerial roles? What is meant by effective *performance* and how is this to be interpreted and measured? What other motives or interests does such a unitarist definition obscure?

What is distinctive about management development?

In a study of four European countries, nearly 500 managers were asked the question: 'What was your most developmental experience last year?' These are some of their responses: 'Being given the responsibility to implement redundancies; setting up a new business unit; having to grapple with an ambiguous management strategy; coping with the loss of an excellent colleague; opening an office in a new country; involvement in an industry think-tank; managing a multi-racial work group' (Tamkin et al., 2006). Do these examples constitute training, education, development, learning or all four?

Management development and management training

Training and development tend to go hand in hand in organizational terminology and are difficult to disentangle at a practical level. However, they arise from distinct theoretical perspectives. According to Warr (2002) in the UK and Laird (1985) in the USA, training refers to job-specific skills improvement in a current job role and is associated with the traditional, stable and long-term psychological contract (Rousseau, 1995). Here the onus rests with the employer to train their workforce and address their skills gaps. Training is a widely researched area within occupational and organizational psychology because the instruction and acquisition of job-specific skills is seen as crucial to both organizational and individual effectiveness (Goldstein, 1993). To illustrate, some studies have focused on the impact of training at the individual level, showing that training results in enhanced learning, increased motivation and positive work attitudes (Tannenbaum and Yukl, 1991; Colquitt et al., 2000). Other studies have pointed to the important role of a supportive environment to facilitate the effective transfer of learning (Rouiller and Goldstein, 1993; Tracey and Hinkin, 2001). Because training is job-specific, it generally relies on a predictivist perspective, which views jobs as relatively stable to which certain skills need to be matched. By contrast, the wider-ranging objectives of development invoke a more mutual perspective. Here the organization is seeking to cultivate leadership talent and the manager is taking increasing responsibility for engaging in life-long learning and possibly developing multiple careers. This has resulted in a growing body of research on employee and management development, which has sprung from a range of theoretical orientations, such as organizational and individual competence, adult learning and the efficacy of different off-the-job and on-the-job development approaches. For all this, we still know little about the effects of a diverse range of development activities, such as development centres, developmental appraisals, multi-source feedback, coaching and mentoring on individuals and organizations (McDowell, 2005). Clearly, the fields of management training and management development, while different in emphasis, overlap considerably.

Management development and management education

Another sister discipline to management development is that of management education. Fox (1997) writes of two contrasting approaches to the development of managers that have emerged since the 1960s. The first is management education, which is largely provided by university and management schools. As such it is subject to the critical rigours of the wider academic and research community. The second is management development driven more by market mechanisms. This is a subset of human resource development (HRD) and largely provided by the private sector in the form of in-house training and development and/or assisted by freelance consultants and training agencies. Of the two, management education tends to be more theoretical, emphasizing a body of knowledge in the academic disciplines relevant to management and is predominantly delivered by classroom and distance learning methods. Individuals usually exercise a good deal of discretion over which courses to pursue. By contrast, management development tends to be more practitioner focused, aimed at developing personal knowledge and a repertoire of skills. Although this may involve classroom tuition, the range of methods for developing managers is far more diverse.

Nevertheless, there has been a blurring of boundaries between management education and management development, certainly in the USA and Western Europe. Several factors have prompted this (Fox, 1997; Latham and Seijts, 1998). For example, there has been a growing acceptance, from the 1980s onwards, of business and management studies as a mainstream subject within the university curriculum. The same period has also witnessed the growth in the postgraduate and post-experience market for Masters-level courses, which has required management schools to move closer to corporate expectations in terms of style and syllabus. These two factors have increased the number of academically qualified managers who in turn expect management development practitioners to be appropriately qualified. Fox also refers to the demand for new Masters degrees from independent consultants (especially in areas like training and development, management development, HRD and change management) wishing to maintain their client credibility and professionalism in an ever more competitive market place. Alongside this, more university faculties are offering bespoke consultancy, executive programmes and virtual learning partnerships with private and public sector organizations. Corporate universities, with their concern for high-quality tuition, tailored learning and corporate consonance, are perhaps an epitome of this convergence between management education and development (Paton et al., 2004).

Management development and management learning

A third discipline of relevance to management development is management learning. This has been characterized as a new disciplinary area of knowledge and practice, which is both a subject area and a research community (Fox, 1997). It encompasses management education, training and HRD, as well as informal managing and learning processes. This perspective is helpful in highlighting that 'formal education and development activities are merely the tip of a learning iceberg' (Fox, 1997: 25). It shifts the focus away from a set of practices to be learnt, what Lave and Wenger (1991) term intentional instruction, to understanding the processes by which managers (and indeed, people generally) learn. Management learning also emphasizes the role of the group in learning. This is something which an individualized approach to management education and development often overlooks. By removing individuals from the fabric of their everyday working-learning contexts, off-the-job training maroons them from the very communities of practice which provide such a rich source of experimentation, reflection and learning in the workplace. Viewing management development through the prism of management learning also alerts us to wider institutional, cultural and political cross-currents which influence the definition and formation of management capabilities in a given regional context or knowledge domain.

So while the primary focus of this book is upon the training and development of managers as a corporate activity, understanding the way management development is undertaken and evaluated at an organizational level will necessarily invoke research from other arenas of management learning (Easterby-Smith and Thorpe, 1997). For example, local training delivery cannot be divorced from wider institutional factors like national policies of skill formation and government intervention (policy-education level). The design of firm-level management development will be influenced by industry or sector-specific qualifications' structures (policy-corporate level) and informed by the fruits of research in the fields of training methods, transfer of learning, training and the like (operations-education level). Easterby-Smith and Thorpe conclude that the overall coverage of research in the various dimensions of management learning is 'variable' and 'thin' (1997: 50). Sponsors, whether governments or corporations, have tended to dictate the questions being asked and dominate the methods being used, leading to outputs which bolster establishment thinking. The possible exception is management learning research at the operations-education level: here the focus on the effectiveness of various teaching/learning processes has ushered in more critical and discursive approaches and methodologies. These bring into question the functionalist treatment of management development as an activity that exists primarily, or even exclusively, to build the knowledge, skills and abilities of managers with a view to ultimately enhancing 'performance' at the organizational and the macro-economic levels of analysis.

For the purposes of this book, then, we use management development to refer to the way it is structured, its mode of delivery and its underlying morality.

By *structure* we refer to the means by which organizations devise strategies and establish internal systems for developing managers, including such activities as career planning and arrangements for diagnosis and review of development. Depending on the country concerned, this will be influenced, possibly constrained, by sectoral, professional and governmental policies.

The *delivery* dimension concerns the actual methods used for developing managers, whether formal or informal, whether on-the-job or off-the-job, whether internally or externally delivered. Whereas development of managers is the focus, we take this to largely incorporate management training, to overlap considerably with management education and to be located within the wider domains of management learning (see Figure 2.1). This figure also reminds us that management development is often a key element of wider organizational learning (Starkey, 1996) and organization development (OD) interventions (Oswick and Grant, 1996).

The *moral* dimension is far more implicit. It refers to the capacity for management development to simultaneously promote diversity and discrimination, empowerment and exploitation, inclusion and marginalization.

Although we locate management development in this way we are not discounting a good deal of management learning which takes place incidentally, experientially and/or beyond the boundaries of formal and informal development

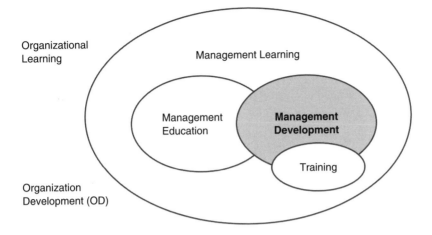

FIGURE 2.1   *The domain of management development*

arranged by the organization. Nor do we imply that training and development activities automatically result in an organizationally, or even personally, productive learning experience. Indeed, these are crucial issues which thread their way through the book.

Why focus on managers?

In one way the task of management might be regarded as a trivial and inglorious occupation, hardly meriting sustained analysis. The profession of management has a serious identity crisis. Other professions have established national if not international credentials, sophisticated routes for continuous professional development, powerful lobbies for policy-making and assessment processes for monitoring quality, standards and accreditation in their respective fields. 'Management' struggles on all these fronts. In the UK, for instance, the last 20 years have seen a succession of ambitious attempts to establish a coherent and credible national approach to improving management and leadership capability. None appear to have had an enduring impact. There is a similar though not identical story in the rest of Europe. European Union (EU) environments are increasingly influenced by a series of general directives on academic and professional recognition; to date, management education and development has remained largely outside this regulatory framework. Especially pressing is the perceived need to create future accreditation mechanisms for management practice for present and aspiring member states, in a manner which supports cultural diversity, subsidiarity and market transparency.

Yet, despite this identity crisis, it could be argued that managers are a pivotal part of the workforce. Let's briefly consider three examples.

Managers as brokers of knowledge. Broadly speaking, intellectual capital refers to the way an enterprise acquires, creates and utilizes specialist knowledge and expertise. One challenge for managers is to make such tacit knowledge meaningful.

Astute management development can help. Perhaps by exploring the necessary skills to systematize and facilitate knowledge-sharing behaviours, by creating conditions of trust for this to happen and by building communities of practice where diversity is celebrated, not ignored, and where non-conformity is valued, not penalized.

Managers as lynchpins of learning. If management can be learned, can learning be managed? A related pivotal role for managers is to help construct a meaningful learning environment around them. Some international firms use their multicultural environment as a growth opportunity. For instance, they plan strategic secondments to promote learning, especially between different countries, areas of technology and between functions such as R&D and marketing, to help their staff to understand the organization from a multiplicity of cultural and functional perspectives.

Managers as makers of meaning. The character and morality of the employee have always been central concerns of managers as they seek to govern and structure organizational life. Thus, under the banner of management development, such 'tools' as ability tests, assessment centres, performance-based reviews, competency-based development programmes may be enlisted. Despite the claims of organizational initiatives to be about improving efficiency, interventions like these often studiously ignore certain key elements of organizational structure and process – the nature and role of power, of conflicts, of exploitation, of difference (Townley, 1994; Bartram, 2005). This, of course, places invidious demands upon middle managers. They may be uneasy about the role cast for them as managers of (new) meaning, but find themselves unable to resist or contradict the rhetoric they find themselves part of. Potentially, management development has a role here to facilitate debate and critiques of 'the way we do things around here'. This calls for courage because of the way senior teams look to such training programmes as the means to usher in, exemplify and legitimize a new cultural order (Kamoche, 2000).

As brokers of knowledge, as lynchpins of learning, as makers of meaning, managers represent a key constituency and their sustained development comprises an activity of supreme significance.

What is 'effective performance'?

The last part of our working definition is that management development will enable individuals to 'perform effectively' in their managerial roles. When presented with a management development activity most of us would have a clear picture of successful outcomes.

Reflection point

Consider a development activity in which you have been involved or one which you have observed recently. What were the expected outcomes? What, for you, were the real benefits, if any? Who were the real 'winners' and were there any 'losers'?

The discussion so far has emphasized that it is easy to presume our personal success criteria will be shared by others (see Rees and Garnsey, 2003). In particular, due to their dominant position in organizations, structurally, ideologically and gender-wise, top teams have a way of galvanizing opinion about the value of a given development intervention around their own interests and drowning out contrary views. But there is a variety of stakeholders: participants, their subordinates, peers and line managers (all of whom will be members of either majority or minority groupings), human resources (HR) professionals, senior managers, business planners, external consultants and government funding agencies. Each has a different interest in, influence over and ownership of, training and development interventions (Garavan et al., 1998; Mabey et al., 1998: 380). Indeed, given the actors involved, the reputations at stake, the budget invested and the proximity of most management development activity to the power nexus of the organization, it is no wonder that it remains one of the most contested of human resource interventions.

Burgoyne and Jackson (1997) discuss the example of a competency-based leadership programme, describing how hierarchically defined stakeholders might support or block the programme for contrasting and congruent reasons. This reminds us that, depending on the particular management development activity, a varying constellation of constituencies will coalesce around a particular issue or group of issues, each with different objectives in mind. 'Different factions can support the same action for entirely different reasons. Support for a particular initiative can be garnered from a plurality of purposes and, therefore, does not have to conform to the same unitarist definition of its purpose' (1997: 63).

Certainly this begins to explain how the very same management development intervention can come to be evaluated quite differently by a range of actors. What it possibly overestimates is the freedom with which these differing views can be expressed and achieve currency. As discussed in the previous section, the degree to which such constituencies are free to act, intervene and shape outcomes will be subject to the prevailing discourse.

Who are managers?

So far we have been talking about managers in the context of development as though they represent a commonly understood, circumscribed and homogeneous group of employees. This is clearly not the case.

Historical conceptions of what it means to manage

In the same way that the definition of management development is not self-evident, neither is the notion of management itself. The roots of the concept are revealing. The French verb *ménager* connotes the comparatively 'humble' role of housekeeping (Grey, 1999), the Italian term *menaggiare* refers to the idea of handling or training horses (Willmott, 1997) and the original Latin word *manus* means a 'hired hand' (Raelin, 2004). The term 'manager' was later extended to war and to a general sense of taking control, taking charge and directing. As Willmott observes, this semantic root is instructive because it conveys 'the social divisiveness of management as a contradictory process – a process in which a person simultaneously takes responsibility for and seeks to control a valuable, yet wilful and potentially resistant resource' (1997: 163). This social division of labour, he argues, is neither universal nor inevitable, but owes its existence to historical and political processes through which managerial work comes to be defined and ascribed to a privileged social group. Grey (1999) also alludes to the distinction between management as an activity and management as a (privileged) category of person. Several writers, keen to become liberated from such modes of colonialist discourse and speech, whether this occurred in the distant past or continues in the present, have critiqued the Western/non-Western divide in management thinking (see Box 2.3).

Box 2.3   Colonialism in management thinking

Colonial theories cast management as a distinctly Western concept. A clear exponent, according to Frenkel and Shenhav (2006: 867), is Drucker, who in his early work argues that management 'is not only a salient product of Western thought, it is also one of the factors that distinguishes the West from other civilizations, and accounts for the West's economic and social superiority'. Like many other 'one best way' theorists, Drucker sees 'other' cultures as exotic and inferior, identifying universalism with Westernization.

Postcolonial theories point out the ethnocentric bias of management practices. Because such ideas were and are shaped in a colonial context, 'they define the West directly or indirectly as modern, rational, and homogeneous, whereas the "other" (the "East", the "Third World", the "native", and the "ethnic") is perceived as less progressive and rational. ... Much like the "classic" colonial project, the neo-colonial project of Americanization meant the introduction of a colonial productivity discourse and its practices in an attempt to bolster and legitimize a cultural and economic hegemony around the globe' (Frenkel and Shenhav, 2003: 1540, 2).

Hybrid theories are a particular stream of postcolonial research which has sought to demonstrate that the binary distinction between Western and non-Western (whether Orientalism or any other) is not sustainable. Rather, it is argued, management discourse should be seen as a hybrid product of the colonial encounter. 'A non-binary epistemology suggests collapsing the boundary between West and non-West and allowing a hybridity to filter in, without denying the asymmetrical power relations between them. From a non-binary perspective we need to show, therefore, how Western and non-Western experiences (and representations) are inseparable; and how binary perspectives may purify the colonial practice and mask its hybrid history. We submit that the binary distinction between the West and the Orient employed by organization and management theorists often masks the hybridity of their origins' (Frenkel and Shenhav, 2006: 860).

What are the implications of this critique for management development? First, it encourages us to explore historical and cultural conceptualizations of who managers are, what they do and how, therefore, they can best be developed. This we consider in a moment.

Second, it alerts us to the way management development activities, perhaps more potently than most other HR practices, can serve to legitimize established priorities and values in the enterprise concerned. Deetz (1985: 127) refers to *legitimation* as the process by which decisions and actions that distort communication are rationalized by invoking 'higher-order explanatory devices'. So, for example, the need for a leadership programme might be justified in relation to a set of core competencies for aspiring managers to become more results-oriented and customer-aware. Quite apart from the potential contradiction in behaviour and psychological stress these two goals may induce for the individual manager, the point about legitimation is that the competency framework becomes an explanatory device and remains beyond examination or question. In a similar vein, Frost (1987) describes *socialization* as a mechanism of learning and orientation that directs and shapes desired attitudes, behaviours and interpretative schemes of some players to the benefit of others. Most of us can identify with this dimension of management development, which is encountered most vividly when newcomers arrive at an organization. Whether explicitly in the guise of training programmes or more subtly in the form of mentoring, buddying and modelling, we discover what is acceptable, tolerated, overlooked and outlawed (Preston and Hart, 1997; Eriksson-Zetterquist, 2002).

Third, and following on directly from the idea that managerial knowledge is historically sectioned and situated, we note that management might also be regarded as a predominantly masculine and Western form of constructed knowledge, or discourse. Since management development is a prime diffuser of such knowledge, its ability to promote diversity must be seen as suspect. We take up these issues more fully in Chapter 9.

Cultural views of what a manager should do and be

The North American model of management has been traced back, not uncontroversially, to the frontier mentality of the early settlers (Prasad, 1997). By contrast, the attributes necessary for senior management and leadership in South East Asia include patience, sincerity, honesty, consensus, flexibility and a willingness to learn. This finding leads van der Boon (2003: 141) to conclude that in the Asian business environment, the 'best man for the job is a woman', noting that women hold key management and political positions, particularly in the Philippines, Malaysia, Thailand and Singapore. Meanwhile, leadership and management in Japan are 'predicated on power and knowledge relations in which the "common instinct" that is generated by long-term interaction amongst insiders guides practice with an elegant simplicity (*wabi-shabi*) that is not commensurate with precious displays of individualism and Anglo-Saxon models of leadership' (Ray et al., 2004: 325).

Even to talk about European models glosses over important differences. For example, while British managers may emphasize the need for communication and interpersonal skills and see the organization primarily as a network of relationships demanding negotiation, influencing skills and image promotion, German managers may be more likely to emphasize individual creativity and to see the organization as based on competence, rationality, knowledge and technical expertise. In contrast, French managers may emphasize the importance of being recognized as 'high potential' and see the organization as based on power, authority and political trade-offs (Laurent, 1986).

Attitudes towards management are naturally forged from political processes and cultural values. For example, Hofstede (1980) describes Turkey as being 'medium high' on the uncertainty avoidance index. He describes how young democracies (which he defines as being those which have developed their forms of government since the First World War, such as Turkey) tend to show higher uncertainty avoidance than older democracies. This notion fits with Ataturk's reforms, which coincided with a Turkish republic salvaged out of the Ottoman Empire in the years following the First World War. A Romanized alphabet, Western dress, and a society no longer founded on religion but on secular values, were among the sweeping changes that patriotic, forward-thinking Turks were expected to embrace. Yet traditional Turkish values, especially around status, remain (see Box 2.4).

Box 2.4   Turkish conceptions of management

The cultural syndrome of status identity embodies the notion that cultural members are stratified into hierarchies or groups based on culturally relevant information. Turkish organizations are distinguished by central decision-making, highly personalized, strong leadership, and limited delegation (Ronen, 1986), together with steep hierarchies indicating the subordination of employees to their leaders; yet also described as 'families' (Trompenaars and Hampden-Turner, 1998). Turkish leaders are characterized by paternalistic attributes (Kanungo and Aycan, 1997). Within this notion of hierarchy versus egalitarianism, Brett and Okumura (1998) inform us, hierarchical cultures like Turkey's favour differential social status, implying distributions of power. Within hierarchical cultures lower-status individuals are respectful and defer to higher-status individuals. Kanungo and Aycan (1997) describe how this status identity syndrome manifests itself in the Turkish context with paternalistic leaders demonstrating parental consideration towards their subordinates (from Ashford, 2005).

This glimpse into the way managers manage in one culture suggests that different countries will have distinctive ways of identifying, grooming and developing their managers. This is partly driven by educational priorities, corporate strategies, historical legacies and cultural values.

What is needed to deepen our understanding of management development?

So far in this chapter we have used a functionalist definition to clarify what is commonly meant by the term 'management development'. But we have also critiqued such a definition from a variety of alternative perspectives. We prefer not to see managers and leaders as distinct entities, but rather to see them on a continuum, with any responsible employee potentially able to operate as a manager and exercise leadership as circumstances demand. We have proposed that to focus on development does not preclude reference to related fields of management learning, education and training, because the boundaries between these domains are relatively permeable anyway. We have also suggested that an elastic use of the term 'manager' is called for, partly because being a 'manager' has quite different cultural connotations in different parts of the world, and in particular, it is helpful not to be constrained by the politico-historical undertones peculiar to the West. For a number of reasons, we believe that managers play a pivotal role in organizations and that a systematic, critical study of the way they are trained and developed is overdue. Finally, we have noted that despite being a hot topic for governments, enterprises and individual managers alike, much remains to be discovered about how and why managers are developed or indeed how and why they even exist (or are socially constructed) as a distinct employee category. In the first chapter we made the case for a multi-discourse approach to the study of management development. Here in the final section we outline four further principles which we believe should guide such an exploration. In order to chart the territory of management development more comprehensively, we propose that such an analysis needs to be international, meso-level, diversity-sensitive and empirically-driven.

International

It is clear that any study of the ways managers and leaders are developed would benefit from an international approach. Not only does this hopefully minimize (if not avoid) ethnocentric bias and assumptions, it also offers the possibility of rich, cross-cultural insights. It might be argued that although governments in different countries pursue quite different goals in their early education systems (Geppert et al., 2002) and adopt varying levels of corporate intervention at a policy level (Noble, 1997), there is a general trend towards regarding management development as market-driven. Globalization and the increasing reach of multinationals are creating common expectations of managers across the world, and corporate cultures are arguably becoming more influential than national cultures. For example, having examined the particular historical emphases of management models in Germany, France, Japan, the UK and the USA, Thomson et al. (2001: 61) note that:

> the general trends are similar. All the models expect something from the individual manager in terms of self-development over and above what might be done by the organisation. All five countries favour development beyond the initial education and induction; in Germany and Japan it is

more formalised, especially in the large companies, than in France, the United States, and Britain. All the countries have problems with management development in small businesses...

But this idea of convergence in the realm of management development, fuelled by the inexorable diffusion of best-practices, has been questioned (Marchington and Grugulis, 2000), particularly where it is assumed that global HR practices are inevitably converging on a US model (Gooderham and Brewster, 2003). Based on extensive survey data gathered over the last decade, Brewster et al. (2004) reach a more nuanced conclusion concerning 23 countries in Europe. They point to directional convergence of HR practices, with increasing training and development as one example of a generic trend. However, they differentiate this from final convergence, noting that there is very little evidence that countries are becoming more alike in the way they manage their human resources. If this is true in the relatively homogeneous arena of the European Community, it is even more starkly the case when we consider approaches to developing managers and leaders in other continents (see Box 2.5).

Box 2.5   Developing managers in China

To understand the nature of management development within Asia, it is important to consider the historical and cultural influences that have formed the system of personnel practices used to ensure the availability of qualified employees for key positions. For countries like Singapore and China, where there is a deep collectivist orientation influenced by Confucian values, the evolution of management development has been heavily guided by planned economies controlled by the respective governments. As Singapore became a self-ruled country under the influence of Lee Kuan Yew and as China emerged after the death of Chairman Mao Zedong in 1976, these governments have aggressively focused on how to ensure adequate managers to support the success of these societies.

The implications on the planned economy within China can be most clearly evidenced through the growth of MBA programmes which are relevant as business schools have become increasingly focused on corporate management development (Beeby and Jones, 1997). In China and Singapore, this focus on business schools by the government has had a significant impact on the practice and policies of management development (Wang, 1999). As the graduates of these programmes facilitated the rapid development of joint ventures and high technology with China, these massive corporate transformations profoundly influenced the structures, social processes and individual behaviours within these firms (Tsui-Auch and Lee, 2003). For example, some of the trends reported within management development in China have included a shift from an academic to professional orientation, from general knowledge learning to competency development, from technical orientation to managerial focus, from a common programme to an adaptive curriculum planning and from 'one-shot' training to strategic distributive development (Wang, 1999).

Meso-level

What the example above (Box 2.5) also demonstrates is that to reach an adequate understanding of management development, we need to engage with and seek to integrate different levels of analysis incorporating both individual and contextual factors (Rousseau and House, 1994). This so-called meso-level analysis indicates a desire, particularly by policy-makers, to move beyond the more traditional macro and micro thinking that has dominated organizational analysis in the past. As Evans (2001: 542) puts it: 'Experience has shown that macro level theories are often too abstract and frequently applied to concrete situations with little attention to the mediating processes, while micro level theories tend to ignore the impact of broader structural factors on micro level decision-making settings.' In fact, theorists in the field of international human resource management have been seeking to address such issues for some time (Harzing and Ruysseveldt, 1995). Jackson and Schuler (1995) propose an integrative framework of international HRM in multinational corporations which maps the twin influences of exogenous factors (industry/regional characteristics and country culture) and endogenous factors (structure and orientation of parent company and competitive strategy) upon human resource management issues, functions and policies. Subsequent attempts have been made to simplify this framework (De Cieri and Dowling, 1999). However, such accounts tend to focus entirely on the multinational corporate experience and lack worked examples. In this book we apply meso-level thinking as an analytic tool for tracing the intricate web of institutional, cultural, structural, organizational and micro-political/agential factors which shape the priority, content, impact and significance of development activities in different parts of the world.

Diversity-sensitive

The notion of diversity management rose rapidly to prominence during the 1990s and continues to gather momentum today. We are now at a point where many organizations devote significant resources aimed (ostensibly) at valuing and leveraging diversity to the benefit of both individual and organization. In many cases, this involves the training and development of managers with a view to sensitizing them to the benefits of diversity and then providing them with the apparent wherewithal to 'manage' it. However, diversity-specific interventions will most likely form only a very small part of a typical manager's development experiences. This begs the question as to how *mainstream* forms of management development (being the main focus of this book) fare when it comes to their impact on diversity. We consider such a question to be all the more pertinent, given that most analyses of *management* (let alone management development!), tend implicitly to take a neutral stance when it comes to diversity and inclusion, which is a polite way of saying that they typically ignore such issues altogether.

At this juncture, we should be clear as to exactly what we might mean when we refer to diversity. This is less straightforward than it may seem. Not only is there much controversy on the issue, certainly within academic circles, but any particular definition will have political consequences for the very people that diversity might be expected to impact (Litvin, 1997; Linnehan and Konrad, 1999; Janssens and

Steyaert, 2003). From a practitioner's point of view, however, the typical pragmatic stance is to adopt a notion of diversity based around essentialist forms of group difference, expressed in terms of, for example, age, disability, race, religion, sex and sexual orientation.

There are many indications to suggest that management development frequently struggles to provide a 'level playing field' with regard to difference along such dimensions. In a sense, this should come as no surprise. Indeed, there are powerful theoretical reasons for a degree of scepticism concerning management development's alignment with diversity. The few authors who have explored the origins and evolution of management have found its knowledge and practices to be dominated by influences that are variously: white/Western (Frenkel and Shenhav, 2003); heterosexual (Parker, 2002b); Christian/protestant (Prasad, 1997); able-bodied and hegemonically masculine (Collinson and Hearn, 1994; Kerfoot and Knights, 1998; Grey, 1999; Vieira da Cunha and Pina e Cunha, 2002). And all this despite the overwhelming tendency for management to be represented as a scientific and value-neutral activity (Alvesson and Deetz, 2000). Theoretically, then, if we consider management development to be a prime diffuser of knowledge and practice that is inherently sectional, should we really expect it to provide equality of opportunity for all demographic groups? An emerging body of empirical evidence supports the view that we should not, and we explore this evidence in Chapter 9. As such, management development might usefully be held (at least partly) accountable for the continuing and lamentably low representation of minority groups within the upper echelons of management (EOC, 2005; Singh and Vinnicombe, 2005). However, we do not wish to imply that all management development deserves automatically to be tarred with the same brush on this issue. As such, our approach throughout the book will be to endeavour, wherever possible, to interrogate management development (on both theoretical and empirical grounds) for its alignment with the assumed interests of those that are traditionally underrepresented within the ranks of management.

Empirical

In its early days, the literature of management development attracted more than its share of prescription, with varying degrees of rigour. In the UK we saw national manifestos and critical success factors for management development being proposed (Holland, 1986; Fonda, 1988; Sadler, 1988; Margerison, 1990), along with typologies of effective and less effective approaches to management development from both British (e.g. Burgoyne, 1988; Wille, 1990) and North American authors (e.g. McLagan, 1989). The following decade saw a growth of more empirically based work, focusing on the education sector and the corporate sector at both policy and organization levels. But as dicussed above, this research was variable in quality, tended to have a strong establishment bias and was invariably conducted to make a political point. Where the focus was on development in the workplace, it was usually descriptive. In order to navigate our way around management development, we are presented with an incomplete map. This is evident from Box 2.6, which briefly traces the contours of European research,

Box 2.6   European research on management development

In Europe research into the education and development of managers is less advanced than research into general education and higher level, technical education and training (Nyhan, 1998). Current knowledge on what constitutes good practice in Europe is inadequate in five respects.

- First, it often deals with training generally (without separating out managers) and is uncontextualized, telling us more about the quantity and types of training undertaken than explaining its quality and effects (CVTS, 1994/1997; Larsen, 1994).
- Second, the few previous studies which have focused exclusively on training for managers have tended to examine specific issues, like the development of competences (Winterton and Winterton, 1997), or the usage of training procedures and practices in different countries (Bournois et al., 1994), rather than the overall significance of management development.
- Third, the favoured methodology has been the use of broad-brush surveys (Brewster and Hegewisch, 1994; Gudic, 2001; Brewster et al., 2004) which lack analytical detail. Exceptionally, in-depth case studies of a few organizations have been conducted (e.g. Storey et al., 1997): these are rich in detail but limited to a small range of sectors.
- Fourth, there have been several country-specific studies of management development, for example in the UK (Thomson et al., 2001); in Ireland (Graham et al., 2000); in Romania (Cseh, 1999); in the New Independent States (ETF, 1997); in Holland (Paauwe and Williams, 2001); as well as non-European studies (e.g. Branine, 1996). Yet cross-national comparative research remains rare.
- Finally, a number of studies have analysed management training and development from an international perspective, but the chosen lens has invariably been that of the multinational corporation (MNC) (Noble, 1997; Tregaskis, 2001).

In many ways, this sets the research agenda and the challenge for this book. We need to move on from descriptive data and prescriptive advice. We need to understand more fully what is happening in the realm of management development by discerning and making more visible the theory/assumptions underlying such policies and practices. To achieve this, what is required is more thorough theorizing and empirical substantiation, preferably in an international setting.

Conclusion

We began this chapter by challenging the dichotomy between management and leadership. We did so by problematizing the essentialist kind of thinking that attributes certain traits or characteristics to managers and others to leaders. Instead, we characterized the divisions between the two notions as discursive or linguistic constructions that can serve a variety of social purposes, not least the differential construction of identity. We then turned our attention to what we will mean by management development as we move through the book. We offered a working definition of the notion, while highlighting and critiquing its functionalist under-pinnings. We then explored the distinctions and overlaps between management development, training, education and learning, before asking ourselves why we should focus on managers at all as opposed to the general organizational popula-tion. We explained our rationale for doing so as being far less to do with elitist or status-oriented concerns. Managers are in our view no more or less important than any other category of employee. However, they frequently find themselves at piv-otal intersections when it comes to brokering knowledge, the diffusion of learning and the manufacture of meaning. We followed this up with a historical exploration of where and how the very notion of management emerged, complementing this with a geographical and cultural analysis of the different meanings it has come to have. We finished the chapter by outlining four overarching principles that will be guiding our exploration of management development as we move through the book. In doing so we align ourselves with Schuler et al. (2002), who call for more qualitative research to study the processes by which international HRM policies (including training and development) evolve, diffuse and become institutionalized. If this can be done in a way which gives equal weight to both macro and micro factors in a given country or region, gives due consideration to issues of diversity, then we will have made real progress in illuminating the arena of management development. As will become clearer, such concerns will come to interpenetrate the multiple discourses (both Grand and meso-level) that we invoke as our analysis proceeds. It is to our four Grand Discourses of management development that we now turn as we move into Part 2 of the book.

Summary

- For a number of reasons, distinctions between leaders and managers (and their development) can be critically challenged. Their substance may lie far more in their rhetorical or discursive effects than in any ontological consistency.
- Management training, management education and management learn-ing are separate fields of enquiry to that of management development but, in practice, the boundaries are becoming increasingly blurred.
- The label 'manager' varies widely in its meaning according to context and, certainly in the West, comes with a good deal of historical baggage.
- Whatever the cultural and historical expectations of what managers should do, they play a pivotal role in organizations and their develop-ment needs to be taken seriously.
- In research terms, the field of management development is relatively immature and would benefit from cross-national, meso-level and multi-discourse analysis.

Part II

Grand Discourses of management development

A key contention of this book is that a fuller understanding of management development is achieved by invoking different/competing discourses (Alvesson and Deetz, 2000). To date, much research in the field has been atheoretical and acontextual. Collectively, studies seeking to theorize management development have drawn on a diverse range of approaches but, individually, each has tended to utilize a favoured methodology, remaining firmly rooted in a single frame, discourse or paradigm. This has led to a fragmented picture, a confusing set of findings and indistinct guidance for those responsible for developing managers. So what particular contribution might a multi-discourse approach to management development bring and to what extent can different discourses be reconciled to inform reflexive practice? Later, in Part 3 of the book, we examine three pertinent meso-discourses to management development: those of best-practice, institutionalism and diversity. First, in the following four chapters, we invoke and assess the contribution of the four Grand Discourses briefly introduced in Chapter 1.

Common-sense logic tells us that the careful development of managers is likely to have a positive influence upon individual capability and organizational performance. Work within the *functionalist Discourse* has begun to identify those variables which facilitate and those which frustrate such impact. Employing both quantitative and qualitative research designs, positivist research therefore has its value in delineating more carefully the linkages between activities and outcomes with the intent of creating a coherent, robust model of management development. However, there are other, equally compelling stories to tell.

The *constructivist Discourse* is well suited to gaining insights concerning the more perplexing, local and emergent processes associated with management development interventions. The approach allows us to privilege participant responses and reflections by attending to their feelings, intuitions and the meanings they ascribe to development activities.

The *dialogic Discourse* helps draw attention to the multiple voices, the local politics and the language that surround management development activities. For example, this perspective problematizes 'self-evident' notions of performance improvement by pointing out that ways of conceptualizing success will be highly contested, fragmented and fragile. And at a time when organization leaders often enlist management development programmes to transmit cultural values and convey corporate 'messages', it is instructive to note from the dialogic that the discursive practices associated with management development help to construct the manager's identity.

Meanwhile the *critical Discourse* brings yet another perspective. For instance, it shows how management development can provide organizations with a means of maintaining order, predictability and control. Its concern with the way corporate orthodoxy prevails helps focus on the way the interests of minority groups may be marginalized. As a domain, management development is concerned with knowledge and power; as an activity, it is usually tied closely to the decision-making nexus of the organization; as a tool, it remains a potent means for regulating employees (or, alternatively, for usurping the status quo and promoting partisan rights).

3

Management development: measurement and performance

'I doubt very much', the old man said, 'if we shall ever learn what significance those numbers may hold.'

It was not, heaven knows, an easy admission for the old man to make. The application of creative intelligence to a problem, the finding of a solution at once dogged, elegant, and wild, this had always seemed to him to be the essential business of human beings – the discovery of sense and causality amid the false leads, the noise, the trackless brambles of life. (Michael Chabon, The Final Solution, *2006: 125)*

After reading this chapter you will be able to:

- Identify the guiding theories of management development which inform the functionalist Discourse
- Discuss some studies which constitute the research domain of the functionalist management development Discourse
- Give an evidenced-based view on the proposition that management development improves organizational performance
- Explain the difficulties associated with evaluating the outcomes of management development
- Assess the strengths and weaknesses of the functionalist management development Discourse

Introduction

Of all the episodes of human resource management (HRM), activities designed to develop managers and leaders are those that probably incorporate the multiple aspirations of organizational endeavour most quintessentially. Take the example of a newly devised middle-manager development programme. Organizational leaders pin their hopes on the new programme to equip a cadre of managers for a period of growth and expansion. Those HR specialists designing and delivering the training relish the opportunity to make a strategic contribution and anticipate ensuing kudos. Individuals participate in the developmental experience as an opportunity to enhance their career portfolio and future employability. Their line managers and immediate colleagues anticipate the positive contribution of newly-won skills and energy. Meanwhile governments, training agencies and professional institutes do what they can to facilitate effective outcomes at national, sectoral and organizational levels (ranging from direct intervention, incentive and accreditation schemes to consultancy support). The collective burden of expectation for management development programmes and activities to 'deliver' is huge. And this takes us to the core of the functionalist Discourse: a pre-occupation with measuring management development. The thinking within this Discourse is based upon a simple premise that well-conceived and well-designed training and development will enhance leadership and managerial capability which will, in turn, lead to improvements in organizational and, by consequence, national competitiveness. How substantial is this rarely questioned premise? In this chapter we examine the tenets of the functionalist Discourse in relation to management development. We do this, first, by assessing the key theories which drive functionalist thinking and then weighing the evidence concerning the tangible impact of management development. Along the way we consider why the pressure to justify its existence is so intense and outline a number of intrinsic difficulties associated with evaluating management development.

Functionalist studies

The functionalist Discourse refers to those studies that are predominantly oriented towards consensus and dualism (see Chapter 1, Box 1.9). Research concepts are treated as objectively existing entities with qualities of constancy and permanence; the primary goal is that of organizational productivity and efficiency. Most usually associated with this Discourse are positivist studies (Johnson and Duberley, 2000). These tend to be primarily quantitative in nature and concerned with testing theoretically grounded hypotheses in the search for regular, generalizable relationships between carefully defined variables. However, many qualitative studies can also be considered functionalist to the extent that they treat research concepts as being largely objective in meaning, broadly stable in nature and consensus-oriented in their pursuit of progress and emancipation. Finally, language within functionalist studies is typically expected to fulfil the 'mirror-like' role of directly representing or reflecting an underlying objective and singular reality (Oswick and Grant, 1996).

Metaphor and the role of management development

Although the term may not be familiar to the majority of managers, the functionalist Discourse is the one that they will identify with most readily, because it concerns the means–end calculation of what needs to be done by an organization to become more efficient and profitable. With regard to developing managers and leaders, an appropriate metaphor is one of a tool-kit, using albeit fairly sophisticated tools designed to deal with complex and subtle problems (see Table 1.1, page 23). Either due to malfunction or new conditions, development tools are required to tinker with, or radically upgrade, the individual and the organization such that they can run at optimum efficiency again (see Box 3.1).

Box 3.1   Individuals and organizations as mechanisms

Various authors invoke similar imagery as a way of addressing the development needs of individuals and organizations:

> 'once the human body became conceptualized as a machine, it was thereafter opened up to mechanical rearrangement and tuning ...' (Burrell, 1998: 19)

> 'As an approach to understanding management [the competencies approach] ... is informed by a mechanical rationale based on the assumption that understanding human performance involves "taking it apart", analysing its basic constituents and then reassembling it.' (Townley, 1994: 61)

> 'The integrated pattern of behaviour of one individual who is perceived to be effective is dissected, whose fragmented attributes are used as a basis for building up the components of the "ideal" person for the job.' (Rees and Garnsey, 2003: 567)

This approach assumes that an 'ideal state' exists in the heads of those initiating and commissioning the development. At its most authentic, the project of enhancement will proceed in a way which deals with current flaws and makes the most of existing strengths, with the intention of creating necessary transformation. However, there is always the danger that the choice of 'tools' will be prompted by fads and fashions. When this happens it is unlikely to deal with real weaknesses and/or to have enduring value. The assumptions underpinning this Discourse are as follows:

- Organizations primarily exist to accomplish strategic goals and objectives.
- In organizations, rationality should prevail over personal preferences and external pressures.
- Performance gaps arise because of a lack of fit between an organization's structure/skill-base and its environment.
- Management development is a primary means to address these gaps and achieve this fit.
- The identification of development needs and delivery methods can be determined in a reasonably non-contestable manner.
- It is desirable to evaluate the performance impact of a management development intervention.

The dualistic nature of this Discourse is revealed by the notion that management training needs can be determined and expressed in a quasi-scientific manner. This may be via graded training objectives and competency classifications; based upon this, it is proposed that subsequent training/learning can be guided by well-defined personal development plans, assessment criteria, performance ratings and the like. All this makes the ontological assumption that there is an objectively definable arena of desirable management development (knowledge, skills, attitudes) which is separate from 'the developing manager'. As we shall see later, this is a dualism which the dialogic, as well as the constructivist Discourse, would seek to collapse. The consensual nature of the functionalist Discourse arises from the fact that such aspirations and definitions of knowledge-gain, skills-acquisition and attitude-shift are deemed to be mutually beneficial for employer and employee alike. As such, it also follows that quantifiable degrees of success (or failure) should be measured in an equally objective manner.

Theories informing the functionalist Discourse of management development

The overriding consideration of the functionalist Discourse is organizational performance. So when applied to management development activities the key questions concern how to motivate, how to develop, how to retain necessary expertise, how to cultivate talent in a way which maximizes the productivity of the firm (Swanson, 2001). Typically, such development activities will be structured, utilizing formal techniques and orchestrated by the organization. A number of theories inform this endeavour. *Intellectual capital theory* accords value-creating importance to human capital (the knowledge, skills, talents and creativity of staff), structural capital (patents, trade secrets, embedded know-how) and social capital, which refers to the way people work together to share knowledge and skills (Stewart, 1997). This has immediate implications for the way an organization structures the development of its managers and future leaders. For instance, is human capital increased by purchasing prized skills in the market or by creating it internally via education or on-the-job training? Is structural capital best leveraged by career systems which reward those who are generous with ideas or do the current organization structure and HR policy encourage talent hoarding? Recognizing the value of social capital will probably lead an organization to invest in cross-functional and cross-hierarchical development activities to facilitate the sharing of tacit knowledge.

Although rarely articulated as such and certainly not confined to the functionalist Discourse, *institutional theory* nevertheless underpins a good deal of normative thinking and action when it comes to management development. Here, the rationality is less about top-down initiatives to address diagnosed skills gaps. It is more about the socially constructed environment, both internal and external, which leads organizations to seek legitimacy and acceptance from multiple stakeholders. For instance, there is a persistent belief that globalization and the emergence of a new knowledge-based economy require the promotion of training and management development. This is illustrated by the Enterprise Management Modernization Programme in China (Branine, 2005) and significant investment in human capital as promoted by the European Commission (2000) (see Box 3.2).

Box 3.2   Institutional pressures to instigate management development

Researchers propose that one reason for the productivity gap in the UK is that its managers are not, on average, up to the quality of their main competitors. This is in part because they are inadequately qualified and with less effective levels of training and education (Campbell, 2002) but is also attributed to insufficient training in 'best-practice' management techniques (Nickell and Van Reenen, 2002). Others indicate that it is only at the level of intermediate qualifications that Britain lags behind European competitors (O'Mahoney and de Boer, 2002), and argue that management capability in the UK and particularly the willingness to adopt 'modern management techniques', is more a consequence, than a creator, of organizational and national performance (Porter, 2003). Despite such counter-evidence, the institutional pressure to invest in management development is strong. Since 2001, the UK government, for example, has focused intensively on strengthening its leadership capabilities as a key aspect of its modernization agenda (Alimo-Metcalfe and Alban-Metcalfe, 2004), mandating the use of 360-degree feedback across a number of departments. It is estimated that the government is investing some £25 million *per annum* on developing its leadership cadre (Cabinet Office, 2005). All mainstream UK government departments now offer external executive coaching support to their senior civil servants as an integral part of their management development programmes.

It is not unlikely that much of this costly investment in senior executive development is driven as much by a persuasive, yet highly speculative, logic which links managerial capability to economic performance as it is by a tailored and careful diagnostic needs assessment of future leadership requirements. It also tends to reduce the calculation to commercial benefits, with little attention being paid to other criteria of success, like individual well–being, social and cultural capital, ecological outcomes and so on. Given the importance of the institutional discourse, we return to consider its influence upon management development in Chapter 8.

Another theory which emphasizes the need for designing structures to fit an organization's environment is *open systems theory*. Again, this has direct relevance to management development policy. From a systems perspective 'skills and abilities are treated as inputs from the environment; employee behaviours are treated as a throughput; and employee satisfaction and performance are treated as outputs' (Jackson and Schuler, 1995: 239). This theory has been widely influential, usually implicitly, in much HRM research. It has also guided attempts to understand training implementation and transfer (Kozlowski and Salas, 1994) and the effectiveness of management development (Garavan et al., 1995; Mabey, 2002). Closely allied to this approach is *contingency theory*. Here, the organization is seen to be responsive to a range of contextual factors, like competitive behaviour, shifting technologies and the external labour market. So, with reference to management development, the argument would be that training systems, by conveying important competencies to staff, are essential resources for aligning organizations to the external environment (Pfeffer, 1993).

In recent years there has been a concerted attempt to demonstrate that HRM systems are strategic assets that enhance organizational performance and therefore value creation. Although often atheoretical, studies in the arena of what we might loosely term *human resource theory*, fall into two categories echoing those already mentioned. First, there are those that seek to demonstrate that HRM systems confer superior performance regardless of the circumstances of the firm, referred to as a 'best-practice' perspective, and, second, those that emphasize contingencies such as the degree to which the firm has aligned its HRM practices with its competitive strategy (Wood, 1999). Also supporting this notion of fit is the *resource-based view* (RBV) of human resources, which highlights the value of nurturing internal talent (Wright and Snell, 1998). This theory underscores the need to retain high performers and to absorb the value of their knowledge, skills and abilities within the organizational routines in order to sustain competitive advantage (Kamoche and Mueller, 1995). From this RBV literature three aspects of organizational fit can be identified: using management development as a means to develop individual potential (rather than just as a means to meet immediate skills gaps) since this helps to create intangible assets which are difficult for competitors to imitate; promoting from within wherever possible in order to cultivate an internal labour market of managerial talent; and, finally, seeking to retain managers over the long term because 'corporate prosperity typically rests in the social architecture that emerges slowly and incrementally over time, and often predates the tenure of the current senior management' (Mueller, 1996: 164).

Having laid bare the roots of research in this area, later in the chapter we move on to consider the fruits, or evidence, arising from studies which have sought to demonstrate the benefits of management development. But, since the functionalist Discourse is preoccupied with performance, we need first to examine the issue of evaluating management development in more detail.

Evaluating management development

As a starting point, we can make the general point that performance improvement, whether at the level of the individual or the organization, is only possible if criteria are established by which that performance can be measured. We should also note that in many organizations those with responsibility for HR practices are coming under increasing duress to justify the cost of those practices and indeed of their own existence:

> On the one hand, CEOs understand the essential strategic value of a skilled, motivated and flexible labor force. On the other hand, the traditional HRM function has not typically been thought of as a strategic asset, and consequently is under pressure to reduce expenses and demonstrate efficiency in the delivery of its services. (Becker and Huselid, 1998: 85)

This leads us to two questions. Why should the effectiveness and efficiency of management development be measured? And secondly, how?

Why measure?

Many organizations face increased environmental factors such as intensified competition, deregulation and, in the public sector, market testing and value-for-money initiatives. Particular targets for cost reduction are resources and activities which do not appear to make a direct operational contribution. Where management development programmes cannot be justified in terms of their monetary value or their contribution to strategic goals, they are likely to be easy targets in any cost reduction exercise. So those responsible for introducing management development are being asked to place a financial value on such practices. Managers with functional responsibility for management development are players in an internal competition for resources: a competition that is conducted in the language of financial contribution (Boudreau and Ramstead, 1997).

Another pressure to evaluate management development policies and practices, not necessarily linked to the profit motive alone, arises from the issues relating to diversity and equal opportunities. Some organizations are attempting to use management development to tackle such discrimination head on (see Box 3.3).

Box 3.3   Using management development to promote diversity

Royal Dutch/Shell is a global organization, operating in 145 countries and employing over 119,000 people worldwide.The company claims to recognize the importance of valuing all employees and maximizing their contribution to the organization. This philosophy sits at the heart of Shell's approach to enhancing performance, and forms one of the Group's 9 Business Principles. The company recently adopted a new global standard on Diversity and Inclusiveness, which sets out the framework for creating a more inclusive workplace culture.

A key objective of this new Standard is to harness the business benefits of having individual strengths, experiences and perspectives at all levels of the company. In 2001, an internal survey at Shell revealed that only 7 per cent of senior executives were female. Based on these results, the company decided to put in place a global approach to actively encourage and assist the rapid development of women's careers within Shell, by giving them the confidence to effectively manage their own personal development.

Putting to one side the questionable assumptions in this approach (see Chapter 9), how can the worth of such management development initiatives be established? Here we briefly discuss two types of evaluation: strategic evaluation, which concerns, among other things, the fit between management development policies and practices and the strategic goals of the organization; and operational evaluation, which concerns how well training and development activities are designed and delivered, either in terms of outcomes or processes.

How to measure strategic value?

What does it mean for management development policies and practices to be aligned with an organization's strategy? Clarity is needed on the following questions:

1   The fit between the goals of the programme/activities and the wider business strategy (external fit) – how well does management development align with the key drivers of success for the organization, and how well does it reinforce messages about strategic goals?
2   The fit between the programme/activities and 'best-practice' principles – for example, how well does management development help the organization build and retain employee commitment, skills and knowledge?
3   The fit between the programme/activities and other management systems and practices (internal fit) – for example, is the management development process integrated with wider performance management policies?

Such issues have generic application. However, the resource-based theory of the firm suggests that the performance benefits of management development will be path–dependent. For example, the success of a customer service strategy calling for high levels of involvement and discretion will depend crucially on the current state of managers' skills, trust relations and the ability to empower their front-line teams. Some organizations use a stakeholder perspective as the basis for the strategic evaluation of management development and wider HR practices. This is based on the notion of the 'balanced scorecard', whereby organizations measure their success with a balanced set of measures that reflect success in satisfying four main perspectives:

- the financial perspective – creating shareholder value
- the customer perspective – satisfaction, retention, market share
- the internal perspective – quality, response time, cost, new product introductions
- the learning and growth perspective – employee skills, motivation and information systems.

It is argued that only by satisfying all four perspectives simultaneously can an organization maintain its capacity to satisfy any single group (see Box 3.4).

Box 3.4   Monitoring the impact of management development at Eastman Kodak

External strategic measures

These evaluate the extent to which HR practices contribute to customer and shareholder satisfaction. Eastman Kodak has used a number of HR-driven processes to target customer and shareholder satisfaction. A programme called 'Champions for Customer Success' sets up opportunities for direct dialogue between manufacturing employees and customers

(Continued)

(Continued)

(e.g. print shops). The goal is to create a learning situation where employees can better understand customers' needs and share best-practice with them in areas such as reducing paper waste, TQM (total quality management), the use of self-managing teams, etc. The intention is to improve customer satisfaction and commitment to Kodak products. Another HR programme has involved changing the bonus system which was formerly an essentially fixed component of compensation each year. Under the new system the bonus is related directly to return on net assets (RONA) for the corporation. The new bonus system was supported by a major communication effort on the part of the HR function to help employees understand RONA and how their own operational area contributes to it. The goal was to produce a change in employee mindset from one of 'entitlement' to one of 'contribution' and focus the whole organization more directly on increasing shareholder satisfaction. The measure of success used by the HR function was change in employee attitudes.

Internal strategic measures

Eastman Kodak have identified three critical organizational capabilities which are essential to the success of their competitive strategy:

- Leadership effectiveness: 360-degree feedback is used to monitor leader effectiveness. It also tracks the diversity of its senior and middle managers in terms of race, gender and nationality.
- Workforce competencies (building customer commitment, market focus, working across boundaries, financial excellence, operational excellence): measured in terms of the number of employees with documented development plans and the number of hours devoted to development. The results of development programmes are measured by participant reaction and planned actions, learning, on-the-job behaviour and business results.
- Performance-based culture is regularly measured through tracking performance commitments and through employee surveys which include questions about management accountability for performance, clarity of performance expectations, adequacy of performance feedback and reward of goal achievement.

Adapted from Yeung and Berman (1997).

This example illustrates the value of: first, having some clearly defined success criteria; second, integrating manager and leader development with other HR policies, such as reward systems, performance tracking and diversity management. It also introduces a dimension frequently overlooked when evaluating management development, that of customer feedback. A potential problem is that these very virtues may lead to a somewhat instrumental approach to the training and development of their management team. Paradoxically, a strategic intervention designed to enhance enterprise and responsiveness to customers *could* lead to goal-bound rigidity and *satisficing* behaviours.

How to measure operational outcomes

Operational measures of management development concern the effectiveness of these practices and the efficiency with which they are delivered.

Reflection point

Consider a recent management development event or activity that you have been involved in. How might the effectiveness of this intervention be evaluated? What aspects of development and learning might be assessed and how valuable is each of these?

A fairly standard way of measuring training interventions in organizations is to track outcomes on four levels (Kirkpatrick, 1958) (see Table 3.1)

In management development, return on investment (ROI) means measuring all the economic returns generated from an investment in a programme or set of activities. These returns are then compared with the true cost of the programme/ activities to determine an average annual rate of return on the investment. All capital assets need to earn a rate of return for the business to make a profit and stay in business. ROI is about judging the investment in management development on similar criteria to other investment in the business. Some returns are relatively easy to measure, such as increase in sales after a sales training programme. Others, such as improvement in customer/employee satisfaction, lower turnover of key management staff and more innovative behaviour, all require conversion of less tangible gains to a monetary amount. Some costs can also be easily accounted for, such as hire of training rooms; others require informed estimates.

It is not surprising that the quest to establish ROI for management development is pursued so energetically. First, it helps to validate training as a business tool: the organization benefits since it becomes more aware of the mechanisms for profitability and the HR department benefits because it is seen as a strategic partner in the business rather than a necessary but non-strategic overhead. Second, employees in the company benefit because the organization validates their personal development and so managers can encourage them to attend training rather than condoning no-shows on training courses due to pressure of work. Finally, it can help to justify the costs incurred in training. This helps HR and training and development (T&D) departments avoid being the victim of cost-cutting in the next economic downturn. If training is seen as one of the levers to achieve revenue growth, then there is no economic sense in reducing training if revenues fall. In fact, ROI can ensure that investment in training is targeted at the programmes which have the most impact on the organization's performance.

TABLE 3.1 *Management development: four levels of evaluation*

Level of evaluation	Benefits	Drawbacks
Reactions: Is the training meeting participant needs? Is the style, pace, content, delivery mode appropriate? Are the materials and documentation helpful? Are the facilities acceptable? Is the administrative support adequate?	Addresses immediate issues of comfort, design and satisfaction. Feedback can help improve the design of future modules and 'nip problems in the bud'.	It is ascertained via self-report and can be influenced by an end-of-course halo effect, where participants are usually (!) in a positive mood. It is of short-term value and does not reveal whether course objectives have been met.
Learning: Is there evidence of enhancement of knowledge? Is training stretching without being overwhelming? Do participants feel they are taking away something of value?	Being questioned can stimulate reflective responses (i.e. get participants into a receptive frame of mind). If carefully designed, can indicate whether the training is *addressing* the stated course objectives.	Individuals are not always the best judge of their own learning (they might report overly positive to look good, or overly negative due to the exposure of unconscious incompetence). Even if learning occurs, this does not inevitably lead to behaviour change, and/or may take time to have an effect.
Behaviour: Is there evidence of improvement in skills? Are participants doing things differently in their workplace? Has their motivation and attitude changed?	If accurately framed, this evaluation can indicate whether the training is *achieving* the stated course objectives. It can reveal transfer of learning issues.	It requires a fairly sophisticated method to assess 'real' change. It is sometimes difficult to attribute changes to the training, as against other factors. Again self-report may be unreliable.
Results: Has the learning and behaviour change had an impact on their performance and that of their team? Are there identifiable improvements that can be attributed (at least in part) to the training? Ultimately, has the intervention led to a positive return on investment (ROI)?	This is the ultimate test, because there is little point (within the functionalist Discourse, at least) in learning and behaviour change unless it positively influences performance. Demonstrating 'bottom-line' impact is probably most valuable for securing future resources/budget.	This is the most difficult to assess for all sorts of reasons. Again, it is difficult to attribute changes to the training, since so many other factors can help or hinder the link between learning and enhanced performance. Some learning outcomes defy instrumental measurement.

Research within the functionalist Discourse

As noted above, a strategic approach to management development implies strong interconnections with other aspects of a firm's strategy. The precise packages or bundles which constitute strategic HRM are defined somewhat differently, depending on the author, and are variously labelled 'high commitment', 'high involvement', 'progressive', and so on. However, all incorporate a dimension of employee involvement, and the majority also involve careful selection, extensive training and contingent compensation. In a synthesis of research in this area,

Becker and Huselid (1998: 2) identify 'management development and training activities linked to the needs of the business' as one of four pivotal, high-performance work systems. For this reason, we now assess the empirical evidence concerning the impact of progressive HRM since this may tell us something about the value of management development.

Management development as part of an HRM package

Drawing on secondary data, from the global automobile industry and other industries, as well as case study evidence of best-practice, Pfeffer (1998) seeks to demonstrate that the ways in which organizations manage their people are enduring sources of competitive advantage. This universalistic or 'best-practice' approach to HRM policies and practices, which are held to attract, then foster and develop superior capabilities, has been purported, among other things, to improve export performance (Gomez-Meija, 1988), increase labour productivity (Koch and McGrath, 1996), enhance employee satisfaction and financial indicators (Bowen and Lawler, 1995), reduce staff turnover, improve productivity and financial performance (Huselid, 1995), and even decrease patient mortality in hospitals (West et al., 2002)!

It is noteworthy that management development specifically, or training generally, consistently features in best-practice research (see Box 3.5).

Box 3.5   Evidence for the universal impact of HRM

- A study of 590 firms in the USA adopting 'progressive' HRM practices, including selectivity in staffing, training and incentive compensation, found these practices to be related positively to perceptual measures of organizational performance. These effects were similar in profit and not-for-profit organizations (Delaney and Huselid, 1996).
- A positive association was found between the use of 'high-involvement' work practices and employee retention and firm productivity in a survey of 190 New Zealand business organizations (Guthrie, 2001).
- A survey of 361 public and private sector firms in the UK found that those adopting 'high commitment' systems, again including training, were positively correlated with good corporate performance (Michie and Sheehan-Quinn, 2001). HRM practices were more likely to contribute to competitive success when introduced as a comprehensive package. Furthermore, firms reporting the low use of progressive HRM practices were 40 per cent less likely to innovate than those scoring highly on the HRM index.
- Using data from two UK Workplace Surveys, four progressive styles of high commitment management (HCM) were identified in a study by Wood and de Menezes (1998). Unlike other research, HCM was treated as a matter of degree rather than an absolute concept. Those firms with exceptionally high scores on the HCM index performed better than other organizations in terms of their profitability and ability to create jobs. However, very low users of HCM also scored highly, suggesting a low commitment strategy can also pay off, at least in the short term.

Despite some impressive linking of progressive HRM to firm performance as expressed by different metrics, such studies have tended to use rather instrumental indicators (e.g. 'number of hours training received in the last year' (Delaney and Huselid, 1996); 'the existence of training focused on future skill requirements' (Guthrie, 2001); 'Are training and development needs assessed' (Wood and de Menezes, 1998)), which tell us little about the quality of implementation and processes used. Other methodological weaknesses include a reliance upon single respondents to make fairly sophisticated judgements (in the first study, for example, HR managers were asked to estimate the proportion of annual sales derived from cost leadership as against differentiation strategies), and the usual pitfalls of cross-sectional data and survey response bias. More fundamentally, the research design employed largely fails to differentiate espoused policy from the actual practice. Aspects of these problems are addressed in other studies.

For example, an analysis of management practices found these to be associated with several performance measures, including productivity, profitability and sales growth across 732 medium-sized firms in the USA, Germany, France and the UK (Bloom and Van Reenen, 2007). This study is noteworthy not only for its cross-national design but also for the way the items were constructed. The researchers explored actual behaviour, rather than intent, via such items as 'Do senior managers discuss attracting and developing talented people?' and 'How would you identify and develop your star performers?' However, these items were just a small HRM subset of 18 practices relating to the broad gamut of management. A study of 360 private and public sector companies in the UK by Guest et al. (2003) was unusual in several respects. It contained both subjective and objective measures of performance, it comprised both cross-sectional and longitudinal data, and the measures relating to planned training included both on- and off-the-job development. It also differentiated that which was concerned with the present job from future development. A strong association was found between HRM and subjective performance estimates (productivity and financial performance). A similarly strong association between HRM and objective measures of labour turnover and profit per employee was found, but this disappeared after controlling for previous years' performance. This underlines the difficulty of attributing performance improvement to the introduction of progressive HR policies.

In an early but revealing study, Fox and McLeay (1991) examined the recruitment and selection, management development, performance appraisal, rewards and recognition and career planning processes of 49 UK companies operating in the engineering and electronics sectors. The research team were careful to distinguish intent (HRM systems), practice (the reality of how staff are recruited, promoted, rewarded and developed) and the internal coherence of such activities. They found a clear positive relationship between financial performance and the degree of integration between corporate strategy and the human resource management functions in practice. In other words, the return on capital of a firm with a higher degree of integration between the human resource management function and corporate strategy is expected to be substantially above the average within its sector. In a sub-sample of 22 firms, there were also significant positive relationships between the return on capital and the degree of integration between human resource management systems when the human resource management focus was development, appraisal and career planning, and in proactive organizations. This study also used industry-controlled measures of performance, which is patently important when drawing inferences about organizational impacts.

In summary, authors adopting a closed or one-best-way perspective suggest that the greater use of progressive HR practices will always result in better performance. Very occasionally, studies trace the mechanisms by which more enlightened people practices translate into improved commitment and, subsequently, enhanced performance (e.g. Purcell et al., 2003). Generally, however, these writers have based their universalist claims on the argument that HR practices are uniquely placed to act as levers for the creation of firm-specific competencies. In other words, while the strategic competencies of firms may be idiosyncratic and situation-specific, it is argued that the HR practices that support them, like management development, are more generic. The closed or best-practice model fails to overcome three inherent contradictions (Legge, 1996). First, how is it possible for a firm to pursue individualized management development policies (e.g. development centres, sponsorship on MBA courses, fast-tracking) at the same time as initiatives to improve teamwork (e.g. action-learning, outdoor development, team-building)? Second, how does an organization reconcile long-term strategies to improve its management cadre with simultaneous requirements to attain cost savings via discontinued career paths and broken psychological contracts? This was an issue raised by Gratton et al. (1999) in their case analysis of seven leading UK-based companies. Finally, how can a firm use management development programmes to achieve a 'strong' culture of shared values and corporate commitment and at the same time radical thinking, creativity and adaptability? The model also seems to imply that a congruence of interests across all members of an organization is both desirable and feasible; this neglects the structural and political reality of such social institutions.

Contingent HRM: the role and impact of management development

Others also operate within the functionalist Discourse but believe it is flawed to believe that there is a single, universal 'recipe' for achieving success. They argue for an 'open' approach which emphasizes the need for a package of HR measures to be appropriate or contingent upon the particular circumstances and strategies of the organization concerned, without prescribing what these should be. Researchers have generally focused on the distinction between 'low-road' strategies that rely on cost reduction and 'high-road' strategies that focus on quality, variety or service. Naturally, management development features more in the latter than the former. The empirical evidence for the open approach is a little less substantial than for the universalistic approach. This is partly because contingent relationships are more complex and more difficult to detect statistically. It is also necessary to have a clear hypothesis about the particular sets of circumstances in which HR practices will be more or less effective in order to test contingency theories. *Resource-based theory* is one which posits that the contingencies will be highly firm-specific; but the very embeddedness and idiosyncratic nature of such

HR practices as management development make them, by definition, difficult to investigate. For all this, a number of studies do offer support for a contingency perspective (see Box 3.6).

Box 3.6   Evidence for the contingent impact of HRM

- In a study of 73 organizations in the US banking sector, Richard and Johnson (2001) found that the use of strategic HRM practices and whether managers believed these programmes were performing satisfactorily, including management and executive development, significantly improved employee productivity and return on equity. However, it was those firms with high capital asset intensity that benefited more from progressive HRM practices.
- While the Bloom and Van Reenen (2007) study reported above generally supports a best-practice approach, the research also found that firms and industries with higher skills (proxied by college degrees and average salaries) have significantly better relative human capital management practices. This leads the authors to support the 'optimal choice model of management practices', whereby firms tailor their practices to the competitive environment.
- Delery and Doty (1996) found the financial performance of those banks adopting three HR practices, namely profit-sharing, results-oriented appraisals and employment security, was 30 per cent better than the average across 219 banks.

> Banks that were able to align their HR practices with strategy are estimated to have nearly 50% higher ROA and ROE than those banks whose HR practices were just one standard deviation out of alignment. Specifically, banks that implemented a prospector strategy involving high innovation, reaped greater returns from more results-oriented appraisals and lower levels of employee participation than did banks that relied on a defender strategy. Banks implementing a defender strategy performed better if they relied less on results-oriented appraisals and gave their loan officers higher levels of participation in decision-making and voice. (1996: 826)

These accounts highlight the importance of first differentiating the strategic intent of the organization and then mobilizing the appropriate HR policies and style to achieve this. So, in the case of the US banks, rewarding innovative behaviour was entirely consistent with the so-called prospector strategy of loan officers locating and exploiting new markets and products. In contrast, the more participative HR approach supported the defender strategy of building a loyal, committed workforce and a customer base which values consistent and reliable service over the long term. A further contribution of the contingent approach is to draw attention to the life-cycle stage of a given organization and the particular strategy it is currently pursuing. In their study, Richard and Johnson (2001: 306) found the strategy to be an important moderator of the HR-performance link: 'Effective HR programmes are costly and time-consuming to implement and may detract directly from bottom-line performance in the short run. However, when these programmes are executed in conjunction with a strategy that particularly meshes with effective HR implementation, then firm performance is more likely enhanced.'

What conclusions can be drawn about management development from functionalist HRM research, whether best-practice or best-fit? There is a number of broad approaches to HRM that can bring performance benefits to most organizations: this much appears well proven. These include policies designed to build employee commitment to the organization, and to acquire, build and retain employee knowledge and skills. However, the way in which these broad approaches are most successfully applied is likely to be contingent on the environment, strategic orientation, operational characteristics and history of each organization. It also appears necessary to employ a number of HR policies/practices in concert, the argument being that it is the very synergy between different HR activities that makes them potentially strategic and powerful in their enhancement of organizational performance. In a study of 319 US business units, Koch and McGrath (1996) investigated whether the amount of formal training undertaken and the extent to which firms promoted from within improved their productivity. They concluded that such effects were indirect because they only occurred when other, more sophisticated HR planning and evaluation, recruitment and selection strategies were used in combination with training.

So, for all the empirical support for performance impacts arising from progressive HR practices, any conclusions concerning the unique impact of management development remain difficult to discern because, by definition, they form part of a bundle of integrated (or at least overlapping) practices. While such integration between development activities and other HR practices is clearly important, it is intriguing to know whether there is a direct link between management development and organization performance.

Direct impact of management development

While much has been written about the broad benefits of investing in management and leadership development, what hard evidence is there concerning the specific impact of training and development of managers? Empirical studies are still few and far between.

Research reporting performance impact

An in-depth analysis of 16 UK organizations found four to be comprehensively adopting 'management standards' as part of their HRD systems and processes. A further three had partially adopted such frameworks and nine had not attempted this or had made little progress in this direction (Winterton and Winterton, 1997). Those in the first category shared certain characteristics: management development and other training was competency-based, job profiles or job descriptions related to the competencies outlined in the management standards (UK's Management Charter Initiative), and appraisal systems were designed to support the attainment of management standards. A major benefit identified was the coherent structure which the standards provided for training, management development and personal development (although the standards were not extensively used for recruitment and selection, nor reward and remuneration systems). Gaps in competency, for example, were more readily spotted through appraisal, training needs were specified more precisely in relation to the competencies required for individuals to meet the needs of the organization, and there were clear criteria for human resource planning and career succession. Also, management development was linked to a qualifications framework. Finally, the researchers report a statistically significant relationship between competency-based HRD systems and both individual and business performance. Some support for these results was found in a study of the UK aerospace industry (Box 3.7).

Box 3.7   Management development in British Aerospace

In a study of 360 British aerospace establishments a significant correlation was found between strategic management capability and business performance, as measured by value added per employee (Thomson, 2000). This was in a context of downsizing, flattening structures and outsourcing (on average 66 per cent had downsized recently). More successful businesses, which also tended to be larger in size, differed in their use of management development in two ways: they utilized personal development plans and succession planning more extensively and were more likely to be investing in leadership skills and developing global managers. It was also found that this investment was strongly and positively correlated with the pursuit of a high-commitment HR strategy and philosophy. In other words, there was senior management commitment to raising management skills, encouraging innovation and investing in development.

In an EC-funded research project analysing management development in six European countries, interviews were conducted with the HRD manager and a line manager in 600 private sector organizations (Mabey and Gooderham, 2005). Findings indicate that 19 per cent of variance in organizational performance is explained by three factors: a strategic approach to HRM, a long-term, proactive and strategic approach to management development and, on the part of line managers, a belief that their employer takes management development seriously. Interestingly, neither the presence of management development systems/procedures, nor the amount and diversity of management training activities enhance performance to a significant effect. This study used a seven-item measure of performance covering the quality of goods and services, the ability to attract and retain essential staff and the quality of relationships in the firm. This subjective index was benchmarked by sector over the previous three years and a mean score reported by HRD and line managers. Causal path analysis revealed that a favourable strategic fit (between the firm's chosen business and HRM strategies) and organizational fit (in terms of a coherent longer-term approach to management development) were significant factors in predicting line manager perceptions of the importance given by their employer to management development. This positive perception distinguished high performers from low-performing companies.

A further analysis was undertaken on a sub-sample of 180 companies where published financial data was available (from the Amadeus database). Again, the perception of line managers proved to be crucial: where they reported positively on their employer's management development strategy, this explained a modest but significant amount of variance (7 per cent) in firm productivity (Mabey and Ramirez, 2005). Again, neither the presence of management development systems/procedures, like policy statements, appraisal meetings, fast-tracking and so on, nor the amount and diversity of training activities enhanced performance to a significant effect. Taken together, these findings lend support to the idea that a contingent approach to management development confers competitive advantage through enhanced organizational performance because of its inimitability. As such, a properly aligned, and therefore distinctive and idiosyncratic, management development system represents a core capability (Becker and Gerhart, 1996). However, the challenge of fitting management development both strategically and organizationally should not be underestimated. Indeed, one should construe these findings as a warning to managers to eschew off-the-shelf management development 'solutions'. A further observation is that the immediate benefits of management development are not necessarily financial. A comprehensive evaluation of the outcomes of management training comes from a government-sponsored research report on the business benefits of management development by the consulting company DTZ Pieda (DfEE, 1998). Of the 127 firms questioned, some 88 firms identified impacts on non-financial business performance following training activities. The types of impact most often mentioned by respondents were: improved morale of staff, an improved response and greater flexibility shown by managers and improvements in quality leading to greater customer loyalty and new business. Indirect impacts were identified to be: an improved management style, better tracking of projects and evaluation of their worth to the firm, and greater understanding of the value of training and human resource development in general.

Longitudinal research

Furthermore, the effects of investment in management development are likely to take time to become evident. Unlike technical skills training, the development of managers often takes place over a sustained period of time and addresses competencies which may take months, if not years, to be internalized and harvested by the organization. For this reason, analysis that spans a number of years is necessary but rare. In a study of insurance salespeople, Frayne and Geringer (2000) were able to demonstrate that self-management skill training significantly improved job performance. Interestingly, these performance effects were sustained and gradually increased over time. Another relevant study here is that of 61 large French firms by Arcimoles (1997), which is unusual in two respects. First, the author uses objective data: HRM data reported in annual Company Personnel Reports and financial results in the form of return on capital employed. Second, the study tracks impact over a seven-year period. Investment in training was found to lead to both immediate and time-lagged economic performance at firm level. Positive correlations remain when not only performance level, but also the change in performance is taken into consideration, which leads the author to conclude that expenditure on training is 'very clearly and permanently associated to an increase in profitability and productivity' (Arcimoles, 1997: 865). However, the study does not isolate the effects of management training in particular, and as the author admits, an index of investment tells us very little about the qualitative aspects or the informal costs and benefits of on-the-job training. Some of these shortcomings are overcome in the following example (Box 3.8).

Box 3.8 Time-lagged outcomes of management development in the UK

Longitudinal data on the link between management development and performance is available from a study of 131 UK private sector companies of all sizes (Mabey, 2005). Three outcome measures were used: (1) organizational performance: a nine-item index of performance benchmarked against competitors over the previous three years, as reported by HRD and line managers; (2) employee engagement, which although not strictly a measure of performance, is an important motivational link in the chain between HR policies/practices and commercial success (Purcell et al., 2003); and (3) productivity, which was operating revenue per employee as derived by factual data supplied by the HRD managers in each firm. Focusing just on time-lagged relationships, three facets of management development proved to have statistically significant impact over a four-year period:

- If development activities were driven strategically in the organization with board support and strong links to business strategy in 2000, then organization performance was greater in 2004.
- If management development was designed to address managers' abilities and competencies, motivation and potential to address business needs (as against being short-term and tactical) in 2000, then organization performance was again greater in 2004.
- If organizations reported a high degree of employer responsibility for manager development in 2000, this was associated with significantly greater employee engagement, a higher organization performance and greater reported productivity, all in 2004.

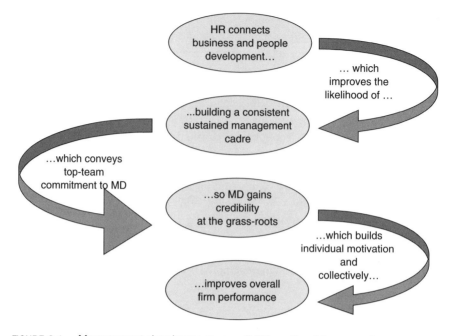

FIGURE 3.1   *Management development: possibilities of a virtuous cycle*

Management development: a virtuous cycle?

Taken together, the studies reported above begin to identify a pathway between investment in management development and improvement in firm-level performance. There is strong evidence that the thought and effort invested in management development at firm level appears to trigger a virtuous cycle (Figure 3.1). High-performing companies are those where those responsible for HR and management development have an opportunity to influence the direction of the business, so that there is a meaningful connection between strategy and people development. This, in turn, improves the likelihood that an internal labour market of managerial talent can be nurtured over a sustained period of time by being consistent, future-focused and with an emphasis on training for potential. Importantly, this conveys to *line managers* that their employers are giving strategic thought and prominence to how managers are trained and developed. As a result, the management development approach begins to gain credibility at grass-roots level.

The effect, over time, is to build motivation among employees which collectively improves the way the organization competes. This will be partly due to the quality of its products and services (because motivated managers will be inventive and want to please customers), partly due to its ability to attract and retain essential staff (because the firm will gain a reputation as being progressive and caring for its staff) and partly due to the quality of its internal relations (because, over time, mutual trust will develop). This tentatively constructed chain of events supports the results of other recent studies in relation to HRM practices generally (Guest, 2001; Purcell et al., 2003). Finally, if it can be demonstrated that this success is due, at least in part, to its approach to management development, then this will enhance the influence of HR and successively reinforce this virtuous circle. The fact that it is the discretionary variables which make the difference, as against those over which firms have no control, should come as some encouragement to HRD managers seeking to justify investment in strategically oriented and thoughtfully implemented management training and development activities.

In what way might this influence practice? For management development to have these kinds of impact, an HR specialist who understands the possibilities (and limitations) of management development needs to be present at a policy-making level, in a position to draw out the connections between strategic intent and managerial capability over the longer term. Once the vision for management development is forged and ownership gained at a senior level, the task is to create a sense of continuity and proactivity in the way management talent is cultivated (with the emphasis on consistency and a long-term focus), which survives the coming and going of key individuals. It is when corporate goalposts appear to shift for no apparent reason and when management development programmes/priorities wither as rapidly as they were previously championed, that weariness and cynicism set in.

The functionalist Discourse: an assessment

There is no doubt that the functionalist management development Discourse has generated a great deal of empirical research (especially in the USA), probably more than the other Discourses combined. The reason for this is not hard to identify. As discussed in Chapter 1, management development is a growth–industry, with many interest groups (government departments, training agencies, senior management teams, HR specialists and consultants, business schools and, not least, academic researchers) standing to gain from studies which demonstrate that the investment is worthwhile. Not only is the volume of research impressive, but there are indications that employing progressive HR strategies like management development can differentiate successful from mediocre firms. Having said this, the quality of studies is uneven, as this chapter has shown. Due to the adoption of very different input measures and outcome indices, it is not easy to compare them (Wood, 1999) and the unique contribution of management development, within a web of other HR initiatives, is difficult to determine. Even where such effects are discovered, the precise reasons for positive outcomes remain elusive (see Box 3.9).

Box 3.9   Do firms evaluate management development?

A survey of 395 UK organizations conducted by the Industrial Society is very revealing about evaluation practice (Tamkin and Hillage, 1998). Most management development appeared to occur on a demand-driven basis:

(Continued)

(Continued)

less than one-third of respondents had a clearly defined development strategy linked to organizational objectives. The most widely used evaluation
method was 'happy sheets' after training programmes. Only just over one
in four actually set objectives for their programmes which they could then
evaluate against. Two-thirds of those questioned rated training evaluation
as very important, yet only a quarter were satisfied with the methods being
used to evaluate training. For all the texts and manuals explaining how to
carry out evaluation of training and development, it seems most organizations admit that investment in management development is still largely an
act of faith.

These low figures of reported formal evaluation perhaps should not surprise us.
A structured approach to evaluation, like that described earlier (Table 3.1), is well
suited to training interventions which address 'hard' skills and which have a finite
time-span. However, most management development, especially that addressing
more senior executives, is very different. The scope of the training and development is often as much about attitude and mindset as it is about on-the-job skills;
the time frame of application may be years, not weeks; and learning transfer, far
from being a discrete activity, will be interwoven with a host of culturally-specific
organizational processes. This is not the fault of a functionalist approach *per se*;
simply that this Discourse has yet to cope with the rich context of management
development activities. However, there are a number of difficulties which remain
inherent to the functionalist management development Discourse.

The problem of assigning financial value

Problematic for this Discourse is that it treats the assignation of financial value to
something like management development as a rational equation:

> Politically, numbers almost always increase HR people's power. Since few personnel people
> have numbers, just coming to the table with cost and benefit analyses 'seizes the high
> ground'. It transmits the message that you care about bottom-line results, and it puts oppo-
> nents in the position of having to respond to your analysis. If the logic of your position is
> accepted, you have already won. You have created the dominant definition of the situation,
> the context of the debate. Others will simply be arguing about whether your numbers are
> right. (Spencer, 1986: 296)

This observation has as much currency today as when first made. Unfortunately,
management development rarely lends itself to such ready quantification. It may be
possible to conduct an ROI on a specific programme, as outlined earlier, but no
matter how much high ground it seizes, this is unlikely to capture the full benefit,
or indeed costs associated with the intervention. Coupled with this concern to
estimate financial impact is that it may cause managers to focus over much on

those practices whose financial impact is easy to measure: 'A weak measure on the right issue is better than a strong measure on the wrong issue' (Yeung and Berman, 1997: 333).

The problem of 'it depends who you ask'

As we have already noted, any management development activity has a number of interested parties or stakeholders, each with their own 'agenda' of what they want the intervention to achieve, and what yardsticks they will use to measure these outcomes. Evaluating management development, then, actually comprises a set of choices, influenced by the values and goals of these key stakeholders (see Box 3.10).

Box 3.10   Split views on the value of management development

An interesting approach to differing perspectives has been taken by Garavan et al. (1998). Although theirs was an exploratory study based on fairly small numbers, it sought the views of a range of stakeholders. One key differentiating issue was utilitarianism, espousing the view that development provision should be of immediate value to the organization and the province of senior and line managers as contrasted to humanism, which emphasizes the priorities of the learner and the long-term contribution of development investment. A similar split occurred with interventionism, with individuals and unions believing that it was the organization's responsibility to develop its human resources, whereas senior managers and HR specialists believed individuals to have primary responsibility for their own development. Other such split-views existed between 'centralism' and 'decentralization', and 'traditionalism' and 'continuous development'. Major differences also existed in terms of the benchmarks used to evaluate development success. Senior managers wanted quantitative measures such as increased productivity and flexibility, and optimal utilization of human resources; line managers wanted development to contribute to cost savings within their area of responsibility. Development specialists placed some emphasis on quantitative measures, such as number of training days and enhanced performance, but also had qualitative concerns that development should be of high quality and relevant, and that it should facilitate change. Individual learners, on the other hand, were essentially concerned with the enhancement of their employability through the level of investment in their personal development, the need for certification and the range of competencies developed.

In the context of such differences, evaluation inevitably becomes a politically negotiated rather than a technically rational process. The very dichotomies implicit within the dualist nature of functionalist Discourse appear to become its undoing.

The reality of evaluation as a political process

Management development, and its evaluation, is always going to be a political activity. Managers, particularly at senior levels, have a preference for information received via their own informal networks and this tends to be far more influential than that produced via more formal channels. This belief of managers in the value of their own assessments is reinforced, of course, by popular management theory which supports an ideology whereby managers are cast as the heroes or heroines who make success possible (Clark et al., 1998)!

   Here again, functionalist management development Discourse is ill-equipped to deal with the non-consensual reality of organizations. There is a need for more receiving-end research to get 'beneath the skin' of organizations and build our understanding of the purposes and meanings that people attach to management development experiences and activities with which they are involved. Methodologies which rely on inflexible research instruments leave little room for pursuing the unexpected and can take only limited account of context. More context-sensitive research methods pay greater attention to interdependencies, settings and complexities of behaviour in organizations because they focus on 'naturally occurring, ordinary events in natural settings, so that we have a strong handle on what *real life* is like' (Miles and Huberman, 1994: 10, italics in original).

Reflexivity

The functionalist management development Discourse can be criticized for its inability to be reflexive, or, in other words, to actually regard itself as a Discourse (or for that matter to even recognize the very notion of Discourse). Reflexivity involves self-questioning by 'turning back' on our own knowledge, truth claims, language and so on in order to scrutinize the various impacts that our research may have on constructions of the social world (Cunliffe, 2003). Those operating exclusively within the confines of functionalism are by definition unable to do this, due to their objectivist stance on reality (i.e. ontology) and their similarly objectivist stance on the production of knowledge about such reality (i.e. epistemology). For the committed functionalist, there is a clear and unquestionable ontological separation between the researcher and the world being researched. So, for example, when the functionalist researcher talks about 'social capital', there is no consideration that the very act of coining such a term contributes to a certain (contestable) construction of the world and the individuals within it (i.e. in accounting terms), or of the effects that such a construction might have. Instead, we have to look to the dialogic and to a lesser extent the critical and constructivist Discourses for such considerations. The dialogic, for example, may choose to 'work with' the notion of social capital but (without necessarily condemning or dismissing it) would treat it as a metaphorical rather than literal description of the social world. Rather than describing something that 'really exists', it would be treated as a label or linguistic device that permits the world (and people within it) to be defined, identified, classified, ordered and rendered predictable, controllable or indeed 'developable'. While its effects may be *experienced as real* by those it impacts, 'social capital' would not be considered to have any ontological substance beyond the language in which it is constructed. This permits the dialogic researcher to reflexively challenge notions such as social capital, while not necessarily rejecting them for the purposes of research. The downside of reflexivity is that, taken to its extreme, it could paralyse the researcher in a never-ending cycle of existential angst.

Conclusion

The concern to attribute organizational benefits to effective management development is understandable. Such activities are expensive, time-consuming and often high-profile. All parties concerned want to be able to demonstrate that such investments are worthwhile. It is perhaps for this reason that the majority of management development research has been directed towards tracking the impact of policies and practices upon organizational performance. As discussed in this chapter, either as part of an integrated HRM approach or as a discrete intervention, there is growing though still modest empirical support for the causal links in this relationship. However, the analysis of management development from a functionalist stance is not without its problems and critics.

Not least, the underlying rationality of this approach has long been questioned as *unrealistic*. For instance, doubts are cast upon the capability of HR departments to translate business priorities into appropriate HRD goals (Huselid et al., 1997) and of achieving timely fit in a turbulent environment (Wright and Snell, 1998). Martocchio and Baldwin (1997) lament the persistent focus of training research upon the content of various management development strategies, at the expense of the processes which shape such strategic planning. Others argue that a focus upon inputs and outcomes is actually *unhelpful* because it diverts attention from the important management development processes which include unanticipated outcomes and informal, more covert episodes of learning (Woodall and Winstanley, 1998). At root, critics of this management development Discourse maintain that researchers are preoccupied with performativity: 'Management is taken as given, and a desirable given at that, and is not interrogated except in so far as this will contribute to its improved effectiveness' (Fournier and Grey, 2000: 17). In other words, this approach is also *incomplete* because its reliance upon positivist methodology and pursuit of quantification leaves no place for moral or ethical considerations (Wicks and Freeman, 1998). Fortunately, some of these shortcomings are addressed by the other Discourses of management development, and it is to these that we now turn.

Summary

- The functionalist Discourse dominates thinking in organizations and much activity in the field of management development is based on functionalist assumptions.
- The functionalist Discourse is informed by a number of theories; while very different in origin they are united in their attempt to explain performance in organizations.
- The commercial pressure to demonstrate the positive impact, if not the financial gain, arising from management development is acute.
- There is some research evidence to suggest that management development can improve organizational performance, either as part of a bundle of strategic HR practices or in its own right.
- Attributing performance outcomes to management development is nevertheless fraught with difficulties and few organizations actually bother to evaluate their training and development activities.
- The functionalist Discourse answers some key questions about management development, but leaves many others unaddressed, not least due to its non-reflexive stance on the very nature of the social world and its own impact upon that world.

4

Management development: narratives, ritual and symbolism

Mma Ramotswe was horrified when she read of people being described in the newspapers as consumers. That was a horrible, horrible word, which sounded rather too much like cucumber, a vegetable for which she had little time. People were not just greedy consumers, grabbing everything that came their way, nor were they cucumbers for that matter; they were Botswana, they were people! (Alexander McCall Smith, In the Company of Cheerful Ladies, *2004: 177)*

After reading this chapter you will be able to:

- **Explain the distinctive features of the constructivist Discourse**
- **Identify the guiding theories which inform constructivist management development Discourse**
- **Discuss how this leads to a particular construction of management development and what this serves to illuminate about such interventions and activities**
- **Identify some insights derived from studies of management development which take a constructivist approach**
- **Provide an assessment of the contribution of constructivist management development Discourse**
- **Point out some of the commonalities and differences between the functionalist and constructivist management development Discourses**

Introduction

The functionalist Discourse of management development, as discussed in the previous chapter, sees the developing of managers and leaders as comprising formal or informal activities, on-the-job or off-the-job, managed by the employer or self-initiated, which lead to improved skills at an individual level and enhanced capability at an organizational level. It might be equally tenable to reverse the logic of this view. For example, starting with the notion of individual and collective learning, we could then explore the conditions which are most likely to bring this about. We might put less emphasis on management positions and more on managerial processes (irrespective of the title-holders involved); less on organizations as instigators of training programmes and more on workplaces, teams, project groups as fertile spaces for learning; less on the control, success and predictability inherent in much management development thinking and more on the learning that arises from risk, setback and spontaneity; less on training and performance and more on learning and reflective action. Larsen (2004) is one author who plays with this reverse logic, and some of his ideas are summarized in Box 4.1.

Box 4.1   Turning management development on its head

- The methods of management development have often been dominated by education and training management, rather than learning to manage (hence emphasizing the sender, rather than the receiver of the development). There has been a reaction to this bias, whereby: 'Learning is now more likely to be viewed as having emergent, natural and personal "inside-out" properties, rather than being the expected outcome from a planned "outside-in" event. Learning is more chaotic and unmanageable than hitherto supposed.' (Storey and Tate, 2000: 196)
- An important part of management development is experiential learning processes in the workplace. But these methods – not necessarily planned, expected, wanted or pleasant – have traditionally been de-emphasized in the management development literature and (conscious) practice. The informal, intangible and spontaneous nature of experiential learning has made these methods difficult to research – and difficult to monitor for organizations.
- What is needed is a focus on managerial processes, rather than on structural features of the organization and/or behavioural characteristics of individuals. The vehicle for management development is organizational learning; however with individual learning as a source of – or consequence of – organizational learning.
- Whether learning is intentional or unintentional, planned or incidental, wanted or unwanted, initiated within or outside the organization, it is there and cannot in most cases be traced back to its many sources of origin. The fact that organizations increasingly break down boundaries to the outside world, join networks or strategic alliances, and exchange information and resources, represents an after-the-fact acceptance of "cross-boundary learning theory", which propounds that learning in its acquisition and application does not respect organizational, geographical or life sphere barriers.

The contribution of such observations is that they begin to create an 'open market' for management development by highlighting the situational dimension of management – and hence management development. In this regard, Storey and Tate (2000: 196) comment: '[A] fundamental issue concerning the theory and practice of management development turns on the question of whether there is a known body of knowledge and set of generic skills which managers should be expected to have, much in the manner, say, of a qualified professional accountant, lawyer or doctor.' To this, the functionalist Discourse would answer in the affirmative: after all, the tool-kit metaphor is predicated upon a picture of finely-tuned completion, managers being developed against a predetermined model (whether articulated or implicit). But it might equally be argued that contextual factors vary from one situation to the next, making building blocks of knowledge and universal lists of generic competencies of dubious value. And even *if* there are such things as generic managerial competencies, these are changing simultaneously with, and as a consequence of, the shifting sands of the business environment. Taking this a step further, it is probable that a defined code of conduct for managers, or a public standard of competency, would itself influence that environment. Take, for example, the pervasive influence of Investors in People (IIP) in the UK, or the Association to Advance Collegiate Schools of Business (AACSB), the Association of MBAs (AMBA) and EQUIS in an international management training context.

There is an important research agenda and need for studies which cross the paradigmatic boundary from (exclusively) looking at individuals and formalized structures to a more informal and process-oriented view on management development. This is precisely where the constructivist Discourse is located, and in this chapter we explore what this reveals about management development. Having explained in more detail what is meant by constructivism, we first explore some of the theories underpinning this perspective and then illustrate how these have been and might be applied to management development. This leads to a very different 'take' on such activities and we close by comparing the relative insights gained from the functionalist and constructivist Discourses of management development. In short, a set of new narratives is provided for management development.

Constructivist studies

The constructivist label is applied to studies oriented towards the consensus and duality-embracing poles of Table 1.1. This Discourse can be considered as emphasizing duality in the sense that 'organizations are regarded as systems of distributed cognition … in which the challenge is to coordinate actions among multiple and potentially conflicting views expressed by individuals who are interested in developing and maintaining their autonomy as well as their unique, personal identities' (Schultze and Stabell, 2004: 557). The functionalist Discourse sees organizational phenomena in independent and mutually exclusive terms. For example, a competency gap is identified and management development is employed to rectify this weakness and 'fill' the gap. In short, competency, like knowledge, is viewed as separable from the knower: an asset which can be owned, bought and sold. By contrast, the constructivist Discourse sees knowledge/competency as less of an objective commodity and more a fluid consequence, naturally arising from, contributing to and being shaped by social practices.

For all their plurality, constructivist studies, like functionalist ones, remain largely consensus-oriented. They are consensus-oriented in the sense that they do seek to portray an 'accurate' or faithful picture of what is going on inside an organization, albeit from a certain, inherently sectional vantage point (e.g. employees as opposed to managers, women as opposed to men etc.). A typical write-up of a constructivist study will contain many extracts from the talk of research participants in order to show their sense-making in action and justify the key messages of the analysis. As such, language is used as a means for both the researcher and reader to access the social constructions of the research participants and gain insight into what might actually be going on from their perspective (see Box 4.2).

Box 4.2   Students or customers?

Why might faculty in a higher education college have misgivings about senior management insisting that students be referred to as 'customers'? Their resistance is not simply associated with linguistic re-labelling. For many lecturing staff their role is to provoke by breaking mental moulds, to stimulate by offering fresh worldviews, to disquiet by asking awkward questions. This mindset is steeped in a long tradition of university education. To replace the term 'student' with that of 'customer' signifies a commercial transaction, an underlying profit motive and a market-led relationship. As such it is regarded as a deeply suspicious and retrograde step, perhaps for reasons not dissimilar to Mma Ramotswe's retort, at the start of this chapter, concerning the comprehensive re-labelling of her compatriots as 'consumers'!

In contrast to functionalist studies, the constructivist emphasis tends to be on the social, symbolic and cultural aspects of organizational life, but for their own sake as opposed to being subordinated to economic and instrumental concerns. Emancipation is not necessarily a prime concern of such constructivist studies, except to the extent that the privileging of research participants' voices and perspectives might be considered an empowering act in itself.

Metaphor and the role of management development

The metaphor of the constructivist management development Discourse is drama, the notion of a 'live' play unfolding on stage. Although initially scripted and rehearsed, the emotional and cognitive impact of the drama is not entirely predictable and a whole range of people, from members of the audience, technical assistants, stage-hands, critics and the players themselves, have material influence over the impact and effects of the emerging drama. Furthermore, each will take away his/her own memories and invest different levels of meaning in the performance. Such narratives and reconstructions will shape future performances.

These may be quite different from those intended by the director and designed-in by the producer. In essence, outcomes are co-created and ongoing rather than prescribed and discrete.

With regard to management development, this Discourse focuses attention upon the interaction between the individual and the organization. If employees are being trained and are developing themselves personally and professionally, the employer organization is likely to gain from their ingenuity, innovativeness and creativity. In turn, this creates a social and technical environment that induces ongoing learning for individuals. But none of this is inevitable. An important issue here is the connection between what is being learnt and developed at an individual and group level, and ongoing organizational processes. The assumptions underpinning the constructivist management development Discourse are:

- Organizations are opportunity-spaces for individual and group-level discovery, development and mutually beneficial learning.
- Organizations tend towards coherence and mutuality: organizations need talent, energy and ideas; people need rewards, careers and ongoing self-improvement.
- Competency is situational and context-dependent so a manager's development arises from his/her subjective framing and experience of work.
- Training and development orchestrated by the organization may contribute minimal learning and be more significant for the cultural meaning/status it confers …
- … While more powerful learning may arise from key, day-by-day, organization episodes and processes which facilitate idea-discovery, fresh thinking and assumption-testing.
- The significance attached to management development arises from shared processes of observation, personal accounts and story-telling.

In contrast to the functionalist Discourse discussed in the previous chapter, here there is an explicit recognition that underlying values and/or embedded cultures are essential elements of organizations. The constructivist Discourse does not ignore strategy and structure, but is more curious about the integration between the needs of staff and the conditions in which they work. Management development activities from a functionalist perspective will usually be highly planned, systematized and documented. More interesting, from a constructivist perspective, are the cultural repercussions and significance of such programmes: the symbolic meaning they come to have for variously situated corporate players. And apart from the usual training methods, any activity (a challenging experience, a difficult project to manage, an inspiring 'mentor', a non-work support group, and so on) might qualify as development. The HRM language is less about return on investment, assessment and performance and more about talent management, building potential and increasing the capability of individuals and teams.

So the constructivist Discourse views the organization as a social site comprising distinct cultural groups, each of whom is expected to have distinct ways of making sense of the organizational world. Viewed from this perspective, the significance of management development – its purposes, implementation and effects – is considered to be a function of the sense-making of these cultural groups.

A principal aim of constructivist research, then, is to provide a voice to such groups and enable the organization (or in this case, management development) to be viewed and interpreted through the eyes of those groups.

Theories informing constructivist management development Discourse

We need to tread a little carefully here. First, the whole notion of authoritative theorizing from a body of well-grounded knowledge is a little foreign to the constructivist worldview; by definition different types of knowledge, interpretation and meaning are distributed across an organization, so any claims to certainty and exclusivity would be treated with caution. Second, not many authors have explored this Discourse in relation to management development, so in order to examine the relevant theoretical underpinnings of constructivist Discourse we need to tease out strands from different and disparate schools of thought, few of which call themselves constructivist.

Actor-network and role behaviour theories

The constructivist management development Discourse, in a sense, works backwards to elucidate how development and learning are produced via a combination of variegated interests in the organization. It is here that *actor-network theory*, or the sociology of translation (Latour, 1987), is helpful because it privileges the way credibility is given to, and energy comes to be invested in, training and development initiatives. The need for and the efficacy of management development are not seen as indisputable; initial justification for investment needs to be secured, significant actors need to be enrolled and the worthwhile-ness of the development intervention needs to be 'translated' to align with the interests of these potential allies. In short, management development is viewed less as a discrete event and more as a series of strategies requiring the 'skills of rhetoric, using conversation, argument, negotiation, persuasion and justification to create a "heterogeneity of alliances"' (Gold and Smith, 2003: 144). This applies not just to the launch of management development activities, but also to their ongoing reputation and evaluation within the organization, as we shall see later.

Role behaviour theory also gives prominence to the organization as a social system characterized by multiple roles, multiple role senders and multiple role evaluators (Katz and Kahn, 1978). In the sense that 'HRM is the organization's primary means for sending role information through the organization, supporting desired behaviours, and evaluating role performances … in ways which are consistent with the system's behavioural requirements' (Jackson and Schuler, 1995: 239), role behaviour theory is fairly central to the top-down view of functionalist Discourse. However, the notion of 'role performances' is consonant with constructivist Discourse. So, for example, the behavioural expectations of all role partners are likely to influence activities in the arena of management development alongside individual agency (see Box 4.3).

> ## Box 4.3   The persistence of informal development processes
>
> Hewlett Packard (HP) is a company that prides itself on 'high performance work practices' like management training and development. Yet in a case study which drew on a wide variety of informants across HP over a two-year period, a more subtle view emerged (Truss, 2001). Fewer than half believed they received the training they needed to do their job well and just one-third were satisfied or very satisfied with their career management:
>
> > What we found in HP was that, although the formal policies turned strongly around the notion of measuring and rewarding individuals' work performance against targets that were closely related to the company's objectives, informally what counted was visibility and networking if people wanted to further their careers. Despite the increased focus at the policy level, ... on formalized career management, the traditional, informal method of career management that had evolved within the company continued to prevail. (Truss, 2001: 1144)

Role theory predicts the conclusion Truss draws. Employees will seek to meet, or at the very least will be influenced by, the expectations of role partners both within and outside the organization. So it would not be surprising to find managers interpreting the value of their management and career development in the light of the cultural and administrative heritage of their employer organization on the one hand, and in terms of clients, professional networks and family on the other. And these informal processes, including networking and achieving professional visibility, have obvious implications for diversity. For example, societies tend to be structured such that women become statistically the primary carers, and are therefore less likely to be available outside office hours. The EU have extended indirect sex discrimination to cover such 'informal' practices that have a disproportionately negative impact on women, as well as men, who are not willing or structurally able to work long hours.

Learning theory

Theories of learning, of which there are many, borrow from a range of insights arising from social psychology concerning individual needs, feelings, predispositions, skills and capacity for learning (e.g. Rogers, 1986). Here the presiding question is: 'how do employees and organizations acquire new knowledge, skills and behavioural repertoires?' This is a subject which has exercised researchers for many years, with slightly different emphases, such as experiential learning (Lewin, 1951), organizational learning (Schön, 1983; Argyris, 1992), action learning (Revans, 1987), communities of practice (Lave and Wenger, 1990). Although few would label themselves constructivist, some strands of these theories inform this management development Discourse. For example, learning theory alerts us to the wealth of on-the-job coaching and unstructured personal development which takes place on a daily basis in all organizations. The field of development in organizations is shifting from a reliance on behaviourism to a broader more transformative conception of learning, spurred in part by the need for continuous learning in the workplace, requiring informal and incidental learning strategies (Marsick and Watkins, 1997; Raelin, 2000). Here development arises from tapping into tacit knowledge, action-centred learning, learning from mistakes, learning-by-doing and as a by-product of other activities (Kamoche, 1996). It is the very embeddedness of these activities into daily work routines (as compared with isolated, formalized training programmes) which makes them 'resource mobility barriers' because competitors will find them difficult to imitate (Mueller, 1996). Indeed, it might be argued that the boundary between knowledge creation and management development is becoming increasingly blurred (see Box 4.4).

Box 4.4   Knowledge creation and management development

In an influential book on the way organizations build their competitive capability, Nonaka and Takeuchi (1995) characterize Western managers as relying upon quantifiable data, codified procedures and explicit information-processing. In contrast, the authors maintain the success of Japanese corporations is based on the fact that managers are encouraged to derive knowledge from intuition, internalize their discoveries and then find ways of migrating this tacit knowledge into the wider organization so that constant renewal can occur. Such a mindset would seem to favour on-the-job learning and informal development as against the programmatic management training so typical in Western organizations.

At one level, this exemplifies the essence of constructivist Discourse. Yet, even Nonaka's notion of knowledge management assumes individual learning takes place primarily, if not exclusively, to serve the current purposes of the organization. By definition, then, the employer remains in control of the learning processes, even though the means used to orchestrate these differ widely from East to West. This is the aspect of learning theory which sits less comfortably with constructivist Discourse. For instance Deci, Connell and Ryan (1989) reason that when managers provide an environment of self-determination, subordinates will trust the context and thus become more active in satisfying their own needs. Their proposition is that if organizations make the external consequences of behaviour clear (with accountability mechanisms and feedback) and present these in a non-controlling way, this will lead to the internalization of external goals: 'People will be intrinsically motivated when they have a sense of self-competence and they believe that they control their own behaviour' (London and Smither, 1999: 6). At the very least, this makes a number of questionable assumptions. That organizations are worthy of their managers' trust; that organizations will not exploit the fruits of learning for ends other than, possibly opposed to, those of the individual; that the external goals to be internalized are inherently correct and worthwhile; and finally, that the self-interest of individual learners corresponds with that of their employer. This remains an endemic difficulty with continuing professional development (CPD) schemes (see Box 4.5).

Box 4.5   How does professional development continue?

The central problem is that – like most discussions of 'education' – the [CPD] guidelines assume that important competence deficits stem from deficiencies in technico-rational knowledge and that these can be rectified by immersion in the ocean of non-knowledge that constitutes the 'knowledge explosion'. Unfortunately, the kind of technico-rational knowledge that contributes to competence consists of idiosyncratic combinations of up-to-date specialist, and usually tacit, knowledge. It cannot usually be specified in advance but is accumulated through feeling-guided adventures into the unknown. ... The key concept here is that of a development environment. ... Effective managers study their ... subordinates' interests and incipient patterns of competence and create situations in which those concerned are able to exercise and develop competencies like initiative, creativity and the ability to understand their organizations and society. (Raven, 2003: 360–1)

Social construction theory

The constructivist Discourse also focuses on aspects of an organization which are routinely missed, or if their presence is observed at all, their significance is underrated. The pertinent theoretical bases here are institutional theory, symbolic interactionism and sense-making. *Institutional theory* maintains that many structures, programmes and practices in organizations attain legitimacy through the social construction of reality (DiMaggio and Powell, 1983). For example, a study by Gooderham et al. (1999) of HRM in six European countries concluded that country-specific, institutional factors were more influential than industrial embeddedness, in determining HRM practices. This, they maintain, casts doubt on rational organizational theory (functionalist Discourse) which implies that organizations and managers make autonomous choices regardless of national setting. Rather, it supports the notion that HR practices, like management development, stem from a firm's attempt to gain legitimacy in relation to government and other public bodies, the law, industry associations, labour unions, other firms and the broader political culture of the host country. In other words, firms 'provide a sense of community by which discourse, coordination and learning are structured by identity' (Kogut and Zander, 1996; 503, quoted by Schultze and Stabell, 2004: 563).

This may explain why certain management development interventions encounter apparently irrational resistance or gain swift approval: due less to their objective efficacy and more to organizational history on the one hand, and/or managerial fads and fashions on the other (Brunsson and Olsen, 1998). From a constructivist perspective, part of the role of management development in organizations is the recovery of integrative values and the generation of mutual understanding. To this end, organizational myths, to take one example, help explain ambiguous events, maintain solidarity and cohesion in times of turbulence, and legitimize and articulate unconscious wishes and conflicts. This is well illustrated by reference to the services of change consultants and gurus, who are often enlisted to initiate and lend gravitas to management development interventions. In some ways, they take on the guise of organizational witchdoctor (see Box 4.6).

Box 4.6   Consultants or magicians?

Many guru performances are focused around programs aimed at changing organizational cultures in order to change how employees feel about their work, their managers, employers and customers. Yet despite their highly doubtful claims to change attitudes, what these programs actually change is behaviours rather than values. They achieve some degree of compliance, not surprisingly, but that they do any more than that is empirically unproven and theoretically unlikely. Yet the programs persist and are highly popular. Behaviour is apparently enough. They are today's version of the rain-making ritual: focusing on ideal connections between events, not real ones – trying to produce causes by producing the results. It is like trying to make it rain by putting up umbrellas. (Clark and Salaman, 1996: 101).

Giving a central role to social actors, and the mediation of meaning through language and symbols is indicative of *symbolic interaction theory* and giving credence to the mutually constitutive nature of unfolding events in organizations invokes *sense-making theory* (Weick, 1995). Although symbolic and highly interpretative, what is taken to be real symbolically is no less real in its consequences. This adds a further dimension to the metaphor of drama.

So, in summary, individuals do not always learn that which is genuinely helpful for organizational progress (or indeed their own!) and organizations do not automatically benefit when employees have learned something. There has to be a mutual behavioural change, a process that is far less manageable than organizations would like to think. Occasionally, activities like management development may be likened to an unfolding drama, providing reassurance, fostering belief in the organization's purposes, and cultivating faith. If 'the corporate message' fails to achieve these things, then, according to Bolman and Deal (1997: 248–9), the imperative becomes to 'change the symbols, revise the drama, develop new myths'. However, we would have to question whether organizations can always 'stage-manage' the symbolic interpretation of events in the way they would like to think they do (Grugulis and Wilkinson, 2002; Keenoy and Anthony, 1992).

Reflection point

Consider a high-profile management development activity with which you are familiar. To what extent have aspects of this entered the folklore or rumour machine of the organization? Do such stories embellish, complement or contradict the official narrative?

In the next section we examine the way some of the issues raised by these theories have been researched.

Research domain of constructivist management development discourse

If we took constructivist thinking to its extreme, we might argue that any organizational experience, no matter how mundane, has learning potential; and any activity might be construed as developmental or deleterious, depending on whose perspective is being sought. This is of little help in understanding management development. Researchers have therefore sought to privilege the experience of different participants to systematically assess the meaning they invest in management development activities. This is conducted in the spirit of *bricolage*, where the researcher recognizes the array of predispositions s/he brings to the study and seeks to understand the deeply held responses, beliefs and values held by the managers being researched as well: 'The bricoleur understands that research is an interactive process shaped by his or her personal history, biography, gender, class, race, ethnicity, and those of the people in the setting' (Denzin and Lincoln, 1994: 3). In some cases the emphasis has been on the organization and at other times the individual, but the common theme is that of co-creation: the constant, unfolding interplay of organizational processes that give rise to insight, discovery, experimentation, new patterns of thinking and working. Others, operating within the sense-making paradigm, are less concerned with intention and more with interpretation. We review studies which take each of these vantage points briefly below.

Social construction of management development

The social constructivist view places emphasis on the way activities conducted under the 'banner' of management development come to be invested with meaning, and how this meaning is jointly arrived at by many parties. Far from being linear, this is an iterative, discursive process, the significance of which is not always apparent at the time. Here we assess some studies which illuminate three cyclical phases of management development. We might characterize these as building a case, gaining currency and telling the story.

Building the case

How do those championing management development activities win the support and active participation of their organizations? Invariably, such activities are costly in time, energy and budgets, require 'extra' work for participants, line managers and HR specialists, and would appear to switch attention away from pressing operational issues and targets.

To answer this question, it makes sense to investigate so-called successful organizations. In the UK, National Training Awards (NTA) are given each year to those organizations across all sizes and sectors deemed to be innovative and effective in training employees (not just managers). Using story-telling technique, Gold and Smith (2003) conducted interviews and collected documentation from 15 winners. The authors make a number of observations about the way individuals and groups sought to mobilize the efforts of indifferent and sceptical colleagues in their respective firms towards a training agenda.

First was how actors within such organizations were able to draw rhetorically upon the resources of talk, thought and action provided by the wider 'learning movement'. This movement is described by Gold and Smith as an array of media attention comprising journals, books, websites, conferences which burgeoned in the 1990s to make learning a hot topic (Contu et al., 2003) and depicted it as an obvious and 'good thing'. And, of course, the very participation in the NTA connoted value since this was emblematic of the emergence and progress of the learning movement.

Second, Gold and Smith found managers in all cases claiming that the ostensible impetus for training and development in their firms was to respond to change in varying degrees. This is an argument which fits well into human capital theory with its concern to increase the net worth of employees' skills and abilities, even though there is little evidence that firms actually achieve this (see Box 4.7).

Box 4.7   The elusive aim of linking business and development strategies

Gratton et al. (1999) conducted in-depth case studies with seven large, UK-based companies, in which they sought to examine the linkages between business strategy, intended HR strategy, strategic HR context, realized HR interventions and outcomes. The outcomes included such measures as organizational commitment ('the ambience of the firm in terms of morale, satisfaction and shared commitment') and competence ('skills needed for new jobs, a positive attitude towards change and learning'). The research team found mixed evidence for the linking of individual performance to business

(Continued)

(Continued)

goals. For instance, training that focused on short-term business needs was pursued by all the companies as a way of creating a flexible and multi-skilled workforce but longer-term embedding of people management processes was far less consistent. In a study of 22 US 'leading firms', Siebert and Hall (1995) found that only two companies, 3M and Motorola, conducted their training of managers in an outwardly focused way in the sense that business priorities were the trigger for development.

Yet, behind this public rationale, Gold and Smith (2003) found more compelling reasons being identified. One was the discourse of personal empowerment: 'giving people a chance that they never had', the opportunity for experienced managers to put something back and the aspiration of improving job satisfaction and job-related safety. A longitudinal analysis of the effects of a life-long learning initiative in a Scottish company arrived at a similar conclusion (Martin et al., 1999). Evidence was found linking the life-long learning programme and employee perceptions of careers and fairness even when the company reduced its previous commitment to job security. All this indicates that the background orientation of significant actors can be highly influential in building a case for training and development. It also suggests a gap between public rhetoric and subjective reality which has been found in other management development research. For example, a study based on interviews with 78 managers in three UK retail banks by Antonacopoulou (2000) is interesting in that it takes a participant view of their training experiences. She found that self-development was hindered by several organizational characteristics: an unresponsive culture (notably a reluctance to encourage innovatory and challenging behaviours), insufficient opportunities for promotion and reward following training, and inadequate connection between the training and other HR activities. This was ironical in that: 'On the one hand, the language used by the three banks emphasises self-development and self-direction, and on the other, the mechanisms set in place to encourage these principles do not always allow the necessary freedom that underpins such initiatives' (Antonacopoulou, 2000: 500).

Stiles et al. (1997) also found a strong rhetoric in the three companies they studied in terms of commitment to manager training and development; in particular, there was a focus on coaching and counselling. However, the organizations were experiencing significant redundancies and the associated pressures of the business were limiting the time available for such development. Where it was being undertaken, the training centred largely on improving within-job performance and participants were unable to put their new skills to work due to the operational demands placed on them. For all this, the researchers also note the potentially positive impact that training and development can have upon employee perceptions of the psychological contract. For example, it conveys that the company values its staff and acts as an inducement to managers to maintain commitment to the organization.

Third, in order to canvass support for investment in training, Gold and Smith (2003) report a quandary in the 'winning' organizations: other players have to be 'enrolled' to actively support the initiatives, but their actions ultimately have to be constrained and limited, typically by budget controls and policy statements, qualifying the value of the planned training and development. This raises the spectre of checklists of standards, competencies and prescriptions of what could and should be learnt (more of this in a moment). In a slightly different context, Newell et al. (2001) report a similar paradox in relation to universities and funding agencies. Based on two case examples, they note the 'the logics used by funding bodies to promote knowledge creation and diffusion are not only at times unrealistic and inappropriate but also contradictory and conflated' (Newell et al., 2001: 113). In both cases there was a push towards outputs that could be diffused directly to industry as best-practice, which while well-intentioned, overlooked the fact that knowledge produced through the research process is not the result of a neutral, scientific and objective process but is socially and politically constructed. This is all the more so in multidisciplinary and multi-institutional research, where the emergent and socially constructed nature of learning is not a by-product but a central gain. So, as the authors point out, the government agency emphasis on ensuring tight control and pre-specified goals, predicated on a desire to arrive at demonstrable 'deliverables', actually subverts the likelihood of innovative knowledge and fresh insights emerging from the research. The parallels when applied to corporate or government sponsors commissioning management development in organizations are not difficult to discern.

Gaining currency

Some management development interventions quickly fade in the collective memory of an organization (which itself establishes lower expectations for future initiatives); others gain immediate currency. Kamoche (2000) uses, in part, an anthropological perspective to understand participant views of an international management development programme at a large transnational. As part of their development, the managers were on secondment to the UK-based head office. Several respondents had recently completed a series of courses at the company's prestigious training institute that was described as resembling a 'mini-MBA'. The stated aims of the programme were all about building skills and competency but this was not how the participants in the programme perceived or made sense of it. They professed to neither learning nor expecting to learn much in the way of formal skills or knowledge as a result of their participation in the programme. Instead, Kamoche reports a general consensus among respondents that the programme served mainly to communicate the expectation that participating managers should be single-minded in their pursuit of career advancement, while also serving as a forum for gaining the insider knowledge required for this. In this way, management development acted to inculcate a common and integrative culture, epitomized by the importance of informal networking, political lobbying and getting noticed by one's superiors. Several respondents admitted feeling uncomfortable about their participation in such a dynamic. They perceived that development within the organization was being artificially restricted to the chosen few so as to maintain a certain cache of exclusivity and status. In summary, viewed through the eyes of the programme participants, Kamoche characterizes the management development programme at this organization as part of a recursive or closed loop of normative control. The loop consists of managers' commitment to the corporate ideology being both manufactured and then secured via the careerist promise of upward mobility. While this may appear unremarkable, Kamoche's point is that development in this organization was serving inherently conservative functions, an elitist socializing process that acted to perpetuate existing structures, hierarchies, rules of behaviour, forms of language and cultural manifestations, with the very notion of 'career' being a central element to all of this. Similar elements were uncovered in a study of executive coaching in a major UK high street retailer (Box 4.8).

Box 4.8 Symbolic dimensions of a coaching programme

Selection for executive coaching was based upon success at an assessment centre, held for those aspiring to, or already holding, senior management posts. It became clear that the way managers came to participate was far from being the open and transparent process initially inferred. Although expressed with differing degrees of cynicism, there were obviously other criteria and dynamics at play: Very often the panel of assessors are not themselves diverse, which has implications for recognizing a diverse variety of attributes, as well as impacting on the psychological process of the minority employee, i.e. no role model, feeling the odds are stacked against them, etc. If the selection panel is not diverse, there's little likelihood that they'll be able to challenge each other's decisions, prejudices and stereotypes. Competencies are also likely to be based on very masculine characteristics.

'So I think you could argue that the coaching we have is a bit elitist and whatever – I don't think it ever really was criticized by the more junior members of the teams, I have never heard any negative feedback about it.' (HR Manager)

'Yeah, it was a bit of a black art I think. People wrote a personal resumé application type form and some screening was done and where people were rejected there was a discussion with their line management, if I remember right, as to some of the reasons why they had or hadn't been ... and it was noticed within different areas how people were influenced to take part, or not take part, made aware or not made aware, and the mystique around whether you could or couldn't put yourself forward.' (E-Commerce Manager)

These comments alert us to structural and hierarchical inequalities, to the views of less senior staff not being voiced (or heard), to screening and the need for 'sponsorship' from those influential in the organization (Ezzamel et al., 1996). There is much of symbolic significance here too. Participation

(Continued)

(Continued)

in the coaching programme appears to connote inclusion in an elite. Seen from this perspective, the assessment centre now takes on a different meaning: that of ritual initiation into senior ranks, with 'expensive' coaching as a reward: a ceremonial status passage serving to certify the manager in their new position (Lees, 1992). And references to 'black art' and 'mystique' add to the drama, perhaps helping to resolve the continual contradiction and problem of why some get promoted and others, of apparent equal worth, do not. The introduction of a rigorous assessment exercise helps to usher in new organizational myths and create new beliefs. The fact that the beneficiaries then have privileged access to external coaches all serves to reinforce such myths and legitimize the new regime. (Mabey, 2003: 445–6)

Such accounts illustrate the range of views, from champion to critic, insider to outsider, enthusiastic to cautious, emotionally involved to distant disinterest, that surround management development interventions. In her account of managers involved in a culture change programme, Turnbull (2002: 126) describes how participants can switch 'sides' from evangelist to cynic when trust is broken through inconsistent behaviours, and conversely some who are initially sceptical relate 'conversion experiences using highly emotive, quasi-religious imagery'. However, having galvanized support, secured budgets and mobilized bias in the organization, such activities tend to take on a momentum of their own. It now becomes difficult to 'break ranks' and criticize a high-profile, corporately endorsed intiative; if anything, the problem now is one of collusion (Clarke, 1999).

As Grugulis (2002) points out, because managerial work is hard to judge quantitatively, managers may be more vulnerable than other occupational groups to being judged on the impression they create on others, the extent to which they are known and the degree to which they conform to organizational norms. In this regard, she provides a fascinating account of the role of humour, an issue which, along with irony and paradox, is assiduously distrusted or disregarded by positivist research (Kilduff and Mehra, 1997). Based on ethnographic participant observation in three organizations over an 18-month period, she collected a rich seam of data concerning manager responses to training they received as they worked towards a National Vocational Qualification (NVQ). Functionalist studies of management development, like that of Winterton and Winterton (1999: 107), have singled out the virtue of NVQs: where management development made 'an unambiguous contribution to improvements in IP [individual performance], this was frequently associated with the use of Management Standards and the implementation of NVQs/SVQs'. Grugulis finds a more subtle discourse at work. Although not a planned part of the original study, which itself is indicative of constructivist Discourse, she found jokes being used to challenge the NVQ, 'presenting it as the impractical antithesis of candidates' own "commonsensical" understanding of managerial work and to question the way they were being assessed (both the

viability of collecting evidence and its function as "impression management")'
(Grugulis, 2002: 391) (see Box 4.9).

Box 4.9   Humour in management development

Grugulis (2002) notes a number of purposes served by humour in the context of management development:

- Testing the limits: simultaneously making a humorous statement about the training but withdrawing it from serious consideration allows managers to test and negotiate the system and the seriousness of its constraints.
- Celebrating pride in the 'real' way to manage as currently practised as against that prescribed in the NVQ. The latter is criticized via jokes, as being naïve, legalistic and poorly written, yet an illusion is maintained that NVQs must be preserved.
- Comic exaggeration of existing practice: the deliberate ambiguity in these jokes means that the risks associated with admitting that work has changed for the worse (due to the NVQ bureaucracy) are defused.
- Venting frustration without endangering a career because direct criticism could indicate to auditors that the candidate is making excuses for shortcomings, demonstrating a reluctance to develop or revealing that he/she is not truly engaged in managerial work.

Not all management development is linked, in this way, to standards, nor is there always such a definite end-point of pass/fail. Nevertheless, most development activities enshrine objectives (whether imposed or jointly agreed) and most paint a picture of effective outcomes. Most also contain a contingent of internal critics. To this extent, these insights apply.

Telling the story

It is perhaps no accident that when asked to explain the worth of management development, most organizations respond by admitting that the investment is 'an act of faith' (Tamkin and Hillage, 1998). This is no different from many other management activities, which are based upon faith assumptions and myths. They contain ritual aspects which exist alongside paradoxes, irrationalities and contradictions (Pattison, 1997: 39). This does not stop organizations telling a good story. Indeed, the spiritual imagery helps to embellish the narrative, which is why the notion of drama is an apt metaphor for this Discourse. To return to the study of 'winners', Gold and Smith (2003) point out that there is an ongoing need for valid information to prove to participants, as well as those still 'outside', that the training is producing outcomes of value. In the organizations they studied, they found evaluation being taken seriously in the form of tracking progress, feeding back results and displaying identifiable benefits, connecting these to external awards wherever possible. Although there was no evidence to prove that training and development was causal in winning awards and the like, this 'evidence', along with anecdotes concerning morale, motivation and very personal success, all became part of an ongoing story to maintain the efficacy of training and to suggest it should be expanded: 'Evaluation therefore had a dual aspect: first to feed a view that there was a causal link between TLD [training, learning and development] activity and measurable outputs and outcomes; second to provide a narrative meaning for the activities, capturing value and uniqueness in a specific time and place' (Gold and Smith, 2003: 148).

This may appear disingenuous, even deceitful. However, as Gabriel (2000) reminds us, the way events are remembered and explained is usually in the form of narratives, especially stories; these provide a way for individuals to reflect their values and interests and to express deeply felt feelings and emotions (see Box 4.10).

Box 4.10   Making sense of management development

If accuracy is nice but not necessary in sense-making, then what is necessary? The answer is, something that preserves plausibility and coherence, something that is reasonable and memorable, something that embodies past experience and expectations, something that resonates with other people, something that can be constructed retrospectively but also can be used prospectively, something that captures both feeling and thought, something that allows for embellishment to fit current oddities, something that is fun to construct. In short, what is necessary in sense-making is a good story. A good story holds disparate elements together long enough to energize and guide action, plausibly enough to allow people to make retrospective sense of whatever happens, and engagingly enough that others will contribute their own inputs in the interest of sense-making.

Sense-making is about accounts that are socially acceptable and credible. Stated differently, 'filtered information is less accurate but, if the filtering is effective, more understandable'. It would be nice if these acceptable accounts were also accurate. But in an equivocal, post-modern world, infused with the politics of interpretation and conflicting interests and inhabited by people with multiple shifting identities, an obsession with accuracy seems fruitless, and not of much practical help, either. Of much more help are the symbolic trappings of sense-making, trappings such as myths, metaphors, platitudes, fables, epics, and paradigms. Each of these resources contains a good story. And a good story, like a workable cause map, shows patterns that may already exist in the puzzles an actor now faces, or patterns that could be created anew in the interest of more order and sense in the future. The stories are templates. They are products of previous efforts at sense-making. They explain. And they energize. And those are two important properties of sense-making that we remain attentive to when we look for plausibility instead of accuracy.' (Weick, 1995: 60–1)

Reflection point

Return to the management development intervention you were considering earlier. What kind of stories has this generated and how were they given legitimacy? How do such narratives help participants and onlookers make sense of the experience?

Interpretative accounts of management development

A variant of constructivist research is that which takes an interpretative stance. It shares with constructivism a concern to understand how people make sense of their situation and to explore the meanings they invest in their experience of organizations. Where it differs is that researchers then express and represent such socio–cultural constructions as objective reality, which is more akin to functionalist writings. A guiding feature of the interpretative research tradition is its phenomenological base, the stipulation that person and world are inextricably related through persons' lived experience of the world (Berger and Luckmann, 1966). Here, there is no place for knowledge, skills and competencies being regarded as separate entities to the manager because this robs them of the unique situational context, tacit understanding and subjective experience through which the individual encounters his/her work. In a quest to understand why some people perform more competently than others, Sandberg (2000) adopted an interpretative approach to study 20 engineers at Volvo. Using intensive interviews and observation, he established that effective performance was not primarily explained by a set of attributes possessed, in different measure, by the engineers concerned; rather the particular expertise demonstrated was 'preceded by and based upon their conceptions of work' (2000: 29). In Table 4.1 this is contrasted to a more functionalist, rationalistic approach.

How might these ideas work out in practice? Take an organization, which in the desire to improve professionalism, introduces a set of competencies which include a number of behavioural indicators. Although derived from consultation with a panel of managers in the organization, these behaviours are generic (modified slightly for three given levels of manager), highly prescribed and relatively fixed. Management development in the form of classroom training and on-the-job development activities, chosen from a menu of options, is provided. This represents a fairly standard rationalistic approach to listing and addressing a set of attributes identified as lacking by an organization. In contrast, the central idea behind Sandberg's research is that competency is constituted by the meaning the work takes on for the employee in his/her lived experience of it and is not reducible to a set of objective standards. So, a good point of departure would be to get managers at different levels to describe their experience of interacting over a variety of issues and to draw out particularly effective behaviours. A relevant technique might be to use repertory grid, because this is designed to identify personal constructs (see Cassell and Walsh, 2004).

TABLE 4.1   *Comparing approaches to competency development*

	Functionalist approach	Interpretative approach	Examples applying interpretative approach to MD
Definition of competency	A set of generic or personal attributes.	My conception of my work and what constitutes effective performance.	Take the manager's frame of reference as the starting point.
Meaning of competency	Attributes (or behaviours) have relatively fixed meanings.	Meaning is context-specific, resulting from the idiosyncratic ways in which I conceive and approach my work.	Use repertory grid to access personal constructs and meanings of 'performance'.
Relevant competency	There is a hierarchy of predetermined attributes, specified for each task/role/level.	I develop necessary attributes, based on a personalized priority of what is most effective in each situation.	Use action-learning sets, OMD, SMD to engage managers and promote personal insight and growth.
Development of competency	Attributes are acquired via the systematic transfer of knowledge and skills from experts to novices.	I develop, deepen or replace present ways of conceiving my work with a new mindset.	Use constructed or reconstructed on-the-job 'encounters' to facilitate manager reframing.

MD   management development
OMD   outdoor management development
SMD   spiritual management development

Sandberg maintains that to move forward, development activities need to be designed and conducted in a way that actively promotes changes in the individual's conception of work (as against having new targets imposed which will simply impel the manager to intensify effort to achieve in the ways she/he has done previously). Action-learning sets may be appropriate here as they can provide a way of learning from the here-and-now (or the gestalt) of intra and interpersonal challenges and break the mould of habitual work patterns. This is done by taking regular time out with a small group of colleagues to question, understand and reflect, to gain insights and to consider a fresh range of options for acting in the future (Revans, 1987; Weinstein, 1995) (see Box 4.11). Coaching or mentoring is another route as this can help an individual identify personal learning blocks and co-devise a wider repertoire of choices/behaviours for situations they find challenging. Sandberg also advocates organizing particular encounters between employees and their work as developmental triggers. This is not unusual and forms the basis of standard work-based development methods such as international assignments, job transitions, creating high-level change responsibilities (McCauley et al., 1994). However, Sandberg proposes that there are two vital ingredients about the encounter. First, it must be organized in such a way that when the individual begins to realize the limitations of his/her present conception, the desired conception presents itself as an alternative. This is similar to the notion of reframing, replacing one familiar frame of thinking with a new, as yet, untried one (Westenholz, 1993). Second, rather than relying on a single encounter, development of the competency is more likely to be reinforced by a succession of encounters which highlight the attributes of the newly acquired conception in different situations.

Box 4.11   Developing managers via action learning

In an interpretative case study the experiences of ten individuals who had participated in a six-month in-house action-learning programme were explored (Wilson, 2005). Those participants who were open to the process of critical reflection and challenge talked about experiencing moments of breakthrough in their thinking. Their accounts highlighted how they had questioned some of their 'taken for granted' assumptions, based on their previous behaviour over the years. Some indicated that this provided them with greater insight into how they could better use their capabilities, and told of the exhilaration felt by recognizing they could take control of their situation; in some cases this led to a decision to quit the company. From the individuals' perspectives, work-based learning focused more on the person than traditional forms of in-house training programmes. For example, they commented on the honest and open dialogue between the action-learning set members, facilitated by a climate of trust and respect for each other. This aspect of psychological safety emerged as a significant factor in enabling participants to explore their mistakes and experiences, and thus facilitate learning (Edmondson, 1999).

Participants were provided with information communication technology (ICT) to facilitate discussions outside the set meetings, but none mentioned the use of ICT as a component that supported the opportunity for work-based learning. Raelin (2000) issues a caution regarding virtual communities in this context because dialogue is restricted by a lack of verbal cues and a reduction in the exchange of socio-emotional information. The result is that virtual teams may handle task-oriented interactions well, but may be slow at developing links between members.

This interpretative enquiry found participants talking of how they had achieved outcomes of considerable personal value, confirming Raelin's findings on action learning (1997). For example, managers described how they had been given the opportunity to grow, not in the knowledge that was immediately job-specific, but in broader areas such as confidence, assertiveness, personal interaction, and freedom to initiate personal change. However, on the debit side, much potential learning was eroded by a perceived lack of time and the pressure of fee-earning activities. First, participants felt that there was no time built into their diaries to free them from the pressures of day-to-day activities, aside from the provision of one day per month for learning-set meetings. Second, that the opportunity to experiment and reflect on their actions was prohibited by the organization's dominant task orientation.

So interpretative studies, as exemplified by that of Sandberg, pre-define competency, much as normative or positivist studies would do but constructivist research would not contemplate. Sandberg is unapologetic about this, stating that pre-defining a research object is unavoidable. He maintains that the crucial difference from normative studies is that rather than being established as an objectively decided set of attributes, 'the desired conception of competence is revealed as an alternative' (Sandberg, 2000: 22) via the conceptions of work expressed by the managers themselves. However, given that the aim of true dialogue is to unearth new insights, the seemingly convergent pursuit of an uncontested outcome, leading to the 'right answer' or the 'solution' would seem to be at the cost of silencing or marginalizing out-of-favour views (Oswick et al., 2000).

In this and the previous chapter, we have explored management development using functionalist and constructivist Discourses. It is perhaps timely to now stand back and assess the fruits of this analysis.

A comparative assessment of functionalist and constructivist Discourses

Utilizing the functionalist perspective, we have found manager and leader development to be typically portrayed as a largely technical activity, the principle purpose of which is to build the knowledge, skills and abilities of management populations. In doing so, the ontological status of both 'management' (as an activity or body of knowledge) and 'the manager' (as a social subject) remain broadly unquestioned and thus taken for granted. Likewise the idea of development, so pervasive and so deeply embedded in Western culture, is represented as a real thing. Ruth (2003: 8) comments that for many it still represents 'the one and only way of thinking'. One has to work hard to detect 'the wider epistemological politics of knowledge [...] where the danger is that knowledge might soon be rewritten to suit the paradigm' (Visvanathan, 2001: 40). Being a manager is an ontological fact and that is that. And surely no reasonable person would question the value of development ... for the individual, for the organization, for society?

The constructivist Discourse turns much of this thinking on its head. Almost ignoring the status of 'manager' and the discrete activity labelled management development (Watson, 2001), the concern here is to identify activities which result in effective managing and to understand how learning and development arise through experiential reframing of work by those engaged in it. This approach helpfully re-clothes management development with its contextual, tacit, irrational and emergent properties. It switches attention from training events to the gaps between them, from one-way knowledge transfer to tacit knowledge exchange, from the planned to the unintended, from the programmed to the processual, from the anticipated to the reconstructed. Most of us can point to examples of training and development activity in an organization becoming invested with multiple-meanings. More difficult perhaps, is how to use this perspective to improve the learning experience. The constructivist Discourse helpfully sensitizes us to the subjective and sense-making nature of management development, but the danger is that we drown in relativism. Sandberg (2000) offers some help here, by pointing the way to a more richly textured understanding of competency development, but such accounts have a way of reverting to normative assumptions. What the functionalist and constructivist Discourses share when it comes to management development, is the predominant value that consensus is ultimately achievable. However, they differ widely in how such outcomes are operationalized and recognized. The majority of functionalist studies are quantitative and survey-driven, because a large number of respondents is required for results of acceptable statistical significance. Functionalist research may also be done using a multiple case study design (e.g. Winterton and Winterton, 1999). Although less prevalent, qualitative work may also fall under the functionalist umbrella (e.g. Anderson, 2004), certainly to the extent that it subscribes to managerialist, objectivist and essentialist notions of the developing manager. Constructivist management development studies, on the other hand, rely heavily on participant observation, in-depth interviewing and ethnographic techniques, but they are far less prevalent at this point in time.

Functionalist Discourse employs a normative perspective which can be critiqued for its claims to objectivity and political/scientific neutrality. The very act of employing a normative perspective must be in itself considered a political one, even if this is not a conscious decision due (perhaps implausibly) to a lack of awareness of available alternatives. It is also an act which has implications for the ways in which we choose to see the world and the people within it. From a diversity angle, for example, it has until recently been rare within normative research for managers to be treated as anything other than disembodied, a-sexual and a-cultural individuals. As such, the results of such research are typically assumed to be applicable to managers in general, irrespective of their within-group differences. Constructivist studies of management development deal with such subjective contexts head-on by elevating the 'lived-experience' of those participating in and being affected by the development activities.

Among other things, this emphasis helps underline the developmental power of such activities as action-learning sets, outdoor management development (OMD), coaching/mentoring, informal on-the-job development, challenging job assignments, and the like. However, herein lies another danger. In a paper which traces some similarities between OMD and spiritual management development (SMD), Bell and Taylor (2004) draw attention to the way the latter prioritizes emotional and spiritual experience over and above theoretical or explanatory frameworks as a basis for self-discovery. By placing full responsibility for change upon the individual, the authors raise concerns about a failure in such development interventions: 'to acknowledge the importance of organizational, social and political structures in defining individual potential' (Bell and Taylor, 2004: 24). Not all constructivist studies are guilty of this, but there is a tendency for constructivist Discourse to assume that organizations are basically coherent and 'relatively unaffected by fundamental conflict and structural tension' (Schultze and Stabell, 2004: 557). We pick up on this potential blind-spot in Chapter 6.

Conclusion

In this chapter we have noted the ways in which the theories and studies under-pinning the constructivist management development Discourse significantly enrich our view of how learning takes place in organizations and helpfully ques-tion many of the assumed benefits of management development programmes. In particular, this Discourse serves to underscore the importance of understanding the manager's frame of reference and construal of the job; the way networks and communities of practice can aid learning and development; the range of factors that can 'interfere' with the learning process; the potent place of informal approaches in the development of managers; the (often irrational) way the case for management development is championed and sustained; and, not least, the sym-bolic currency and credibility management development interventions come to have in organizations which, in turn, shape future expectations.

This kind of analysis helps to counterbalance the functionalist Discourse, which is predicated on the view that development needs can be – and typically are – addressed by the organization, either by arranging some kind of learning activity or facilitating a learning culture. Much functionalist management development theorizing assumes individual learning takes place to exclusively serve the current purposes of the organization, which by definition, remains in control of the learn-ing processes that have been 'constructed'. As we have discussed, this is actually at odds with other conclusions derived from the adult learning literature. For instance, it is known that truly innovative learning is more likely to occur in situ-ations which lack certainty and controllability (Sitkin et al., 1994). It is in high-lighting and amplifying such learning narratives, and the symbolic significance they come to have, that the constructivist Discourse makes its contribution.

Summary

- Rather than taking such concepts as management knowledge and development as objective realities, the constructivist Discourse sees them as highly experiential and subjective.
- The development of managers is not confined to programmes and struc-tured activities, but can arise from, contribute to and dynamically shape all kinds of social practices.
- The theoretical basis of the constructivist Discourse as applied to management development is not clear-cut, but a number of disparate theories offer constructivist and interpretative insights.
- The constructivist Discourse helps attune us to the ways in which narratives, symbolism and sense-making construct legitimacy for man-agement development activities.
- An interpretative perspective leads us away from formal, predetermined development to more experiential, learner-oriented approaches which engage the whole-person.
- The constructivist Discourse is not without its problems, not least in its inability to explain tensions between individual and organizational needs and offer guidance on how to manage the development of managers.

5

Management development: identity and discipline

Many existing linguistic or representational systems are shown to be self referential. ...
They produce the very same world that they appear to accurately represent. (Alvesson
and Deetz, 2000: 105)

Any system of education is a political way of maintaining or modifying the appropriation
of discourses, along with the knowledges and powers they carry. (Foucault, 1984: 123)

After reading this chapter you will be able to:

- **Explain the theoretical and epistemological underpinnings of the dialogic Discourse to management development**
- **Discuss some of the key studies that constitute the research domain of the dialogic Discourse to management development**
- **Identify the distinctiveness of the dialogic Discourse's conceptualization of 'the manager' and the 'developing' manager**
- **Understand and describe the dialogic Discourse's distinctive treatment of management competency**
- **Explain the potential of the dialogic Discourse to contribute to our understanding of gender and diversity issues within the field of management development**
- **Compare and critique the dialogic Discourse in relation to the functionalist and constructivist Discourses to management development**

Introduction

Listen to conversations about management development in the boardrooms, training centres and corridors of any organization and invariably the focus will be on the 'development' side of the equation: how can staff be encouraged to 'grow' as managers? Likewise, read the training policy statements and websites and the 'management' side of the term will go unquestioned. The manager is assumed to be a largely self-evident entity, needing only to be improved upon or 'developed' to the mutual interests of both the individual and the organization. As such, there is a tendency to gloss over questions such as:

- What constitutes being a manager in the first place?
- What distinguishes managers from non-managers?
- Who decides on such issues?

- Where, how, why and to what effect did the very notions of 'management' and its 'development' originate anyway?
- What today can we learn about management development from an investigation of the emergence of management, both as a concept and as a category of person?

What also tends to get glossed over is the language in which people or documents express themselves, the metaphors they draw upon, those they leave out and the implications thereof. Take, for example, an HR Director who might typically refer to the 'ROI of development' or 'people as assets', etc., despite the fact that her/his main area of expertise relates to people as opposed to numbers. Can you imagine for example the Finance Director doing the converse? These are all issues that, in our view, are worthy of attention and upon which the dialogic Discourse to management development is well placed to shed light.

We begin, however, by situating the dialogic along Schultze and Stabell's (2004) two poles, as set out in Chapter 1 (Table 1.1): duality/dualism and consensus/dissensus.

1   Duality versus dualism

As we saw in Chapter 3, the functionalist Discourse relies very much on a dualistic ontological separation of the knowing subject (e.g. the manager) and the known object (e.g. managerial knowledge). In common with the constructivist Discourse, the dialogic rejects any such separation. In contrast to functionalism's 'ontology of being', various authors (e.g. Watson, 2001; Cunliffe, 2003) have characterized the dialogic as subscribing to an ontology of becoming (see Box 5.1).

Box 5.1   Comparing ontologies – 'being' versus 'becoming'

Orthodox, dominant or 'functionalist' thinking looks at the person or the organization as a 'thing' or an entity which has various properties – characteristics, goals, motives, and so on. This emphasis on 'thingness', when applied to individuals, sees them as relatively fixed beings, each with a certain personality, certain attitudes, etc. When applied to the work organization, this perspective presents a picture of a relatively coherent system. Goals, motives, strategies, cultures, personalities and so on are properties of these entities, whether they be persons or organizations. Within the dialogic, instead of seeing individuals or social groupings as entities, organizational and individual identities are seen as the ongoing achievements of human interaction. Persons and their worlds are continuously in process. Through institutionalizing much of that interaction in cultures and discourses, humans are constantly creating (or 'socially constructing') a knowledge or 'sense' of who they are, of what they are doing and of where they are going. Individuals and organizations are constantly in a process of 'becoming'. There 'is' no organization. There is 'organizing' – brought about through relating and talking. There is no 'management' as such within this ontology, there is only 'managing' – brought about through talking and relating.

Adapted from Watson (2005: 223).

This ontology has profound ramifications for management development. Far from being a rational/technical process of merely developing managerial capability, it becomes a key resource in the very constitution of managerial identity (we say more on this later in the chapter). In just the same way as the dialogic rejects the dualism or ontological separation between subject and object, it also challenges other dualisms that are typically taken for granted within functionalism. So, again like constructivism, the very separation between managers and non-managers is questioned, as is the notion that to become an effective manager there is a predetermined body of knowledge or repertoire of skills to be mastered. It is not that the dialogic rejects such things entirely. It is just that it refuses to accept them as ontologically verifiable, preferring instead to see them as phenomena that are linguistically and socially constructed. This facilitates a focus on the effects such constructions give rise to (rather than their 'truth' or 'falsity') and a consideration of how these constructions are socially contingent, rather than natural and inevitable.

2   *Dissensus versus consensus*

Functionalist and constructivist Discourses take a broadly consensual stance towards the social order, albeit in different ways. Functionalism is consensual in the way in which it privileges the notion of scientific knowledge as an ostensibly value-free, politically neutral and enlightened route towards emancipation for all. Constructivism is consensual by tending to privilege shared notions of reality, concentrating on how meaning is mutually created among research participants (Cunliffe, 2003). In stark contrast to this, the dialogic Discourse views the scientific as just one form of knowledge among a multitude of viable alternatives. Furthermore, the dialogic rejects any notion of singular, objective and universally applicable truths. It views any attempt to produce or privilege such truths (even socially constructed ones, as in the constructivist Discourse) as hegemonic, inherently open to challenge and ripe for 'deconstruction'.

Metaphor and the role of management development

Schultze and Stabell (2004) employ the metaphor of discipline as a means of epitomizing the dialogic Discourse. While we would not disagree with this (and will be exploring it in some depth in our section on theory), we suggest that any attempt to tie the dialogic too closely to any single metaphor goes against the very spirit of the Discourse itself. Drawing on Alvesson and Deetz (2000), we would add the metaphor of 'carnival' as a further means of encapsulating the approach the dialogic might take to the study of management development. There are several reasons for this. First, seeing the dialogic uniquely in terms of discipline renders it too negative, pessimistic and restrictive in our view. The metaphor of carnival reminds us of the often 'playful mood' (Calas and Smircich, 1991) of the dialogic but also of the way in which this Discourse regards identity as multiple, shifting and negotiated. You will probably notice the similarity of the dialogic Discourse's carnival metaphor to the constructivist metaphor of drama, as explored in Chapter 4. It is worth spending a little time contrasting these (see Box 5.2).

Box 5.2   Contrasting management development metaphors: carnival versus (dramaturgical) performance

While sharing similarities, the dialogic metaphor of carnival differs from the constructivist one of drama in a number of ways. First, as we highlighted in Chapter 4, the drama is largely scripted, rehearsed and controlled. The carnival is anything but and always liable to veer off into unplanned or unanticipated directions. Participants have more freedom in terms of the roles they can take on, stepping into and out of roles or identities as the mood might take them. Carnivals often involve a degree of cross-dressing, most notably in gay pride events where men might dress up as women. In applying this to management development the converse is often the case, where the feminine all too often becomes subordinated to the masculine, obliging women to metaphorically 'dress up' as men as a condition of participation (more on this in Chapter 9). While often playful in its unpredictability, the carnival can also degenerate into a scary, sinister and sometimes violent place to be. What is more it can be difficult to extricate oneself from at the best of times, never mind the worst.

A further metaphor is that of 'reproduction'. Here we draw on Calas and Smircich (1990: 698), who describe how management development can be analogous to a form of 'inbreeding'. They characterize the rhetoric of management development as promising much in terms of change and transformation but often ending up reproducing a largely masculine form of sameness when it comes to managerial identity. Such a view is echoed by Covaleski et al. (1998) in their investigation of the ways in which development (specifically mentoring) can function as a device for the metaphorical 'cloning' of managers, all in the service of corporate homogeneity. Our final metaphor for the dialogic study of management development is that of 'dressage' (see Box 5.3).

Box 5.3   Management development as dressage

'Dressage' is a French word in origin and has complex connotations, encapsulating the twin notions of discipline and training. It is associated with the verb *dresser* in French, which in turn has various related senses: to render straight, to bring into proper order, to manage and to direct. The most common usage of 'dressage' in English (which also commonly applies in the French) is to denote the mastery of a horse, that is its training in deportment and response to controls. The horse is trained to perform unnatural movements and to obey commands for the pure sake of control and the gratification of both rider and audience. As such, equestrian dressage is in

(Continued)

(Continued)

part a non-utilitarian behaviour for the benefit of its master or mistress and any spectators. Applying such a metaphor to management development would direct our attention to its non-productive and non-utilitarian aspects; at the extreme, these might include the inculcation of unnatural behaviours for little other purpose than the public display of compliance and obedience to disciplinary corporate norms.

Adapted from Jackson and Carter (1998).

So far in this section, we have employed four metaphors, those of discipline, carnival, reproduction and dressage, in our exploration of the dialogic view of management development. It is no coincidence that these are to some extent contradictory. For example, the metaphor of dressage, with its connotations of non-productivity, seems directly at odds with that of reproduction (the very epitome of productivity). Meanwhile the metaphor of discipline seems at odds with the chaotic connotations of carnival. It is also by no coincidence that each of these metaphors might be seen as polemical exaggerations of 'what really goes on' within the sphere of management development. Indeed, the dialogic Discourse is nothing if not playful, provocative, ambivalent and paradoxical. It is replete with metaphors and the four we have highlighted above are far from exhaustive. Others will crop up as the chapter progresses, for example management development as 'government' within our section on competencies.

Reflection point

Cast your mind back to one or more management development initiatives you have participated in or been witness to. Which, if any, of the above metaphors can you relate to your experiences and in what respects? If you have difficulty in drawing any parallels, try it again at the end of the chapter to see if you have any more luck.

Assumptions underpinning the dialogic Discourse to management development would include the following:

- Although managers are often described in terms of essential and hence developable traits, these are to be regarded as social constructions as opposed to ontologically verifiable properties.
- Managerial identity (how managers think and speak of themselves and the image they portray to others) is inherently fragmented, multiple, shifting, negotiable and in process, albeit within the limits of available discourses and power relations. As such, so is their 'development'.

- The dialogic study of management development gives prominence to language, as this is the principle means by which we *construct* reality (i.e. as opposed to being the means by which we *represent* it).
- The knowledge that is generated, transferred and exchanged within management development, is socially constructed and historically situated and does not reflect a world 'out there' just waiting to be discovered.
- Management itself is not an inevitable or natural concept whether in terms of management as an activity or management as a category of person. Managerial identity needs to be continually performed or accomplished, with the notion of 'development' often providing a prime vehicle for such accomplishment.
- Management development is inevitably a political activity; power is relational (as opposed to something possessed), bound up in the construction of knowledge and competency and vice versa.
- Organizations, just like 'management', are not considered to be ontological entities but ongoing social processes (i.e. of organizing, of managing).

Theoretical underpinnings of the dialogic Discourse to management development

We draw on two bodies of theory (Foucauldian social theory and Derridean deconstruction) that we feel best encapsulate the theoretical underpinnings of dialogic studies of management development. In his work on organizational discourse, Deetz (1996) was an early adopter of the term 'dialogic', which covers approaches that might elsewhere be labelled as either postmodern or post-structuralist. Notions of 'dialogue' also have a role to play in other Discourses, especially the critical and perhaps more implicitly the constructivist. But in the sense that we use it in this chapter, the term 'dialogic' encompasses the idea that all discourse can only exist both in relation to prior discourse and in anticipation of future discourse (Bakhtin, 1981; Fairclough, 1992). Any text or utterance is therefore inherently 'intertextual' (Kristeva, 1986) in that it forms part of a dialogue that establishes the conditions of, and the potential for, all meaning (Wehrle, 1982).

Foucauldian social theory

In their theoretical exploration of the dialogic in relation to knowledge management, Schultze and Stabell (2004) draw almost exclusively on Foucauldian social theory. Foucault himself is perhaps most renowned for his theorizing around the inseparability of knowledge from power. For Foucault, knowledge is not 'out there' in the world just waiting to be discovered but is always socially constructed. The concept of 'discourse' is central to such processes of construction in terms of how regimes of knowledge and their corresponding social practices come to be produced, taken for granted and part of everyday common sense (Mama, 1995, cited in Dick and Cassell, 2002). Foucault's method for uncovering such processes is known as 'genealogy'. In a nutshell, Foucauldian genealogy is concerned with historical analysis, not so much to understand the past but rather to interpret and critique the present (Burrell, 1998; Townley, 2002). It aims to render intelligible the processes by which we come to regard things in the present as unquestionably 'natural' or 'objective', including our own selves. It does so by seeking to analyse the conditions in which discourses emerge and come to be sustained (Townley, 1994). In our own case, genealogy can help us understand the historical *development of management* (Grey, 1999) as a means to better comprehend the contemporary workings of *management development*, with the latter being viewed as a pervasive contemporary discourse.

For Foucault, discourse is not just a form of representation but also a powerful form of action, hence Foucault's linking of knowledge to power and of power/knowledge to discipline. When alluding to the disciplinary nature of power/knowledge, Foucault consciously does so in relation to the dual meaning of the term 'discipline'. First, knowledge is disciplinary in the sense that it brings into existence the very possibility of professional expertise. Without the socially constructed boundaries around different strands of knowledge, we could have no basis for being able to identify different professional disciplines (see Box 5.4).

Box 5.4   Management in its 'disciplinary' aspect

The very notion 'management' has historically been rather vague and amorphous. As such, it has struggled to assert any kind of identity as a profession, especially in the face of other more formalized professions, such as accountancy, surveying, engineering, etc., each with their own institutes, standards, examinations and accreditations. More recently, the UK has witnessed the emergence and growth of the 'Chartered Management Institute' (CMI). From a Foucauldian perspective this can be seen as disciplinary form of power/knowledge in action. The CMI offers a means for management to be regarded as a professional discipline in its own right. It publishes a set of standards that serve to set it apart from other disciplines and offers development mechanisms to enable its members to continually improve their own performance and achieve 'chartered' status. This also enables its members to exercise power as managers by invoking the formalized knowledge, status and identity that would formerly have been unavailable to them.

But knowledge is also disciplinary in another sense. In order to conceive ourselves (or indeed accomplish our 'selves') as managers, we have to abide by certain rules or social conventions, right down to talking a certain language, respecting certain dress codes and rules of self-conduct, all of which constitute what we might call the discourse of management. To stray too far away from the observance of the discourse may call into question our status or identity as managers. This last point is what is meant when the dialogic Discourse refers to the collapsing of the subject/object dualism; a separation which is unreflexively taken for granted within functionalism. For Foucault, as social subjects we are both (re)producers of discourse and (re)produced by discourse:

We must cease once and for all to describe the effects of power in negative terms: it 'excludes', it 'represses', it 'censors', it 'abstracts', it 'masks', it 'conceals'. In fact, power produces; it produces reality; it produces domains of objects and rituals of truth. The individual and the knowledge that may be gained of him [*sic*.] belong to this production. (Foucault, 1977: 194)

Foucault coined the term 'technologies of the self' to describe the concrete ways in which the individual comes to be constituted through the power of discourse. He goes on to make an explicit link between such technologies and management development in acknowledging that the former involve the 'training' of individuals, not only in the obvious sense of acquiring skills and abilities but also in the correctional sense of acquiring new attitudes (Foucault, 1988), or in other words becoming a re-formed kind of self. Two specific elements to these technologies are particularly identifiable within the domain of management development. These are the 'examination' and the 'confession' (see Box 5.5), which respectively have the effect of rendering individuals both objects of and subjects of knowledge at one and the same time (Townley, 1998).

Box 5.5   The examination and confession in relation to management development

The examination

In the realm of management development, Foucauldian examination might comprise the processes of selection to participate in a given programme or course and assessments or appraisals that take place either during or after the programme (formally or informally). Prime examples would include 360-degree feedback and psychometric tools such as Belbin's team roles, the Occupational Personality Questionnaire or OPQ and the Myers–Briggs Type Indicator or 'MBTI'. What these practices serve to achieve is to objectify managers, by providing ways in which they can be rendered visible, knowable, calculable, discussible, and hence governable.

The confession

Confessional practices refer to episodes where the manager actively participates in a discussion or assessment of the self according to the organizational norms, categories and rules that emerge from the examination. By doing this, employees participate in the constitution of their own 'subjectivities' (see Box 5.6) by embracing, to the point of taking for granted, technologies that become part of their basis for self-knowledge and identity. This typically happens via methods that purport to reveal supposedly innate qualities of the managerial self as opposed to producing or constituting them (du Gay et al., 1996). Forums for this might include appraisal and career discussions, job interviews, coaching and mentoring. It also includes the kind of self-revelatory or psycho-therapeutic development that we explored in Chapter 1 (Box 1.2).

All in all, such processes of examination and confession permit individuals to be calibrated and quantified via systems of precise categorization and measurement, the scientific aura of which typically belies their constructed nature. In Foucault's own words, 'power is exercised by virtue of things being known and people being seen' (Foucault, 1980: 154, cited in Townley, 1993).

Box 5.6   Subjectivity in the Foucauldian sense

The notion of subjectivity in the Foucauldian sense is close to, while transcending, that of identity. It is described by Foucault himself as a process in which disciplinary power/knowledge:

> applies itself to immediate everyday life which categorizes the individual, marks him [*sic.*] by his own individuality, attaches him to his own identity, imposes a law of truth on him which he must recognize and which others have to recognize in him. There are two meanings of the word subject: subject to someone ELSE by CONTROL and DEPENDENCE, and tied to his own identity and conscience or self-knowledge. Both meanings suggest a form of power which subjugates and makes subject to. (Foucault, 1983: 212, original emphasis; cited in Starkey and McKinlay, 1998)

Importantly, when Foucault refers to notions such as identity and individuality, he does not use these in any realist or essentialist sense but as products of discourse. More colloquially, subjectivity can be thought of as our sense of 'who we are and how we think about who we are [which] emerges through our engagement within the practices, discourses, moralities and institutions that give significance to events in our worlds' (Fenwick, 2005: 34).

Deconstructionist theories

In a later section we will go on to explore some management development-related studies that have developed the above themes more fully. Before doing so, however, we explore a related but rather different strand to the dialogic Discourse, but one which perhaps surprisingly remains untouched by Schultze and Stabell. This relates to the deconstructionist approach to organizational analysis as developed by the French post-structuralist philosopher Jacques Derrida (see Box 5.7).

Box 5.7   Derridean deconstruction

Deconstruction begins from the premise that language has no fixed meaning. Therefore, we cannot assume we know what words mean, either to ourselves or anyone else. Instead, we should acknowledge written or spoken language (and therefore attempts to communicate through it) as continuous

(Continued)

(Continued)

processes of struggle that are never fully clear in their meaning or amenable to final closure. Accepting this argument means we must see texts as unstable and open to infinite interpretation. Derrida goes on to argue that the meaning of words is always constructed with reference to what they do not mean – so we understand what 'day' means by referring to what it does not mean and in particular what any opposed terms (e.g. 'night') might imply. Meaning can only be deferred through the process of establishing temporary *différance*, a term Derrida created to emphasize that meaning is produced by the 'difference' between words and by 'deferring' to other unstable meanings. A further implication of a deconstructionist approach is that context is central to meaning. Therefore, if the context of a word is changed, then its meaning is also changed.

Adapted from Taylor (2007).

Deconstruction is duality-oriented in the sense that it will always seek to dismantle dichotomies by showing how each side of any dualism will rely on the other for its very 'existence'. For example, 'management' only has meaning in relation to what it is not (most obviously non-management) and the same goes for 'development'. Deconstruction is dissensus-oriented in the sense that it focuses on suppressed conflict in order to undermine all claims to a singular or objective truth (Martin, 1990). It is often associated with feminist post-structuralism (Agger, 1991) and employed as a means of exposing gender conflict within organizations that often goes unrecognized within the hidden sub-texts of what people write, say and do (Martin, 1990). One way in which it does so is to expose the inherent hierarchy within any dualism, such as 'male' and 'female' or 'masculine' and 'feminine' (see Chapter 9 for more on this). Equally as important as what is said in a text, however, is what remains unsaid and the implications of such omissions (Cunliffe, 2003). As Taylor (2007) points out, Derrida's own work is generally acknowledged as exceptionally difficult, dense and somewhat resistant to authoritative interpretation. Perhaps because of this, there remains very little in the literature in the way of deconstructionist analysis of management development.

A final point to be made within this section is that theory within the dialogic Discourse plays a very different role from the one it plays within functionalism. Functionalist or 'grand narrative' theories, which offer universal explanations of the social world, only have a place within the dialogic in as much as they provide a basis for critique. Typically, this would involve exposing the implicit hegemony within the truth claims inherent in such grand narratives. Apart from this, explanatory theory within the dialogic Discourse can only be based on locally situated understandings (in both time and space) that are context-specific, inherently sectional and representative only of one 'truth' among many.

Research domain of the dialogic Discourse of management development

Wherever we refer to individual papers within this section, it is not necessarily the case that the whole work fits neatly or squarely within just the dialogic perspective. Indeed, it is not unusual for any one paper to span (more or less reflexively) two or even more Discourses. This is particularly the case for the dialogic and critical Discourses where there can be a fairly high degree of overlap (Alvesson and Deetz, 2000). Our aim here, purely for illustrative purposes, is to draw out the particular aspects of various management development-related papers that can be identified fairly directly as dialogic and that we ourselves have found illuminating. As such, you may well spot the same works cropping up again in our next chapter, where we will be focusing on their salience to the critical Discourse.

Dialogic research in the area of management development can perhaps be divided into the following sub-domains: first, genealogical/historical analyses of management and associated concepts; second, the contemporary production of managerial subjectivity via management development; and third, deconstructionist analyses of management texts. Here we discuss these in turn with particular reference to various dimensions of management development: careers and career development, mentoring, graduate development and competency-based management development (noting, especially, the potential for gender bias).

Genealogical/historical analyses

> I was styled a 'manager' and my wife ... was a 'housewife'. I can remember well the blessed relief of leaving my house and its attendant chaos each morning to go off to my oh-so-demanding 'management' job. In what sense ... was my wife not 'managing' and in what sense was my work ... more essentially *managerial* than hers? At work I had another woman to make sure I managed properly. ... This one wasn't styled a manager either, but the same essential question held good for her, in what sense is the work of a secretary not managerial. (Mant, 1977: 1; cited in Grey, 1999)

Du Gay et al. (1996) make the point that what it means to be a manager varies historically and does so in relation to the techniques and practices that constitute (what is generally regarded as) the 'material reality' of management activity. In a similar vein, Willmott (1997) highlights the constructed, contextual and disputed nature of the diverse meanings that the term 'management' has come to have. As we saw in Chapter 2, he traces the term back to the Italian *maneggiare*, the original meaning of which was 'to handle a horse'. For Willmott, this semantic root remains indicative of the social divisiveness of contemporary conceptualizations of management, connoting as it does the efforts of some to control an often resistant 'other'. There is also an intriguing connection here to the equestrian metaphor of dressage we introduced earlier. In building upon the social divisiveness aspect, as our opening quote to this section indicates, Grey (1999) points out that activities typically thought of as 'managerial' are far from restricted to those commonly identified as 'managers' and that a diverse array of people, both within and without the 'work' place, do in fact carry out managerial activity (the obvious gender dimension in this is something we will be developing later within this chapter and beyond). As such, there is nothing natural or inevitable about the status of those deemed to actually *be* 'managers' and so we need to look at alternative explanations for the existence of their distinctive status. Grey favours a political view, referencing Foucault's theorizing around the role of disciplinary power: the discourse of management permits not just the subordination and control of non-managers by managers, but also the auto-disciplining of managers by their own constructed selves. But what are these disciplinary 'techniques and practices'? How, where and why did they emerge and what is their legacy for contemporary management development and its participants?

Given the close connection between management development and career development, an analysis of the very notion of career helps throw light on such questions. Two authors, Savage (1998) and McKinlay (2002), have each employed Foucauldian genealogy in identifying the 'career' as a disciplinary mechanism. Savage traces the origins of career back to the large railway companies of the mid-nineteenth century. Interestingly, he analyses how the very notion of the career replaced physical inspection and punishment routines by serving to internalize self-regulation. Similarly, McKinlay (2002) has observed how the career was invoked as a novel device to secure compliance and commitment among banking employees of the late nineteenth century. For McKinlay (2002: 596), the career 'speaks of a promise, a vow that an organization makes to an individual that merit, diligence and self discipline would be rewarded by steady progress through a pyramid of grades'. For an example of this, see Box 1.4 and the ensuing discussion in Chapter 1. Within McKinlay's analysis, however, career implies much more than an economically instrumental exchange. It is a life-long moral project for the individual and is always subject to validation by the organization (and, we would add, society at large): 'The very idea of the career epitomized the reflexive self at the heart of the modernist project: we are what we make of ourselves' (2002: 597).

Both McKinlay and Savage draw attention to the way in which previously chaotic labour markets within both industries became gradually more internalized and structured, such that 'progress through the ranks' came to be even thinkable as a concept. Intriguingly, the subsequent achievement of such progress relied not so much on technical task performance but on strict conformity to behavioural and attitudinal norms that were often peripheral to the task at hand. Note how this resonates with the metaphor of dressage that we introduced earlier. What also becomes clear from both these analyses is the extent to which the career (and its role in constituting contemporary notions of organizational hierarchy) is rooted in a time when the clerical/managerial work environment truly was an exclusively 'man's world', where unbroken service and steady progress through the ranks was a model accessible to the whole (i.e. male) workforce.

Contemporary production of managerial subjectivity

Career and career development   Obviously, organizations today are very different environments from the nineteenth-century workplaces studied by Savage and

McKinlay, not least in their gender composition. Despite this, however, a study by Grey (1994) indicates that the concept of career in the late twentieth century was fulfilling many of the same organizing, disciplinary and regulatory functions that Savage and McKinlay discerned to be operating over a century previously. His study was of graduate trainees in a large UK accounting firm. What he found was that via various processes of organizational socialization (including management training), graduates came to discipline themselves via the social construct of 'career'. Career provided the discursive lynchpin around which graduates rapidly learnt the importance of appearing: ambitious, committed, presentable, acquiescent, well-networked, enthusiastic (even when doing the most mundane of tasks) and generally compliant to a variety of other social norms of the organization. One such norm was the expectation that family life would serve as an adjunct and support to work life rather than the converse. For example, one participant in the research alluded vividly to anyone of partnership potential being expected to have a 'well packaged wife'. As such, career and all it entailed went well beyond what was needed for efficient work performance within this organization (another example of development as dressage). For Grey, career became the basis for a 'moral' and all-encompassing project of the self which, while not entirely negative, presented anything but a level playing field for all organizational members. For example, while Grey, by his own acknowledgement, only touches on the gender and diversity implications of his analysis, it is not difficult to appreciate how subjectivities other than those which revolve around masculine heterosexuality are at odds with the careerist ideal that appears to reign within the organization he studied. As a final comment, it is not that management development *per se* dictated the importance of things like a 'well packaged wife' within the Grey study. The point is rather that development often serves to inculcate the importance of careerism which, in turn, can serve as a discursive resource for the more informal and often discriminatory socialization that goes on.

Mentoring   Much of Grey's analysis is supported by a more recent study of management by objectives (MBO) and mentoring practices within 'Big Six' accountancy firms in the USA (Covaleski et al., 1998). The authors found such practices to be constructing managerial subjectivity around careerist norms to the extent that one ex-partner of the firm attested to feeling extreme 'grief' at the loss of his tenure within the firm, likening the event to the loss of a child. Like Grey, the authors also drew attention to the gender implications of such dynamics. For a start, women within the firm had fewer opportunities for mentoring, given the dearth of senior females within the organization combined with the sexual innuendo that often surrounds mixed-gender mentoring relationships. What was more, however, women tended to be judged according to different standards than men when striving to adopt the mentoring-inspired careerist subjectivities required for 'success' within these organizations. The most flagrant example of this revolved around a lawsuit against one firm for denying promotion to a female employee on the basis that she was 'too macho' and needed to 'walk, talk and dress more femininely'. Another conclusion of the authors (resonating with our 'reproduction' metaphor) was that mentoring in combination with MBO was instrumental in producing 'corporate clones' in the sense that the organizational form was discernibly duplicated within the managerial subjectivity of each individual. The most vivid example of this comes from a manager who talks of having become more identifiable as a 'revenue stream' than as a living, breathing individual.

Graduate development   Fournier (1998) takes the notion of corporate cloning a step further in her Foucauldian analysis of graduate development processes within a large UK service sector organization. She explores how career discourse within this organization operated to engender the dominant notion of 'self as enterprise', an enterprise which just like any other became an object needing to be 'assessed and evaluated' (typically via appraisal) and then 'invested in' (typically via training and development). This often involved considerable 'sacrifice' on the part of the individual, all with the aim of becoming more 'marketable', thus generating the highest possible 'returns' in terms of the increased status and material wealth that flow from this type of 'career development'. But Fournier also makes the point that any discourse, including the entrepreneurial careering discourse above described, can only achieve and maintain dominance in the face of its deviant, pathological, irrational and ultimately negative 'other'. In her case, this 'other' comprised a more militant discourse of resistance and exploitation, emanating from those who perceived themselves as either unable to access the dominant discourse of enterprise due to structural and political factors and/or those who laid claim to what they perceived as being their more authentic, uncorrupted and integral selves. This is where Fournier's analysis admirably illustrates the duality-embracing aspects of dialogic thinking in as much as 'enterprise and militancy, power and resistance, core and margins, only exist in relation to each other, rather than independently of each other'. For her, wishing for a world where everyone can and should fit in with entrepreneurial/careerist ideals is futile, not least because such a discourse 'can only govern by invoking and constructing its "other" and by delineating the space within which the reprehensible other may legitimately be bound i.e. the margins' (Fournier, 1998: 72–3).

Having said this, Fournier is careful to avoid any condemnation of the discourse of careerist enterprise or indeed its opposite. She merely makes the point that each needs the other for either to have any meaning, arguing for discursive plurality and warning against the potentially colonizing influence of enterprise discourse to all forms of life. Among the implications of this is that any call for management development to be rendered more democratic, more inclusive and less discriminatory (for example by doing away with 'fast track' or 'high potential' development schemes), while well intentioned, may simply lead to elitist social divisions cropping up elsewhere within the organization if, as may be the case, they are integral to the (dominant) discourse of management. This of course does not preclude the consideration of alternative, perhaps as yet unimagined, discourses of management.

Competencies, power/knowledge and the disciplined self

So far we have only alluded in rather general terms to the role of management development in constituting managerial subjectivity and without entering into the specific micro-practices of management development in their disciplinary aspect. In this section we draw on the concept of management competencies in order to illustrate how these micro-practices of disciplinary power/knowledge can be seen to operate within the field of management development. In doing so, it is important to remember that, for Foucault and dialogic researchers more generally, the human subject (managerial or otherwise) is not 'given' but is produced historically by the power/knowledge effects of discourse:

> When the individual loses his or her privileged epistemological status, it becomes possible to see the individual as a product of the social techniques of power, a perspective that highlights the importance of both identity and identity-securing strategies in the reproduction of power relations (Knights and Willmott, 1985). The focus of analysis becomes the 'knowability' of the individual. (Townley, 1993: 522)

Examination and confession   From the dialogic perspective, competencies are one way in which this 'knowability' of the managerial subject is produced. Competency formats may be many and varied but they will typically be arranged in clusters with each cluster presenting a set of images that managers are encouraged to emulate (Townley, 1998). In most organizations, the competency development cycle will commence with some form of evaluation or appraisal exercise, perhaps in a one-to-one session with a superior, perhaps in the context of an assessment and/or development centre, or perhaps via 360-degree appraisal. Whatever the precise forum, all of these appraisal activities entail elements of Foucauldian 'examination' and 'confession'.

Townley (1994) describes examinational practices as systems of marking and classification, often constructed around a battery of questions and documented answers. They provide a basis for measurement and hence judgement by their facilitation of hierarchical ranking around constructed (albeit often statistical) norms. They also serve to render individuals (in our case managers) visible in the first instance and hence knowable in the second. In other words, such things as a manager's apparent performance, character, disposition or personality are calibrated by scores, grades or marks, thereby differentiating them from other managers. For Foucault, it is via such practices that the individual comes to be constituted as an object of power/knowledge. Furthermore, as Townley also points out, such practices have become so widespread within society that their effects are barely noticed or remarked upon. It is only when we refuse to take managerial subjectivity as a given that we can appreciate how these practices operate to render individuals (in our case managers) not only visible and hence knowable, but also calculable, measurable, rankable, discussible and therefore judgeable, all of which are necessary precursors to an individual becoming both 'developable' and ultimately governable (see Box 5.8). It is also when we refuse to take managerial subjectivity as a given that we can critically reflect on the (inevitably arbitrary) criteria against which we, as managers, are rendered both developable and governable as objects of constructed knowledge.

Box 5.8   Competency development as a form of 'government' or 'governance'

Rees and Garnsey (2003) explain governance in the Foucauldian sense as being not simply about the ordering of activities and processes but as being intimately concerned with the internalization of discipline. Discipline is most effective when it is least visible, for example by operating through the internalization of norms and the development of subjectivities in keeping with a certain form of conduct. They relate this to competency development in as much as powerful interests may promote the notion of the 'competent' manager in line with their own aims and aspirations for the organization. Managers are then encouraged to 'take responsibility' for their own 'development' or 'self-fulfilment' but according to constructions (of competency) that are not of their own making.

However, it is not just a case of managers being passively constituted as *objects* of constructed knowledge. Examinational practices become *confessional* when the individual actively participates in a discussion or assessment of the self according to these same norms, categories and rules. It is here that managers also become *subjects* of knowledge. They do so by embracing, to the point of taking for granted, a technology that becomes part of their basis for self-knowledge and identity. In other words, they actively participate in the constitution of their own subjectivity. Confession operates through avowal or the opening up of oneself (one's strengths, weaknesses, thoughts and actions) in front of an authoritative interlocutor. The 'confessor' may come in various guises: often it will be someone who is deemed more experienced and more expert, perhaps a mentor or a coach, who can act as a 'guide' or 'master' to the confessing 'novice' (Townley, 1994; Covaleski et al., 1998). Or, it may be an inanimate entity, such as a psychometric test or structured questionnaire, a tool which nevertheless embodies the expert knowledge of a distanced authority (Brewis, 1996). The more such knowledge takes on an aura of scientific neutrality, the more powerful its effects.

Competency-based development as pseudo-science   Du Gay and Salaman (1996) carried out a series of case studies within seven UK organizations in order to assess the ways in which specific competencies were identified and used and to explore the kinds of problems or conflicts that might surround their implementation. In terms of the identification and clustering of individual competencies, they found that such processes were often characterized by qualitative negotiation and arbitrary judgement and sometimes even imposed by diktat from on high. However, this did not seem to prevent organizational respondents from talking about their own competency development as if it was a largely scientific and value-neutral activity. Such a finding was echoed in a more recent study by Finch-Lees et al. (2005a), where one manager in a large UK-based multinational commented as follows on the outcome of his competency assessment (carried out by a firm of external HR consultants):

I said you know this is a good way of me just stopping and thinking and testing myself against sort of world-class benchmarks so I had real energy for it. And the bit of the process I was a bit disappointed with was the robustness of the benchmarking bit of that process. I pushed them on it but it was explained as 'it's based on our experience of dealing with leaders'. And they *have* got *huge* experience I mean don't get me wrong. They are expert occupational psychologists so it's not that I don't trust their judgement.

From the Foucauldian perspective the kind of trusting acquiescence we find above is understandable, as to do otherwise would call into question the knowledge upon which a manager's sense of developing self is being founded.

Brewis (1996) performed an empirical study of competency-based tuition within the context of the 'Personal Effectiveness' module of the UK's Certificate in Management. She focused in particular on the diagnostic phase of the module, drawing parallels with Foucauldian processes of confession. Confession in this context took the form of an initial questionnaire-based self-diagnosis followed up by an ongoing self-development diary designed to track progress against the competency profiles. Alternatively, some students preferred to self-diagnose by way of 'confessing' to the tutor running the session. Brewis found that this resulted in students often expressing feelings of deep contentment at having revealed or unveiled the 'truth' about themselves. It enabled them to get a sense of 'where they were' and where they needed to devote their developmental attention. Similar sentiments were expressed by a number of managers in the previously mentioned study by Finch-Lees et al. (2005a):

> By using the capability frameworks you can really focus in on what you're great at, and build upon those and leverage those.
>
> I've got a report on me from [the psychologists] which I do refer back to around both assessing me against, you know, desired leadership capabilities, where I'm at at the moment.[1]

As in Brewis's study, these managers talked in terms of the competencies having helped them 'reveal', 'unveil' or 'unearth' some kind of singular and essential truth about themselves, and this despite some simultaneous misgivings (see earlier extract) as to the actual origins of the competency frameworks themselves. This tends to reflect the language in which much company documentation surrounding management development is itself couched, sometimes actively preparing the participant for the confessional experience:

> To get the most out of the [management development] experience you will need to be open-minded and be prepared to open up and take a few risks. This won't always be easy or comfortable but is likely to enhance the quality of feedback and learning you gain. The first session will focus on mapping out your experience and functional skill base and your leadership capabilities. Where psychological assessments are used they will be fully explained. The second session, which will take place shortly after the first, will focus on drawing out your strengths and development needs. The process outlined above allows effective diagnosis of the factors that underpin capabilities and development needs. (Extract from company documentation, Finch-Lees et al., 2005a)

---

1 In this extract and elsewhere, respondents sometimes employ the term 'capability' (rather than competency), as that was the term favoured by the organization in which they worked. The full paper from which the extract is drawn explores the differences between the two terms but, for our purposes here, they can be regarded as synonymous.

Far from revealing any kind of absolute truth about the managerial self, the dialogic Discourse regards this pseudo-scientific, essentialist view as being just one among the inherently multiple 'knowledges which supposedly tell [individuals] who they are' (Brewis, 1996: 78). We now explore some of the gender implications of such a view.

Competencies and gender bias   Rees and Garnsey (2003) reviewed competency practices in six UK organizations with a view to appraising the gendered nature of such 'knowledges'. They draw attention to how the managerial function has predominantly been theorized as a gender-free construct, despite the fact that managers themselves have historically been primarily male. Pointing to the fact that the proportion of women in senior management in the UK showed little increase in the decade preceding their analysis, they speculate that competency frameworks, despite their aura of scientific neutrality, may actually be maintaining gender imbalances in management. One aspect of their analysis was to divide the competency statements they encountered along a 'nurturing' versus 'directive' continuum, the former being primarily associated with femininity and the latter with masculinity. What they found was that the competencies in five of the six organizations were skewed towards the directive end of the continuum, with prescribed behaviours tending to privilege independence of self and control of others. This, for the authors, was a reflection of the dominance of male managers and masculine values within these organizations in as much as the competencies they encountered reflect 'constructs and categories that are already defined in the minds of senior managers or consultants. ... The language of such discourses tends to reproduce itself and draw on existing categories, rather than bringing in anything new' (Rees and Garnsey, 2003: 564). Referring back to our earlier section on metaphor, note how Rees and Garnsey draw upon that of *reproduction* here. Only in one of the six organizations did nurturing qualities (such as those associated with cooperation, connectedness and democracy) comprise a significant element of the competency statements. This organization happened to be one where women made up a far higher proportion of the management population than in the other five organizations.

Rees and Garnsey also open up a gender perspective to the confessional aspect of competency development. They cite evidence from the literature to suggest that women typically engage less in self-promotion than do men and are more likely to 'confess' to weaknesses as opposed to touting their strengths. If, as others propose, participation in management development signals vulnerability as well as power (Ackers and Preston, 1997), then Rees and Garnsey's analysis suggests that when it comes to the examinational and confessional aspects of management development, there is anything but equal opportunity when it comes to gender. In fact, women, it seems, are faced with at least a double bind. When it comes to examination, they are rendered visible, measurable and rankable according to predominantly masculine criteria. Then when it comes to confession, the tendency is to construct self-truths focused around 'weaknesses to be remedied' rather than 'strengths to be leveraged'. Taking this a step further, a recent study by Finch-Lees et al. (2005a) suggests there may even be a *triple* bind to consider. They argue that even if a competency statement could be value-neutral *on paper* (which from a deconstructionist perspective is contestable in any event), its representation would nevertheless be inherently subject to interpretation in practice. Where the organization itself is a predominantly masculine environment, then the dominant interpretation is also likely to be a masculine one. This was vividly reflected in the views of one female manager who stated:

> If you actually look at what it says about 'Edge' [i.e. one of the competency clusters], it's actually quite a broad definition about umm getting stuff done essentially. But its *interpretation* in [the organization] has been actually quite focused around the kind of courage to put your head above the parapet.

She later went on to build on this:

> Some of [the competencies] have kind of taken prominence over others. And I think some of that's been around the interpretation that they've been given by the [organization's exclusively male] executive themselves. There are certain capabilities that are kind of quite prevalent in individual members of the board. So there was a kind of a tension in myself in thinking through my own development around, well, 'am I gonna have to change myself so fundamentally as a human being kind of thing in trying to address this behaviour that's kind of expected within [the organization]?' And, er, I actually came to the conclusion that actually what I need to do is to be true to myself.

But it is not just in the area of gender that the disciplinary aspects of the competency approach might work to flatten, suppress or marginalize difference (Ackers and Preston, 1997; Fournier, 1998; James, 2001). In the same organization from which the above extracts were taken, Finch-Lees et al. interviewed a manager on secondment from a different continent. This manager was subject to the 'examination' of 360 feedback, not just from colleagues but from the external supplier agencies with whom he was closely working:

> Because I understand fully that I'm here to develop myself, I constantly have to check back and say, if my weakness or my development area was say communicating clearly, at every opportunity when I'm going to a meeting for a presentation or my meeting with agencies, I always have to have that at the back of my mind, to say I need to work on this. Two reasons for that is that every end of month I would have feedback, conversations with the person I report to. But then every three months I've got a formal written feedback from the agencies.

The above provides a vivid illustration of the all-seeing or 'panoptical' (Foucault, 1977) potential of competency development. The manager is permanently subject to the 'normalizing gaze' of the examination (Townley, 1994), even to the point of being rated against the competency standards by an *external* agency with whom he was closely working. What's more, he later confided that while the behaviours he was being measured against might be enabling him to fit in within his UK host environment, they might actually disadvantage him when he later returned to his home country.

> The capability development process in my view needs not be brought across as 'this is the only path through which you know you can progress in the organization'. Because if you do that, then human beings are only human, then people come across differently. They will behave differently, or you may actually end up identifying the wrong development areas.

He went on to recount how several of his colleagues had already suffered career-wise for taking the UK-centric competency statements too literally within his home country, where they were deemed to be counter-cultural and a consequent threat to the hierarchy. This illustrates how identities that are constituted through the power/knowledge of competency are also made vulnerable by the same (Townley, 1998). We can also see how competency development has the potential to produce superficial and self-fulfilling performance effects at the individual level, in as much as stakeholders may simply 'surface act' (Clarke, 1999) against the competencies for purely instrumental ends such as career progression or mere survival.

To conclude this section, our intention is certainly not to condemn competency development for its disciplinary functioning (nor indeed to condemn technologies of the self in general, such as those mentioned in Box 5.5). In fact, it is this very functioning that provides the means for dealing with existential doubt, doing so via the productive creation of self-knowledge. Indeed, the very basis for this may frequently be the adoption of an ideology which portrays competencies as scientifically neutral and pre-existent properties of an objectively measurable self. Notwithstanding the fact that such claims to scientific neutrality rarely stand the test of closer scrutiny (and even if they did, they would still be epistemologically suspect for the dialogic), the resulting self-knowledge can undeniably perform productive identity work for managers. Along with this comes an optimistic and energizing sense of being, belonging, orientation and purpose. Furthermore, the notion of an objectively knowable, visible, measurable, discussible and calculable self (for which a competency approach is admirably suited) provides the very basis for, or 'foundation' for, development. Without such a foundation, albeit a discursive one, how could any manager embark upon (or, to use dialogic parlance, engage in a discourse of) professional learning and personal growth, not to mention the material rewards that might go with all this? To pretend, however, that such a dynamic does not produce both winners and losers, often along diversity lines, would be disingenuous to say the least (and this is something we explore further in Chapters 6 and 9). As such, the repressive aspect of competency development might, in many respects, be understood to be the flipside of the productive side, since an adherence to any one representation of the self (e.g. the 'entrepreneurially competent self') inevitably suppresses or marginalizes a multitude of potentially legitimate alternatives. In other words, the productive capacity of the capabilities to constitute identity via constructed self-knowledge brings with it an equal capacity to render such identities vulnerable, by subjecting organizational members to all-seeing, normalizing and potentially discriminatory forms of regulation and control.

Reflection point

Cast your mind back to any competency-based development you have personally experienced or observed. In what ways did this impact, not only on conceptions of 'development', but on what it might actually mean to be 'a manager' in the first place?

We now turn to a related but somewhat distinct dimension of the dialogic, that of deconstruction.

Deconstructionist readings of management development

One of the few deconstructionist readings of management development in the literature was carried out by Bell et al. (2002). These authors sought to deconstruct the ostensibly intended meanings of the UK's Investors in People (IiP) initiative. This is a state-sponsored accreditation mechanism that at the time of their paper covered over 9 million employees in the UK or 39 per cent of the workforce. It was also being piloted and/or licensed to governments overseas, including the Netherlands, Germany, France and Denmark. Organizations accredited as an 'Investor in People' need to pass an assessment according to four main criteria:

1   The organization's commitment to developing its people in order to achieve its aims and objectives.
2   The organization being clear about these aims and objectives and what its people need to do to achieve them.
3   The organization developing its people effectively in order to improve its performance.
4   The organization understanding the impact on performance of its developmental investment in people.

Accredited organizations are permitted to display their status in a number of ways: by displaying the IiP logo on company materials (brochures, letterheads, etc.); by flying an IiP flag outside the premises; by prominently displaying a certificate (e.g. in the reception area); by encouraging employees to wear lapel badges, etc. The authors conducted a series of interviews with employees of six participating companies, complementing this with analysis of documentary materials from both the companies themselves and IiP. Their study explores the multiplicity and ambiguity of meaning that the IiP award carries within the different organizations. While there was some support for the intended principles of the initiative, there was also much talk of IiP as little more than a badge, either an end in itself or a symbolic means to differentiate the company from other, supposedly inferior organizations.

Deconstruction was used as a means to explore the 'oppositional characteristics', or in other words, the internal contradictions discernible within the award process and related texts. As part of this, the authors draw attention to the 'paradox of fashion', which dictates that while satisfying the need for differentiation, a simultaneous need for uniformity based on imitation is satisfied. Because of this, a process of 'serial badging' can ensue where signifiers (such as the IiP award) become detached from their originally intended meaning. The whole IiP process becomes 'hyper-real' in as much as the official or intended language used to describe it becomes totally divorced from local organizational experiences. As such, IiP whether as a process, sign or symbol carries potentially infinite alternative connotations. Via the paradox of fashion, the authors use deconstruction to show how a discourse (such as that of IiP) can undermine the very philosophy that it simultaneously seeks to assert, along with the hierarchical oppositions on which it depends. This, they claim, can partly explain why the images and signs associated with 'quality' in organizations continue to proliferate and how the growth of badging as a contemporary organizational phenomenon is secured.

Elsewhere, Garrick and Rhodes (1998) propose deconstruction as a means to challenge the dominance of economic instrumentalism within research on organizational learning. Calas and Smircich (1991) employ deconstruction to expose and overturn masculine sub-texts within a number of classic management texts on leadership.

A comparative assessment of dialogic, constructivist and functionalist Discourses

The dialogic and the functionalist Discourses

Whereas the functionalist Discourse takes the concept of 'management' or even 'the manager' as pre-constituted foundation points for 'development', the dialogic focuses on the socially and historically situated ways in which these foundations have come to be conceived of in the first place. This opens the way for alternative understandings of the activities associated with management development. For example, as well as *development* being understood as a means to improve personal and organizational effectiveness (as in functionalism), it also becomes a means for the production of identity, subjectivity and thus for social differentiation. By way of illustration, our chapter on functionalist Discourse devotes a significant amount of space to an exploration of whether and in what circumstances management development can lead to improved outcomes, typically expressed in financial terms such as ROI (return on investment). The dialogic perspective to such matters is much less interested in the veracity or falsity of ROI claims as it is in exploring their discursive effects. For example, the HR manager who embraces the language of ROI (or indeed of accounting more generally) is, from the dialogic perspective, adopting a certain subjectivity, one that affords a legitimacy that alternative subjectivities may not. It is also one that may bring personal benefits (such as psychological and material security) that alternatives may not. This may go some way to explaining the conundrum mentioned in our opening chapter: that so much functionalist-inspired management development activity persists despite the relative paucity of demonstrable evidence for the 'success' of such development.

Many authors have claimed that the dialogic is epistemologically at odds with functionalism and in many respects we would agree with that. However, in one limited respect we would beg to differ. If we regard functionalism as a Discourse in and of itself (i.e. as opposed to a fixed worldview or 'paradigm'), then we can also regard the ontological and epistemological objectivity of functionalism as a truth effect of that Discourse and a potentially productive one at that. We use the term 'truth effect' in opposition to any notion of absolute truth located outside discourse. We also use the word 'productive' here to simultaneously refer, *inter alia*, to the production of organizational social relations, managerial subjectivities and material outputs in terms of goods and services. In sum, what we claim here is that one does not have to subscribe to the ultimate 'truth' of functionalism's ontology and epistemology to acknowledge that their effects can nonetheless impact people's lives in ways that are experienced as very 'real' indeed. Despite the rather suspicious tone of this chapter, we believe that such effects can be positive as well as negative. Furthermore, in the spirit of reflexivity we need to acknowledge that the arguments we put forward here regarding the subjectivity-producing power of discourse apply as much to our own writing as they do to management development. While from the dialogic perspective we may be understood to be doing little more than accomplishing our 'authorial selves' by the very writing of this book, we would also hope that any truth effects we create in doing so might be of at least some (including, dare we say it, functionalist) material consequence to our readers.

The dialogic and the constructivist Discourses

Although the dialogic and the constructivist Discourses are similar in adopting a subjective epistemology, they differ quite markedly in terms of what they do with this. While constructivist approaches accommodate the possibility of multiple social constructions of a phenomenon, they are always on the lookout for the processes by which communities might arrive at shared and therefore relatively stable understandings, albeit context-specific ones. In contrast, dialogic approaches are just as interested in the *deconstruction* of meaning as they are in the processes by which meaning comes to be *constructed* in the first place. In other words, from a dialogic perspective, the constructivist act of recovering meaning is, in itself, another creation of meaning (Calas and Smircich, 1991), and thus ripe for deconstruction in itself. Another key difference is the starting point for analysis. Recall the example in Chapter 4 where Sandberg (2000) employed a constructivist/ interpretative approach to uncover shared meanings of competency among a group of managers. While his analysis called into question prevailing conceptions of competency, it stopped short of deconstructing the very identities of his research subjects. In this sense, constructivism is similar to functionalism in taking the 'management' part of management development for granted. We hope in this chapter to have shown how this is anything but the case for the dialogic Discourse. Indeed, the dialogic is a Discourse which rejects any claim to solid epistemological ground, including that on which 'the manager', as a form of social subject, is based. Instead, it regards the self (managerial and/or otherwise) as a multiple, fragmented and discursive accomplishment, one that is continually in a state of becoming as opposed to anything more fixed or stable.

Conclusion

In this chapter we have sought to explain the key theoretical and epistemological tenets of the dialogic Discourse to management development, most notably its non-foundational treatment of the individual (including the individual as manager). We have also discussed some of the key studies that constitute the research domain of the Discourse. In doing so, we have drawn particular attention to dialogic analyses of management competencies, including their implications for organizational diversity. We believe that the dialogic Discourse inevitably has a critical tone or feel about it, calling into question as it does any notion of a fixed or stable sense of self. This is not a comfortable perspective for those designing and implementing management development activities. For example, even the best-intended of programmes will, according to the dialogic Discourse, be inherently disciplinary leading to potentially negative outcomes as well as positive ones. Furthermore, the deconstructionist angle implies that whatever the sponsors of a development programme might intend for it, and however they might explain it to organizational members, the potential for multiple interpretations always remains. Also, the very labelling of a programme as being a 'management' programme perpetuates socially and historically constructed divisions which may not always be helpful.

Management development (as with all discourses) will always present a paradox in terms of its capacity to produce subjectivity while at the same time restricting it. Life would be meaningless without the means to discursively construct our senses of self, but as soon as we allow our subjectivity to be constructed in any particular way (for example, by our participation in, and adoption of the language of, management development), we simultaneously create the conditions for repression, marginalization and exclusion, alongside those for emancipation. An example covered in this chapter is the way in which the notion of competency both enables managers to act, speak and conceive their own 'self' according to certain norms or conventions while at the same time restricting their freedom to do so according to others. An important point to remember here is that the dialogic denies any ultimate notion of the true or 'essential' self.

But all this also presents an interminable quandary when it comes to questions of ethics, human agency and change. If all knowledge is relative, then on what basis can we make moral or ethical judgements about what is better or worse for us, our communities and our world? On what basis, for example, might we even choose to sponsor or participate in management development as against other activities, let alone choose between different types of development? By the same token, if all meaning (including our own sense of self) is constituted by discourse, then to what extent is that same self capable of exercising agency when it comes to making a difference in the world? These are questions that we shall revisit as we turn our attention to the critical Discourse to management development, the topic of our next chapter.

Summary

- The dialogic considers language (via the notion of discourse) to be the principal means by which reality is socially constructed. Language cannot be merely regarded as a neutral means to represent or mirror reality.
- Reality itself is therefore a subjective notion (in the sense of being contingent, multiple, shifting and fragmented), in direct opposition to functionalism's objective ontology and epistemology.

- The dialogic regards management development as a discourse in and of itself, thus caught up in the social construction of reality.
- As such, management development has as much to do with the very constitution of the 'manager' as a social subject as with any 'development' of that same subject.
- This does not preclude management development (as a discourse) from having effects (including functionalist effects, both positive and negative) that are experienced as eminently 'real' by its participants, sponsors and other stakeholders.
- This insight provides scope, albeit limited, for a potentially fruitful dialogue between the dialogic and the functionalist Discourses to management development.

6

Management development: power and control

We seek merely to surface the implicit, often unspoken agendas of power, exploitation and control that often lie beneath the cozy, overly humanist and unitarist surface exterior of much HRD discourse and practice. (O'Donnell et al., 2006: 6)

After reading this chapter you will be able to:

- **Explain the theoretical underpinnings of the critical Discourse to management development**
- **Understand and explain the key concepts of the critical Discourse to management development, including dialectical reason, ideology, hegemony, false consciousness and commodification**
- **Discuss some of the key studies that constitute the research domain of the critical Discourse to management development**
- **Compare and critique the critical Discourse in relation to the dialogic, functionalist and constructivist Discourses of management development**
- **Draw on the critical Discourse to mount your own critique of the management development that you have observed or experienced**
- **Develop and reflexively critique your own ideas as to whether, and how, management development might be rendered more equitable, more inclusive and less reliant on dominant Discourses of instrumental reason**

Introduction

Dominant or functionalist approaches tend to evaluate management development uniquely on the extent to which it leads to beneficial outcomes, either for participants, for organizations or even for nation states. The criteria used for assessing 'benefit' will typically be utilitarian, economic or financial. For example:

- For the individual: How has management development improved career prospects, job performance, satisfaction, commitment or employability?
- For the organization: What kind of return on investment is it receiving from its efforts to develop its managers? Has the culture been positively impacted by such efforts?
- For the nation state: What impact on national competitiveness derives from the different types and aggregate levels of management development taking place throughout the economy?

Within this approach, management development is implicitly considered to be a 'good thing' and the answers to the above types of question are those that dictate the extent to which it is 'working'. Increasingly, however, a more critical strand to the study of management development has begun to ask different types of question:

- Is management (and therefore its development) as universally beneficial as it is commonly assumed?
- What are the moral or ethical considerations when embarking on a programme of management development?
- When we talk in terms of 'benefit' or 'positive change' deriving from management development, from whose or what perspective are we talking? Are there other perspectives being silenced in the process?

It is with questions such as these and more that we will be dealing in this chapter on the critical Discourse to management development.

The term 'critical' has been used and interpreted in a variety of different ways in the organizational literature (Alvesson and Deetz, 2000; Fournier and Grey, 2000; Johnson and Duberley, 2000; Fenwick, 2004; Valentin, 2006). Our use of the term throughout this chapter refers to approaches that variously seek to:

- expose situations of oppression, marginalization and subjugation arising from the presence or absence of management development.
- question whose or what interests are being either served or neglected by management development interventions.
- champion the cause of those groups which might arguably be disadvantaged by management development practices. This extends to challenging the established order (hierarchical, cultural, etc.) within organizations, certainly to the extent that management development might be contributing to the maintenance of such order and the inequalities it implies.
- decentre the organizational imperative of economic efficiency by paying equal if not more attention to ethical issues of social justice and equity.
- extend critique beyond the boundaries and micro-practices of any one organization and direct attention to macro-societal or structural causes of inequality mediated by management development.
- pursue an activist, change-oriented agenda, ranging from a 'small wins' approach (e.g. Meyerson and Fletcher, 2000) to the radical overturning of accepted societal or structural norms (e.g. Brookfield, 2001).
- embrace 'reflexivity' which extends the notion of critique to one's own knowledge and truth claims. This requires that all those involved in the development of managers (including the managers themselves) be constantly and critically aware of their own presuppositions, values, motivations and social positioning.

Duality versus dualism

The critical discourse can be described as dualist (see Table 1.1) in the sense that it tends to represent the world in terms of analytically (if not ontologically) distinct divisions, the most common of which would include:

- Truth/falsity
- For/against
- Oppressors/oppressed
- Agency/structure
- Knowledge/ideology
- Individual/collective

We take each of these in turn in a bid to tease out the distinctive features of the critical discourse, particularly in relation to our previous analysis of the dialogic in Chapter 5.

Truth/falsity

To qualify as critical (in the sense we use the term in this chapter), analyses will take an ontologically realist stance on the nature of the social world, even if only implicitly through their use of language (Parker, 1999) and even if only as a strategic or tactical manoeuvre (e.g. O'Doherty and Willmott, 2001). Although the critical Discourse does not necessarily deny processes of social construction (Rusaw, 2000; Brookfield, 2001), and hence multiple images of reality, it nevertheless tends to treat these as no more than images. This is in contrast to the dialogic Discourse which makes no distinction between *images of* reality and what it considers to be the inherently multiple *nature of* reality in itself. Ontologically, therefore, the critical Discourse lays claim to the objective existence of ultimate and singular truths about the social world. Epistemologically, however, the critical Discourse considers that our means of accessing such truths will always be socially, historically and politically mediated, *inter alia* via competing ideologies (Carr, 2000). Struggles over the truth or falsity of representations of the social world will therefore never be totally resolvable and it is this that gives rise to the critical Discourse's dissensual stance towards the social order (which we examine later). It is also this which gives rise to one of the main concerns of the critical Discourse, which is to expose what it sees as the 'false consciousness' of individuals whenever they unthinkingly acquiesce to social dynamics or ideologies that do not serve their own 'true' or 'real' interests (Rusaw, 2000; Garrick and Clegg, 2001).

For/against

As we saw in Chapter 5, the dialogic Discourse's ability (in its archetypal form at least) to make moral judgements about social phenomena is problematical (e.g. concerning their ultimate goodness/badness, desirability/undesirability, etc.). We began to see this, for example, in the way in which the discourse of competency was appraised as being *both* productive *and* repressive at one and the same time. The same would be the case with a dialogical analysis of any social phenomena, due basically to the 'judgementally' (Fairclough, 2005) or 'ethically/politically' (Parker, 1999) relativist stance of the Discourse, which holds that all representations of the world are equally legitimate. In contrast to this, the critical Discourse sees no problem in taking a moral or ethical position with regard to the desirability of social phenomena, examples being Parker's (2002a) stance against the very concept of 'management' and Contu et al.'s (2003) stance against the discourse of learning.

Oppressors/oppressed

Schultze and Stabell (2004: 558) characterize the critical Discourse as assuming society is 'made up of antagonistic factions i.e. a powerful group that is evil and guilty of oppression and a powerless group that is pure, innocent and helpless'. Albeit a deliberate caricature, perhaps the starkest example of this dualism within the critical Discourse comes from orthodox labour process theory (O'Doherty and Willmott, 2001) and its distinction between the oppressive holders of capital (including their supposed agents, i.e. managers) and the sellers of labour (i.e. mere employees). More generally, critical Discourse tends to demarcate in terms of dualisms based on class, gender, age, race/ethnicity and sexuality.

Structure/agency

A key tenet of the critical Discourse is its ontological distinction between structure and agency. This is in stark contrast to the dialogic, which has been heavily criticized in some quarters (e.g. Reed, 1997) for its 'flat' or 'horizontal' ontology which has a tendency to merge both structure and agency into localized or micro-level discursive practices. We again turn towards labour process theory for a typical example of the structure/agency dualism within critical Discourse, where capitalism is treated as an overarching structural mechanism that is largely independent of (while governing the relationship between) antagonistic social agents, that is the owners of capital and the sellers of labour.

Knowledge/ideology

The critical Discourse can be considered to be modernist in the sense that it maintains the Enlightenment aspiration that knowledge can lead to emancipation and progress. In this sense, the critical Discourse draws a distinction between scientific and ideological forms of knowledge (Fairclough, 1992). This is in stark contrast to the dialogic which, via Foucault's notion of power/knowledge, rejects the assumption that ideologies can be demystified, thus regarding the pursuit of undistorted, scientific truth as misguided and futile (Diamond and Quinby, 1988). For Foucault, all knowledge is irremediably ideological.

Individual/collective

The critical Discourse takes a self-avowedly collectivist view of the social in both its analytical privileging of group (e.g. class) interests and in its frequent critiques of the individualizing nature of modern society. In relation to management development, for example, this can be seen in Brookfield's (2001) critically-informed view of adult development as an inherently collective process, since one person's humanity cannot be realized at the expense of others' interests. As such, opportunities for development must not remain the preserve of the privileged few, for example, managers *per se* or managers of a certain level or type. The dualism can also be seen within critically-informed assessments that reproach certain forms of management development for over-emphasizing personal responsibility for learning, progression and development, thus detracting from the collective or structural constraints that put certain groups at a disadvantage to others. Examples include the works of Fenwick (2004) and Bell and Taylor (2004) that we shall be referring to later in more detail.

Consensus versus dissensus

The critical Discourse is dissensual in the sense that it considers conflict and power struggle to be natural facets of the social order. Any appearance of ordered harmony is considered to be the hegemonically stabilized outcome of power (Contu and Willmott, 2003), or in other words, a 'manufactured' kind of consent (Burawoy, 1979) rather than a natural state of affairs. The critical researcher will see his/her role as being that of exposing the taken-for-granted processes by which the status quo has come to be accepted as the natural order. The aim is to show how such status quo produces exploitation, imbalances of power, distorted communication and false consciousness, all of which prevent people from genuinely understanding, let alone acting upon, their own real interests.

Role and metaphors of management development

Schultze and Stabell (2004) describe the critical Discourse as aligning itself with the interests of workers and against those of management. Viewed in this way, the role of management development becomes that of maximizing the effectiveness of management in their role as privileged agents of capital. The inherent assumption is that the workers, if left to their own devices, would act in ways that are detrimental to those of both managers and shareholders. Under this scenario, the critical researcher's role becomes that of exposing the manipulative and exploitative nature of the knowledge or ideology being imparted to managers (within processes of management development) *vis-à-vis* the oppressed ranks of the workers.

While we would agree that the above certainly forms one strand of the critical Discourse to management development (e.g. O'Donnell et al., 2006), like Fenwick (2004) we would contend that it is a fairly narrow and to some extent superseded one. This is due to Schultze and Stabell's over-reliance on modernist/orthodox labour process theory (O'Doherty and Willmott, 2001) to the exclusion of other important theoretical dimensions to the critical Discourse (see our section on theory for more on this). It is equally as plausible, from the critical perspective, to regard managers themselves as open to manipulation, exploitation and oppression (Willmott, 1997; Johnson and Duberley, 2000; Garrick and Clegg, 2001) from their participation in management development. From this perspective, the role of management development becomes not so much to empower and build capability but rather to produce vulnerability and anxiety (Willmott, 1994b; Ackers and Preston, 1997), thereby ensuring order, predictability and control within the ranks of management (Hopfl and Dawes, 1995). Under this scenario, as well as retaining a concern for the interests of workers, there is a concern to raise managers' own consciousness of the less than benign nature of the practices they themselves are subject to, all in the name of development (Finch-Lees et al., 2005a).

There are a number of metaphors we might use to characterize management development from a critical perspective. Schultze and Stabell (with their particular focus being that of knowledge management) propose the metaphor of power.

At first glance their conception of 'knowledge as power' seems to resonate with Foucault's 'power/knowledge' approach of the dialogic Discourse. However, it is important to appreciate that power within the dialogic is seen as relational and rooted in discursive practices, thus not amenable to being 'held' as a possession by any particular individual or group. By contrast, both power and knowledge within the critical perspective are indeed conceptualized as possessions. These are possessions that can be exploitative in the hands of the dominant but which also have the potential to be emancipatory in the hands of the oppressed. Extending the power metaphor, Burgoyne and Jackson (1997) suggest that, exploring management learning from the critical perspective, the organization as a whole could be likened to a 'battlefield' where rival forces such as management and unions strive to achieve incompatible ends. Management development thus becomes a 'weapon' within the 'armoury' of management that serves to keep such rival 'forces' at bay.

Box 6.1 sets out a number of other metaphors invoked by various authors who have sought to analyse management development from a critical perspective.

Box 6.1   Critical metaphors of management development

- Turnbull (2001a) describes the ways in which some managers come to internalize the values and beliefs transmitted via management development, likening this to the kind of enculturation processes one might encounter within a religious sect.
- Ackers and Preston (1997) demonstrate how management development can invoke and exploit the emotions in attempting to remould personality in a way that mimics the 'religious conversion' process.
- Johnson and Duberley (2000) use the term 'cultural doping' in drawing attention to the ways in which many organizations use various socialization techniques in order to inculcate employees into adopting prescribed attitudes, values and expectations.
- The drugs-related imagery of cultural doping is vividly and somewhat polemically extended by O'Donnell et al. (2006). Their assessment of HRD recounts how employees, under a false illusion of empowerment, can become 'addictively obsessed' with the notion of self-development within what they describe as a 'psychologically warped value system' that seeks to transfer the entire burden of maintaining employability on to the employee him- or herself. They evoke vivid imagery that talks of line managers becoming the 'regulated dealers' of development who have the power to either provide or withhold the 'HRD-fix' to 'addicted employees'.

All of this imagery feeds very much into the critical Discourse's concern with ideology and the role that it can play in producing forms of false consciousness. On a more optimistic note, there are some who argue that while management development certainly *can* work to invoke false consciousness, it can also serve as a vehicle to combat it. Both Rusaw (2000) and Brookfield (2001) argue that management development can, under the right circumstances, play a role in rendering ideologies visible, comprehensible and therefore open to critique. This is something we explore further on pages 144–8.

Assumptions underpinning the critical Discourse would include the following:

- Organizations are composed of multiple, shifting and conflicting coalitions of interest, a fact that is often obscured by dominant yet taken-for-granted managerial ideologies.
- Management development has the potential to be an emancipatory force for good by educating managers in the identification and critique of organizational ideology.
- More often than not, however, management development serves merely to obscure the ideological nature of managerial knowledge by presenting it as neutral, apolitical, and universally beneficial.

Theoretical underpinnings of the critical Discourse to management development

In this section we set out a far from exhaustive discussion of critical theory as used within studies that are relevant to management development. On occasion, we find it fruitful to stray into the areas of adult learning and HR development as these have a longer tradition of critical analysis than does management development.

Critical theory: ways in which it has been mobilized within the critical Discourse to management development

The term 'critical theory' is sometimes used in a broad sense to denote any form of self-conscious theorizing aimed at emancipatory social change. However, it is also frequently used more narrowly to refer to the body of theorizing emanating from the Frankfurt School of critical theory (Carr, 2000; Johnson and Duberley, 2000) and it is with this more narrow meaning that we are primarily concerned here. We do not aim to enter into anything like a full discussion of critical theory as this is an area of extreme complexity and much debate. Instead, we selectively draw on various authors to briefly explain how some of the theory's concepts have been mobilized within critically informed analyses of management development. Such concepts include: dialectical reason, ideology, hegemony, false consciousness and commodification. An examination of these concepts will then lead us into a discussion of Habermasian critical theory and its relevance to management development.

Dialectical reason

... today's wisdom, culled from the latest findings of science and clothed in our latest vocabularies, is provisional and represents just another possibility out of the infinite number of possible vocabularies in which the world can be described. (Case and Selvester, 2002: 231)

The Frankfurt scholars developed their notion of dialectical reason in response to what they saw as the cultural dominance of positivism and its exclusive focus on instrumental reason (Rusaw, 2000). Instrumental reason caters only for means–ends calculations and positions itself as apolitical and value free (Johnson and Duberley, 2000). This stifles any consideration of justice and ethics as legitimate ends in their own right, subordinating them instead to notions of economic efficiency, production and growth. What is more, claims Agger (1991), positivism's correspondence theory of the truth (i.e. the notion that knowledge can simply *reflect* the nature of the world without making political assumptions or value judgements about it), leads people to uncritically accept the world 'as it is', thus unthinkingly perpetuating it. Rusaw (2000: 251) draws on various Frankfurt scholars to claim that positivism and instrumental reason work to reduce humans to objectified status or mere 'touch points of progress'. As a result, people come to see themselves in one-dimensional organizational terms, unquestioningly conforming to norms and practices, either out of fear, or as a result of being seduced by the perceived material and psychological benefits of capitalism.

In a nutshell, the Frankfurt scholars opposed positivism's instrumentalism along with its claim to be the ultimate arbiter of truth. Their alternative notion of dialectical reason sees truth as historically, socially and politically situated. For them, what we come to accept as the truth is never anything more than temporary and unstable syntheses of previously contested ideas. Over time, such *syntheses* break down into new *theses* as they are countered by new *anti-theses* and so the never-ending dialectic cycle begins once more (see Box 6.2).

Box 6.2   Dialectical knowing and project-based learning

Raelin (2001) coins the term 'dialectical knowing' in relation to project-based learning, distinguishing it from other, less radical forms, that is 'propositional' and 'practical' knowing. Propositional knowing involves the mechanical implementation of actions based on theoretical formulations and research findings. Such knowing is underpinned by instrumental reasoning in the sense that it seeks merely to replicate practice that empirical research has found to be effective in other contexts. Practical knowing goes one step further by deliberating among competing versions of effective practice and by taking account of the importance of context. Managers thus develop practical knowledge or 'rules of thumb' concerning how to act in particular situations. Dialectical knowing goes even further by challenging, reconstructing and thus transforming taken-for-granted assumptions that underpin the very notion of effective practice. It might, for example, ask such questions as 'effectiveness for whom' or 'effectiveness for what'. In sum, dialectical knowing involves not just a search for answers but a reflexive search for alternative questions. It is inherently concerned with the 'common good' as opposed to the good of just certain sections of society. Crucially, it is also a form of knowing that both encourages and depends on open, inclusive and democratic dialogue and debate.

Although Schultze and Stabell (2004) do not present things in such terms, it is this notion of dialectics that provides the theoretical underpinning to their characterization of the critical Discourse as dissensual. It also provides an important qualification to their characterization of the critical Discourse as dualist. While we would agree that the critical Discourse *can* be described as dualist, it is a very different kind of dualism from that which we find within positivist-inspired functionalism. Within the latter, dualisms are considered to represent real, immutable phenomena of the social world. In other words, they are *ontological* dualisms. In contrast to this, the dualisms we encounter within the critical Discourse need to be seen as *analytical* and *recursive* ones (Parker, 1999). Rather than claiming to represent an underlying, ontological reality, they are deployed as strategic or epistemological devices in furthering the cause of critical understanding and emancipation. For the sake of completeness, but without wishing to introduce undue confusion, Parker describes this critical form of dualism as 'post-dualism'.

Ideology

Critical theory's notion of dialectical reason leads us directly to the notion of ideology. If truth is never anything other than a temporary stopping off point between dialectical cycles, then the notion of ideology helps us understand how new cycles can be disrupted or delayed. Ideology from the critical perspective has been defined and applied to training and development in a number of different ways (see Box 6.3).

Box 6.3   Definitions and applications of ideology in relation to training and development

- O'Donnell et al. (2006), in their critical assessment of HRD, define ideology quite succinctly as knowledge that serves particular sectional interests.
- Rusaw (2000: 249) in her critical assessment of training resistance describes ideology as 'a set of systematic norms, beliefs, values and attitudes that labour [i.e. her focus of analysis] is socialized into accepting unquestioningly as guides to everyday thinking and behaviour'.
- Brookfield (2001: 14), in his critical theorizing of adult learning, is even more expansive in describing ideologies as 'broadly accepted sets of values, beliefs, myths, explanations, and justifications that appear self-evidently true, empirically accurate, personally relevant, and morally desirable to a majority of the populace, but that actually work to maintain an unjust social and political order. Ideology does this by convincing people that existing social arrangements are naturally ordained and obviously work for the good of all.'

It is rare to find management development activities in organizations which facilitate the identification and critique of ideology. For Brookfield, one of the most important extensions to the understanding of ideological control is the Gramscian notion of hegemony.

Hegemony

Hegemony describes the way in which people learn to understand and accept an unjust social order as being natural and in their own best interests. In linking this to adult learning, Brookfield (2001) draws on Gramsci's (1995: 157) assertion that 'Every relationship of hegemony is necessarily a educational relationship'. In other words, the processes by which people come to take ideologies for granted inherently involve those of learning. An important facet of hegemony is that it works via consensus rather than coercion. A hegemonic state of affairs is achieved when an ideology becomes accepted as the natural order or, in other words, when it becomes incorporated into a community's notion of 'common sense' (Fairclough, 1992). Brookfield (2001: 17) uses the notion of hegemony to explain how people become willing partners in the active promotion of their own oppression: 'The dark irony, the cruelty of hegemony, is that adults take pride in learning and then acting on the beliefs and assumptions that work to enslave them.' The same might be said of many management development interventions. By their active participation, managers enthusiastically imbibe the underlying values, in a form of 'orchestrated consent' (Valentin, 2006: 23). Brookfield's characterization of this as 'enslavement' is perhaps an overstatement, but managers can nevertheless become complicit in a social order which may arguably serve others' interests more readily than their own.

False consciousness

It should be now fairly clear as to how critical theory's notion of false consciousness fits in with these related notions of ideology and hegemony. Agger (1991: 108) describes false consciousness as 'the inability to experience and recognize social relations as historical accomplishments that can be transformed. Instead, people "falsely" experience their lives as products of a certain unchangeable social nature.' Commodification provides an example of how various writers theorizing management development and HRD have built on this notion of false consciousness at work.

Commodification

Brookfield (2001: 9), writing from the critical HRD perspective, defines commodification as 'the process by which a human quality or relationship becomes regarded as a product, good, or commodity to be bought and sold on the open market'. As such, in the modern capitalist economy, it is not just products and services that are deemed to have a commercial exchange value, but one's own organizational self. Brookfield builds on this by reflecting on how the language of 'capitalist investment' has extended even to our personal and emotional lives: 'We talk of making emotional investments as if emotions were things we could float on the stock market of significant personal relationships' (2001: 11). But if this is true for our personal lives, then how much more is it so for our organizational ones?

Reflection point

How often have you come across the notion of management development being described as an investment for both the organization and the individual (see Box 6.4)?

Box 6.4   Research accounts of management development as 'investment'

'The programme represents significant investment in [the company's] leadership. ... This is an all too rare opportunity for our leaders to really invest in themselves.' (extract from company documentation, Finch-Lees et al., 2005a: 1199)

Participant extracts from Finch-Lees et al. (2005b):

'Just from my personal point of view, I would feel that the company is not going to invest money in you or send you on a course for no reason.'

'And I think if the company is prepared to invest in an individual and the individual can see that, the company can see the individual grow and actually takes probably more notice of that individual.'

'My pay since I've joined has gone up 70% in four and a half years ... partly I guess because the company feels confident in the individual that they're investing in. Now that has got to be because I'm also taking part in growing myself as an individual.'

For Brookfield, metaphorical allusions to management development as investment are symptomatic of how the *exchange value* of learning (i.e. how learning will improve one's success in the job market) has come to overshadow its *use value* (i.e. the degree to which learning can help us draw new meanings from life, become more open to new perspectives on the world and develop the capacity to imagine more congenial and humane forms of collective existence). Writing in a similar vein, Fenwick (2004: 198) holds out the hope that a more critical theorizing of HRD can help reverse the dominance of positivist or functionalist theorizing that she sees as 'complicit in unjust, inequitable, or life-draining commodification of human minds and souls'. She specifically alludes to the ubiquity of human capital theory as an example of such complicity. She goes on to contend that a critical HRD must aim not to develop humans' exchange value but to actually liberate them from exchange relations in the first place. She suggests that such liberation cannot be conducted through the kind of imposed techniques typical of much management development but through 'participatory dialogue in dialectic

with collective action'. What this amounts to is a call for a critical and emancipatory form of action learning, something that other writers, such as Willmott
(1994b), have long been arguing for. It is also a call that implicitly connects with
many of the ideas developed by Habermas, one of the more recent directors of
the Frankfurt School and whose ideas have been drawn upon by several authors
in the critical theorizing of management development.

Habermasian critical theory

Habermas is best known for his theory of communicative action. While Habermas
does accept the ultimate existence of a reality independent of our constructions of
it, he contends that any and all attempts to represent such reality cannot be divorced
from the subjectivity of those making such representations. As such, claims to truth
will always be impacted by the fundamental interests of those making such claims.
It is on this basis that Habermas rejects positivism and its *correspondence* theory of
truth. In order to avoid any descent into limitless relativism, however, he argues for
a *consensus* theory of truth instead. Consensus-based truth would be one in which
all participants in a dialogue are able to reach some kind of agreement (even if this
be an agreement to disagree) without resort to 'systematically distorted communication'. Examples of such distortions would be force, coercion, or duplicity but they
might equally (and perhaps be more likely to) include the more subtle means of ideology combined with hegemony. It is when communication and dialogue are free
of such distortions that, according to Habermas, an 'ideal speech situation' can be
said to exist. The route to attaining such a situation lies in a specific form of knowledge, based on self-reflection. In the words of Johnson and Duberley (2000: 119),
Habermasian self-reflection 'demystifies previously unacknowledged distortions and
enables awareness of the link between knowledge and interest'.

A number of authors have drawn either explicitly or implicitly on Habermasian
ideas in theorizing how management and HR development might be rendered
more democratic, transparent, inclusive, just, equitable and emancipatory. Most
such authors (e.g. Willmott, 1997; Coopey and Burgoyne, 2000; Brookfield, 2001;
Raelin, 2001; Fenwick, 2004) tend to advocate more 'critical' forms of project-
based, action or organizational learning. These are areas we will be exploring in a
later section on research domains of critical theory. However, Habermas's theorizing, especially his emphasis on inclusion and democracy, also calls into question
the very notion of management development. It does so by problematizing development aimed exclusively at managers, thus distinct from the kind of development available to non-management. In this manner his theorizing dovetails with
the concerns of labour process theory.

Labour process theory

Education is a liability to the employer. (Braverman, 1974: 441)

Schultze and Stabell (2004) exclusively propose labour process theory as theoretical underpinning to the critical Discourse. While this may or may not be acceptable

for their specific focus of enquiry (i.e. knowledge management), we hope to have already demonstrated via our engagement with the wider field of critical theory that this would be far from adequate for any critical treatment of management development. Nevertheless, labour process theory does have an important role to play in our assessment. As Delbridge (2006) points out, however, since its inception within Braverman's *Labour and Monopoly Capital* (1974), the whole field of labour process theory has been characterized by schism and fragmentation. This presents a problem (unacknowledged by Schultze and Stabell) in terms of summarizing exactly what qualifies as labour process theorizing and where its boundaries or limits should be deemed to lie (see Box 6.5).

Box 6.5   Delineating the boundaries of labour process theory

Jaros (2005) proposes that the 'core' of labour process theory should comprise the following:

1   The consideration of labour as an important source of surplus value within capitalism.
2   The necessity for constant evolution of the forces of production, including those related to labour skills, all due to the profit imperative inherent within capitalism.
3   A related control imperative over the labour process in order for capital to be competitively successful in extracting surplus value from the production process.
4   An assumption of inherent power imbalances which create the structural tendency for antagonism between labour and capital. Responses of labour can include resistance but also accommodation, compliance, consent or even active cooperation.
5   Research that involves acting politically to ultimately eliminate such imbalances, or, in the short run, to at least ameliorate their effects. This includes critical reflection on one's own ethical stance towards the subjects of one's research to avoid reproducing the kind of domination the research is aimed at undermining.
6   An open-minded approach to methodology to include both quantitative and qualitative methods and both dialectical and non-dialectical reasoning.
7   Recognition that other forms of domination (i.e. transcending those of class, and extending to issues such as race and gender) are also manifest in the workplace.

Labour process theory questions both the naturalness and the effects of the division between labour and capital. It laments the way in which modern capitalism has evolved to find ever more ingenious ways of extracting surplus value from the workers to the benefit of both the owners of capital and to a lesser extent their supposed agents, that is the managerial class. According to labour process theory, this involves a systematic deskilling of the workforce and deliberate (including state-sponsored) policies to prevent the workers becoming too educated, lest they wise-up to their true position within the labour process equation.

A labour process perspective to management development can therefore take us in at least two directions. On the one hand, it can be used to cast both management and, by implication, management development as the problem. This might involve exposing the ways in which managerial knowledge and ideologies can be put to exploitative use in extracting surplus value from the workers. Classic examples would include the culture/excellence movement, Total Quality Management and Business Process Re-engineering etc., which have variously been critiqued from a labour process perspective by the likes of Willmott (1993a, 1994a) and Knights and McCabe (1998). Each of these initiatives relies, at least in part, on the development of managers in order to equip them to usher in and sustain the new regime which, *vis-à-vis* the workers, is arguably more exploitative than its predecessor. On the other hand, a labour process perspective can also be used to cast management development as a potential solution. This would involve an assessment of how managers as well as workers can be subject to the exploitative side of capitalism and how a critical form of education and development might improve not only managers' own awareness of this but act as a catalyst to more social responsibility in the workplace. This might involve not just a focus on the micro-dynamics of exploitation within individual organizations, but a critical focus on institutional or macro-societal systems and the role of management development and education within them (e.g. Willmott, 1994b; Clarke, 1999). Among others, these are issues we go on to examine in our next section, which explores how the critical theorizing of management development has been applied empirically.

Research domain of the critical Discourse to management development

In terms of research domains, the critical Discourse to management development can usefully be divided up according to the following broad areas:

- Power, control, resistance and acquiescence
- Ideology critique

    — of specific or 'micro' development initiatives
    — of wider-scale discourses

- Critical management pedagogy:

    — emancipatory action learning
    — reflections on attempts to critically educate managers

Power, control, resistance and acquiescence

Various authors have sought to investigate the ways in which management development can either support or disrupt interests of power and control, and how such functioning can provoke responses ranging from outright resistance to unthinking acquiescence. For example, Hopfl and Dawes (1995) investigated action learning-type development programmes in two separate UK organizations. Each programme was designed to empower middle managers, giving them greater autonomy to both identify and resolve key operational issues. However, both initiatives were summarily curtailed when senior management felt that the type of learning emanating from them was becoming a threat to their own managerial prerogative. In a similar vein, Rusaw (2000) studied a development programme in a US university, designed to bring about higher levels of trust, fairness and openness of communication. The programme spanned all levels of the organization, stretching from top management down to non-management grades. It sought to involve the participation of all these levels in the development of new values and norms. It combined this with a range of techniques designed to enhance assertiveness, conflict management, speaking openly and honestly, networking and mutual support. An evaluation of the programme revealed those lower down the organization reporting positive results within their peer groups. This was accompanied, however, by frustration at a perceived absence of behavioural change at senior levels. Despite this, the dean of the university took no action to address such concerns, eventually abdicating all responsibility by taking early retirement. The climate rapidly deteriorated to a point where levels of dissatisfaction were even greater than had existed prior to the programme. These two examples show how learning that threatens to break out of the tight confines imposed by senior management can rapidly come to threaten the interests of the latter, thus supporting Braverman's (1974) labour process-inspired thesis that too much education of the masses can become a liability to those in charge.

These studies also illustrate how potentially emancipatory forms of learning for those lower down the organization can meet resistance from those further up, since such learning can *disrupt control* within the organization by threatening existing power structures. It is just as likely, however, that management development (of a more directive nature) can be used to *strengthen control* by reinforcing existing power structures. In such cases, overt resistance (this time from those lower down the organization) is perhaps less likely to be the outcome than acquiescence (see Box 6.6).

Box 6.6   Management development and conformist acquiescence

Kamoche (2000) conducted a study of management development at 'IP', a large multinational. The development initiative covered international managers on secondment at IP's UK headquarters and involved a programme of education (resembling a mini-MBA) at the company's prestigious training institute. The programme was seen as a means of socialization and enculturation for the managers in the sometimes mysterious social and corporate workings of IP. It was also seen as a crucial rite of passage for any

(Continued)

(Continued)

manager seeking to transit from the 'profane' world of middle management to the 'sacred' terrain of the senior ranks. Through the analytical lens of ideology, Kamoche was able to delve into the largely unspoken assumptions about the 'right' way to behave within IP, whose interests were being served by the programme and why participating managers largely acquiesced in the supposedly integrative values it espoused. In his view, embedding such values within a development programme that simultaneously determined career advancement effectively emasculated potentially deviant and non-conformist individual interests.

Kamoche is not alone in claiming that such a closed or recursive loop of control can implicate management development in the suppression of difference and plurality all for the sake of conformity, predictability and control, often revolving around disciplinary notions of 'career'. Grey (1994),[1] writing from a labour process perspective, reflects on how career can act as an organizing and regulative principle in securing self-disciplined subjects in the workplace. His particular focus is the socialization and development of young trainee graduates in the UK accounting profession. In his study he highlights graduates' ambivalence towards the development process, which they perceive as *both* controlling *and* benevolent at one and the same time. However, overt resistance to the control aspect is largely absent due to the negative consequences this would have on career advancement. He also notes how instrumental reason predominates, with the career becoming a moral project to which all else, including family life, is subordinated. In other words, career becomes an end in itself rather than a means to an end.

Ackers and Preston (1997) make the related point that managers who have been singled out for development are highly unlikely to be openly critical of it, even when the ethics of the practices in which they participate are questionable. These authors studied a management development programme that sought to evoke and then manipulate strong and sometimes painful emotions among its participants, all in the service of provoking deep personal change. In their view, the processes involved were of the type more commonly found within the realms of religious conversion. While some managers *did* question the intensity and ethical currency of the programme, many others professed to enjoying precisely those aspects which, in the opinion of the authors, crossed the border between skills enhancement and 'revelatory psychological or religious experience' (Ackers and Preston, 1997: 694). Turnbull (2001b) echoes these findings in her research into a management development programme designed to engender commitment to a new set of

---

1   We should point out that Grey's paper combines the critical/modernist inheritance of labour process theory with the distinctly dialogic or post-structuralist insights of Foucauldian social theory. This is why we also have alluded to other aspects of Grey's study in Chapter 5. It also serves as a useful example of how the critical and dialogic Discourses, while not being totally commensurable, to a certain extent can be combined and to good effect.

corporate values. She identified similar processes of emotional manipulation but then went further than Ackers and Preston in identifying several types of religious conversion process at play, including a coercive variety. Her overall assessment was that while programmes of this type may appear liberating to their participants, they can also be viewed as an 'insidious form tyranny by seeking to govern the very "soul" [of] organizational members' (Turnbull, 2001b: 27).

In summary, accounts of overt resistance to management development from within managerial ranks are relatively scarce. From the critical perspective, this is considered more likely to be the result of hegemonic processes at play than any authentic meeting of the needs of managers. In the light of this, a number of authors have turned to ideology critique in order to gain insight into the less obvious workings of management development.

Ideology critique

The field of ideology critique within management development can be distinguished by studies which seek to critique the micro-practices of development within specific organizations and those that seek to instigate a more macro-type critique at the institutional level of analysis.

Micro-critique

An example of the first type of critique is a study by Bell and Taylor (2004). The study extends the themes of religiosity examined in the previous section by investigating the ideological assumptions underpinning a number of management development courses that either explicitly or implicitly invoke notions of spirituality. The authors' main conclusion is that, by focusing exclusively on deep personal transformation as the route to development, such courses deflect attention from political and structural barriers to organizational change. As such, these kinds of programme need, in the authors' view, to be seen as potentially repressive rather than enlightening. See Box 6.7 for another example of ideology critique at the micro-level of analysis.

Box 6.7   Ideology and simultaneous acquiescence and resistance

Finch-Lees et al. (2005a) delved into the ideological character of a competency-based programme of a large UK-based multinational by exposing how the programme's documentation:

- represented, as factual, claims that could never be reliably proved
- sought to naturalize shareholder interests as being in the universal interests of all
- relied exclusively on economically instrumental reasoning in getting its message across (e.g. the documentation implied that all decisions within the company needed to be justified by reference to shareholder

(Continued)

(Continued)

value, including individual managers' decisions on whether and how to 'invest' in their own development)

- portrayed competency development as a scientific and politically neutral technology, designed neatly and unproblematically to enable managers to maximize their own performance as individuals and consequently that of the whole organization as a collective.

Having distilled the ideological character of the company documentation, the authors went on to confront this with managers' evaluations of their development experiences within the overall programme. This phase of the research showed managers to be in many respects ambivalent towards the implicit ideology of the programme.

- On the one hand, they appreciated the way in which it gave them an uplifting and optimistic sense of being, belonging, orientation and purpose with respect to their organizational existence.
- On the other hand, some managers expressed a degree of scepticism about the 'scientifically neutral' status accorded to the competencies. This was associated with a certain reticence about conforming to a somewhat arbitrary stereotype of what it means to be a developing manager within the organization.

But ideology critique at the organizational level of analysis fails to explain how ideology can also regulate society at the wider or institutional level of analysis. For this we need to turn to macro forms of critique.

Macro-critique

What we have chosen to categorize as macro-critiques are those that reflect critically on wider trends or discourses within or related to the field of management development rather than presenting empirical work from individual organizations. For example, there is a small but growing critique of the discourse of organizational learning, and it is to this that we now turn our attention.

Contu et al. (2003) subject the whole discourse of learning (as typically used in the terms 'organizational learning', 'life-long learning' etc.) to provocative critique. In doing so, the authors consciously acknowledge that theirs could be seen as a heretical move given the difficulty of making the case against a concept that has come to be regarded as universally beneficial, benign and apolitical. However, they argue that it is precisely these properties that render the discourse of learning a significant and hegemonic ideology with real practical force. In their view it has achieved this by conjuring up a nebulous but seductive futuristic vision in which 'old' conflicts (such as those between capital and labour) are rendered invisible within the new and supposed knowledge economy. Like Bell and Taylor (2004), they characterize the learning discourse as both individualizing and individualistic in as much as it transforms social subjects into 'learners' who become uniquely responsible for their own employability. Historical and structural causes of social exclusion are thus obscured, rendering any prospects for their alleviation more remote.

However, while Contu et al. provide an eloquent critique of the learning discourse, as with much work within the critical Discourse, they propose little in the way of alternatives. In contrast, Ortenblad (2002) draws on Burrell and Morgan's (1979) four paradigms for social research in highlighting the predominance of functionalist and interpretivist perspectives to organizational learning. He puts forward his own theoretical vision for what a radical and critical perspective might look like. He makes a range of proposals, including that of organizational members having genuine freedom to decide for themselves what they should learn, rather than having the agenda dictated for them by those at the top of the organization. Perhaps paradoxically, he also alludes to the need for rules and norms to guarantee such freedom and ensure that learning remains democratic. But as Ortenblad himself acknowledges, there remains much work to be done in coming up with a truly critical (and workable) vision for a radical/critical perspective to organizational learning, not least of which is the degree to which such a perspective might depend on a replacement to contemporary forms of capitalism. Ferdinand (2004) extends the above critiques by drawing attention to the role of the state in influencing and indeed restricting what might actually count as learning. He characterizes the UK government's sponsorship of national vocational qualifications (NVQs) as a hegemonic attempt to direct the development of individuals within the confines of a neo-liberalist ideology. For Ferdinand, this results in the commodification of learning, combined with an undue restriction on managers' and employees' freedom to learn whatever they might consider appropriate to their own needs. The dangers of such a restrictive and prescriptive approach to development are brought home by Grugulis (2000) in her study of the competency-based management NVQ, the content of which she considers to bear very little relevance to what managers actually do in the workplace. As an interesting aside, Ferdinand is fairly dismissive of other authors (Coopey and Burgoyne, 2000; Butcher and Clarke, 2002) within the field of organizational learning who self-style themselves as critical. He criticizes their calls for organizational democracy with respect to learning as being neglectful of context and simplistic in their conceptualizations of power, thus presenting a danger that such calls may lead to little more than the reproduction of state hegemony within organizations.

There have been a number of other attempts to formulate a vision of what might constitute a critical form of management learning and development. These are often referred to under the collective heading of critical management pedagogy.

Critical management pedagogy

Within this body of literature there are some who advocate specific forms of critical learning and others who reflect on their own attempts to instigate a critical form of learning among practising managers and/or management students. In terms of the former, a frequently advocated means of engendering more criticality within the field of management development is that of emancipatory or critical action learning (Fenwick, 2004).

Emancipatory and critical action learning

Willmott (1994b) makes the point that critical management academics have tended to be more concerned with preparing scholarly publications, establishing alternative journals, organizing conferences and writing monographs than with the incorporation of a critical approach to the education of practising or student managers. At the same time, he characterizes traditional approaches to the education and development of managers as doing little to challenge 'the personally degrading, socially divisive and ecologically destructive consequences of modern economic development' (1994b: 110). Management development for Willmott is largely *done to* managers rather than *done by* them, via processes that treat them almost like patients as opposed to agents. He cites the capitalist labour process as being a substantial constraint to change but also claims that periodic crises within capitalism (provoked by its inherent contradictions) also present opportunities for change. Allied to this, he urges those involved in the development of managers to search for new methods that will permit the latter to become more socially and critically active and aware when it comes to their own learning. If Grey (2004) is anything to go by, Wilmott's concern remains just as pertinent today as when he expressed it well over a decade ago (see Box 6.8).

Box 6.8   Models of management education and pedagogy

Grey (2004) has criticized business schools for their almost universal adoption of a scientific and politically neutral stance to the discipline of management. Management is taught as if it comprises a body of facts and techniques that can be reliably applied to real-world situations with predictable effects. For Grey, what this obscures is that the discipline of management is characterized by a plethora of values that cannot be divorced from the facts to which it lays claim. As such, management is inherently to do with issues of morals, ethics, politics and philosophy. Despite this, business schools continue to follow an educational model derived from those of engineering and medicine. These are disciplines characterized by techniques that are far more amenable to cross-context generalization and where any non-separation of fact from value is of less consequence. In contrast: 'management cannot be adequately formulated on the basis that others are "objects" to be manipulated through some "people-management tool kit"' (2004: 184). Grey therefore calls for business schools to adopt a pedagogy based more around the context-specific lived experience of management students themselves. This would go beyond relatively established (and not necessarily critical) models such as experiential learning, interpersonal relationships and self-awareness to examine structural issues of power, control and inequality. Grey refers to the University of Leicester in the UK, which is one of the few to have set up a management faculty based around critical principles.

TABLE 6.1   *Putting the 'critical' into critical action learning (adapted from Willmott, (1994b; 1997)*

	Traditional management education	Action learning	Critical action learning
Worldview	The world is something to learn about.	The world is somewhere to act and change.	The world is somewhere to act and change.
	Self-development is unimportant.	Self-development is very important.	Self-development and social development are interdependent.
	Some notion of correct management practice established by research defines the curriculum.	Curriculum defined by the manager or organization.	The interdependence of beings means that no individual or group can gain monopoly control of the curricula.
Modus operandi	Managers should learn theories or models derived from research.	Managers should be facilitated by a tutor to solve problems.	Managers should be receptive to, and be facilitated by, the concerns of other groups, in addition to individual tutors, when identifying and addressing problems.
	Experts decide on what should be learnt, when and how much.	Experts are viewed with caution.	Received wisdom, including that of experts, is subject to critical scrutiny through a fusion of reflection and insights drawn from critical social theory.
	Models, concepts, ideas are provided to offer tools for thinking and action.	Models, concepts, ideas are developed in response to problems.	Models, concepts, ideas are developed through an interplay of reflection upon practice and application of ideas drawn from critical traditions.

Willmott (1997) proposes that a critical form of action learning might allow this to happen but in a manner that avoids the *imposition* of a critical perspective. Table 6.1 sets out what he means by critical action learning, contrasting it first with conventional action learning and also with traditional approaches to management education.

Since publishing his paper, Willmott's call has been echoed and built upon in various guises and by various authors. Both Raelin (2001) and Garrick and Clegg (2001), for example, advocate 'project-based learning' as a critically oriented form of action learning. Raelin in particular draws on Habermasian critical theory in arguing that a public, participatory and democratic form of project-based reflection provides a route to unlocking a critical form of learning. Crucially, for Raelin, this needs to include 'premise reflection' (2001: 12), which challenges the very questions being posed within the particular project at hand, along with the fundamental beliefs or societal norms upon which these questions are based. This will typically entail a 'dialectical' form of knowing that can lead the learner towards an awareness and subsequent challenging of the social, political and cultural conditions that give rise to taken-for-granted assumptions that in turn constrain self-insight. So, for example, if a project entails the search for a cost-effective way of reducing headcount, premise reflection would question not just the solutions proposed but the very assumptions upon which headcount reduction is assumed to be necessary in the first place (see also Willmott, 1997, who makes a similar point). Raelin links these processual concepts to the kind of outcome that others have described as triple-loop learning. In doing so he stresses the need for the critical reflection he describes to be not just a public activity but a shared, social and mutually supportive one. This requires that all participants in the process become reflexively aware of how they might each use power, privilege and voice to exert influence and suppress dissenting views. The aim is to ensure that all views are heard within a dialectic that leads to new ways of thinking and acting. While all this sounds admirable in theory, and despite Raelin's view that his ideas are practical and fully realizable, we share Fenwick's (2004) concern that such 'inspirational hypotheses' can prove difficult to put into practice. Despite these concerns, however, Fenwick does allude to empirical evidence which suggests that such an approach can, under certain circumstances, lead to emancipatory and socially beneficial learning. Some of her sources are briefly expanded upon in the section that follows.

Reflecting on attempts to critically educate managers

Occasionally, the academic literature will throw up a 'success' story from those employing a critically-informed approach to the development of managers. One such example comes from Meyerson and Fletcher (2000), who recount how they have employed a form of action learning in addressing issues of gender inequity within a range of different organizations. They maintain that this form of learning can be effective in allowing organizational members to discover for themselves previously hidden forms of gender discrimination (often of a subtle, systemic nature) and then taking sometimes small but eminently practical steps to address them. Their argument is that this 'small wins' approach can cumulatively add up to larger-scale systemic or societal change.

More typically, however, the literature is characterized by ambivalence and sometimes outright pessimism on the part of those attempting to draw upon the critical Discourse in the education and development of managers. Interestingly, an example of the former comes once again from Meyerson (Meyerson and Kolb, 2000), in which this time the writers acknowledge the various barriers and difficulties they have encountered in bringing about positive change via their action learning approach. One of the main difficulties emanated from their dual-pronged approach of aiming to alleviate gender discrimination while simultaneously seeking to improve organizational effectiveness. This resulted in the gender aspect constantly 'getting lost' as the natural tendency within the project teams was for it to be subordinated to performance imperatives. For some, however (e.g. Fournier and Grey, 2000; Hearn, 2000), this is an eminently predictable consequence of attempting to deploy a critical approach without letting go of functionalist performance concerns. For Hearn (2000), it is entirely plausible that modern capitalist organizations actually derive an aggregate financial benefit from gender inequities. If this is indeed the case, it is functionalism itself (along with its economic and instrumental reasoning) that needs to be called into question rather than it being accommodated within attempts to engender a critical form of management learning (a similar argument is made by Litvin (2002) in her critique of the 'business case' for diversity). Furthermore, Hearn makes the important point that many sources of gender discrimination are actually macro-structural in nature and therefore not necessarily amenable to a 'small wins' approach that relies on local interventions at the organizational level of analysis.

Any attempt to instigate a critical approach to the development of managers brings with it a number of risks, dilemmas and responsibilities (see Box 6.9).

Box 6.9   Risks, dilemmas and responsibilities of critical management development

One inherent dilemma for the tutor or trainer is that of finding a way to impart critical knowledge (and as we have seen there is a substantial body of critical theory on which to draw), without setting oneself up as 'the authority who knows best', as this would reproduce the kind of hierarchy, hegemony or dominance that critical discourse seeks to resist (Reynolds, 1999). A common risk is that of participant resistance which, for Reynolds, is hardly surprising given the critical Discourse's emphasis on confronting vested interests, power differentials and the inequities to which they give rise. Managers typically look to education and development in order to reduce uncertainty in terms of both self-knowledge and dealing with others' expectations of them as managers. Far from reducing uncertainty, however, a critical perspective is likely to increase it by introducing a new set of social problems, which are considered by some to be anathema to the managerial remit, let alone part of it. As such, managers who are prepared to engage with a critical agenda often find this to be an unsettling experience and a source of disruption on both the domestic and the work fronts. In this regard, Reynolds cites a study by Brookfield (1994) where the participants in a critical management programme found the experience to be in some ways liberating while at the same time experiencing dissonance with regard to their current roles. For some, engaging with a critical agenda amounted to 'cultural suicide' given the resentment and hostility they faced when critically questioning accepted practice back in the workplace. Partly because of risks and dilemmas such as these, Reynolds calls for a high degree of reflexivity on the part of those involved in the critical development of managers.

Fenwick (2005) voices similar concerns when drawing upon her own experiences and ethical dilemmas of being a critical management educator. Her own approach is to constantly 'model reflexivity' by openly confronting her own position of authority, power and influence *vis-à-vis* the student population. Echoing Grey's (2004) call in Box 6.8, she also expounds the need for critical management education to both begin and end with students' own organizational experiences of inequity and oppression along with their own transformative ideas. Here the educator's role becomes one of mediator in terms of both problem-posing and championing voices alternative to those espousing the dominant ideology. Such an approach is not without its own dilemmas, however, as alternative voices by the very act of 'being championed' may be inadvertently constructed as weak and deficient. By the same token, Fenwick also points out that the problematizing of students' personal experiences of privilege, merely to arouse public defensiveness or shame, is not ethically justifiable for any educative reason. Furthermore, she claims that this kind of personalized blaming is not productive in any event as it leaves structural inequities and complex power relations unchallenged.

In summary, the critical Discourse to management development, while rich in theoretical underpinnings, is complex, controversial and wracked with its own ethical dilemmas and implementation issues. Before concluding, we now set out some key critiques of the critical Discourse to management development, with particular reference to the other Grand Discourses we have encountered in previous chapters.

A comparative assessment of critical, dialogic, constructivist and functionalist Discourses

As we hope to have demonstrated, the critical Discourse has much to offer that is distinct from the other Grand Discourses examined in this book and affords intriguing options for our understanding of management development. In this section, our aim is to briefly recapitulate on the main differences between the critical and the other Discourses but also to explore some similarities, overlaps and potential synergies between them, particularly when it comes to the dialogic Discourse.

Critical Discourse and functionalism

In terms of differences, the Discourse with which the critical is perhaps most at odds is that of functionalism. As we have seen throughout this chapter, critical Discourse takes issue with many of the key tenets upon which functionalism is founded, the main ones being its performative intent, its managerialism, its positivist commitments, its instrumental reasoning, its correspondence theory of truth and its portrayal of management knowledge as scientific and politically neutral. In fact, the main target of the critical Discourse to management development tends to be functionalist conceptions of management development itself, which the former views as being laden with ideological content masquerading as scientific and benign neutrality.

Furthermore, while functionalism tends to focus on the 'development' aspect of the management development equation, the critical Discourse seeks to problematize the very notion of 'management' instead, calling into question the motives behind a separate form of development for such a category of person. For example, the critical Discourse regards the division of labour between managers and non-managers to be inherently artificial and motivated by concerns of power and domination, not least the capitalist imperative to extract surplus value from the workers. So critical/emancipatory action learning, for example, would arguably cease to be either critical or emancipatory if the activity was restricted to include just those enjoying the formal status of manager within the organization. However, as we shall see on page 152 below, such aspirations to collapse categories and dissolve social divisions generate an internal tension when set against the critical Discourse's emphasis on shared group interests.

Critical Discourse and constructivism

When it comes to comparing the critical Discourse to the constructivist, one important point of difference is the treatment of participant accounts of the development process. As we saw in Chapter 4, the constructivist approach to researching management development tends to draw heavily on participants' own interpretations of the activities they are involved in, with a view to drawing out the diverse meanings these activities might hold for such participants. The researcher's role is more one of foregrounding the constructions of participants but for their own sake rather than for the sake of judgement or critique. The critical researcher may also draw heavily on participant constructions of the development process but will not be taking these at face value. Instead, such constructions will be critiqued from a variety of angles with the researcher asking such questions as:

- What is the participant trying to achieve by expressing themselves in this way?
- Are their views indicative of support or resistance to the dominant ideology underpinning development in this organization?
- What do they stand to gain or lose by such support/resistance?
- Are they acting in their own or their identity group's real interests, or are they in a state of false consciousness?
- How can my own critically-informed analysis make the hidden dynamics of the situation more visible?

From this we can begin to appreciate how the critical Discourse opens itself up to accusations of elitism. By what right, for example, do critical researchers claim to have superior insight to those they are researching? And what is wrong with taking the latter's views at face value? Such challenges are launched by Guest (1999) in presenting his own research, purporting to show that workers actually support the kind of HRM practices that have been widely challenged (supposedly on their behalf) in the critical literature. Guest's challenges are echoed by Caven (2006) in her interpretative assessment of women's HRD experiences. She takes critical researchers to task for the 'totalitarian' way in which they automatically assume false consciousness when women fail to acknowledge structural sources of gender discrimination. Such an assumption in her view runs counter to any emancipatory intent and merely inflicts its own form of oppression on women. If women report being 'content' with their lot, then we should just accept that:

> This paper reports the stories of the women who took part in this research study. It has given them their own voice and presented their interpretations of their accounts rather than having explanations provided on their behalf. ... The women are exercising choice ... [and] ... report that they are content. (Caven, 2006: 51–52)

A critical response to researchers such as Guest and Caven might be that not only are their respondents susceptible to false consciousness, but so are the authors themselves. And if it's not false consciousness to which they are prone, then perhaps they are merely being disingenuous by taking participant accounts at face value and have some political motive or identity-stake in seeking to de-legitimize the critical perspective. Also, to be fair to critical researchers, their critiques are by and large informed by an extensive body of critical theory which can perhaps be expected to afford them a form of insight not necessarily available to research participants. Reflexivity is an important part of the critical process and entails a degree of explicit self-questioning of the researcher's own motives, choices, assumptions and ethics, things that we suggest are noticeably absent from papers such as Guest's and Caven's.

The critical and dialogic Discourses

There tends to be a good deal of tension between the dialogic and the critical, much of which stems from the former's attempts to deconstruct the latter's analytical dualisms. So whereas, for example, the critical Discourse makes clear epistemological distinctions between, say, freedom and oppression, free will and structural constraint, the dialogic regards each side of such dualisms as mutually constitutive of the other. In response, the critical Discourse's assessment of the dialogic position is that, taken to its extreme, there is ultimately no point in struggling towards a 'better' social order as any supposedly emancipatory alternative will only result in different forms of oppression (Parker, 1999). For an example of this, recall our dialogic treatment of competency in Chapter 5. The dialogic stance, for the critical researcher, denies itself any basis for a politics of ethical change, rendering the Discourse socially irrelevant even if it could ever be proved to be epistemologically 'correct'. Furthermore, as Parker (1999) points out, the only way in which those of a dialogic persuasion can assert their own position is by refuting those of the critical persuasion, thus falling into the kind of dualist language they themselves seek to reject. It is to avoid such circular and perhaps irresolvable arguments that Parker calls for a retreat from debates around ontology and epistemology as a starting point for research, suggesting instead that research might usefully begin with ethical problems and then take an epistemologically pragmatic (rather than dogmatic) view on what is to be done about them. This is not to say that questions of ontology and epistemology do not matter, but they perhaps matter less, in Parker's view, than the material conditions in which people live out their lives. This is a view with which we ourselves have a good deal of sympathy, being the spirit in which this book was conceived in the first place.

Other dialogically-inspired critiques of the critical Discourse would include its rather inflexible view of human subjectivity, which once again is partly the result of its dualist commitments. The critical Discourse tends to work at the level of group interests (e.g. workers, middle managers, senior managers, labour, capital, etc.) and conceptualize power as some kind of possession or commodity. In contrast, the dialogic tends to reject the notion of ontologically stable or common interests at the group level and views power as a relational/discursive phenomenon. As such, the notion of 'interests' is inherently more complex and unstable for the dialogic (see Box 6.10).

Box 6.10   The problematic critical notion of shared group interests

Two middle managers may ultimately have very different interests, depending on the subjectivities they either adopt for themselves or find themselves being pigeon-holed into by others. It is fairly evident that a young, black, male, heterosexual manager may have substantially different interests and power relations than a middle-aged, female, white, bisexual manager. However, it is unlikely that the critical Discourse will be able to easily accommodate such considerations given its focus on shared group interests. However, the dialogic (in its ideal type at least) tends to go to the other extreme by deconstructing subjectivity to such an extent that any notion of a collective politics becomes difficult, if not impossible, to sustain. It is perhaps for this reason that, in practice, much research tends to span both the critical and the dialogic, oscillating between the two even if only implicitly via the non-reflexive use of language.

A comparison of the dialogic and the critical is further clouded by the way in which the 'critical' label is often attached to both perspectives. Indeed, the field of 'Critical Management Studies' (despite its name) is somewhat of an umbrella term for studies that draw from both Discourses, whether explicitly or implicitly, and sometimes within a single piece of work. Notwithstanding some difficult questions of epistemological 'correctness', we share the view expressed by others that there is much to be gained from an approach that combines elements of both these Discourses, whether in the field of management development specifically (e.g. Garrick and Clegg, 2001; Valentin, 2006) or the field of organizational analysis more generally (e.g. Parker, 1999, 2000; Alvesson and Deetz, 2000).

Conclusion

In this chapter we have noted the ways in which a variety of concepts and theoretical positions underpinning the critical Discourse can help provide a radically alternative understanding of management development compared to the dominant functionalist and the increasingly prevalent constructivist traditions. We have also explored how the critical Discourse exists in a state of productive tension alongside the dialogic. In summary, the critical Discourse to management development helps re-orient attention towards issues of power, politics, domination, exploitation and oppression within the field of management development. It also provides a means by which alternatives to the status quo can be both envisioned and potentially enacted via forms of learning that hold out the promise of being more inclusive, more democratic and more emancipatory. However, it should also be evident from our account within this chapter that the critical Discourse does not present any kind of neat road map towards the achievement of a more equitable, inclusive and democratic approach to management development (or indeed to society more generally). Indeed, one major unresolved dilemma within the Discourse itself is one of how to bring about (what it regards as) positive social change without itself becoming a universalist and thus totalitarian form of prescriptive oppression.

This brings to a close the middle section of the book which has examined four Discourses to management development, namely the functionalist, the constructivist, the dialogic and the critical. It is important to stress that these are meant to be taken as no more than 'ideal-types' or heuristic devices, with somewhat arbitrary boundaries, in order to facilitate as full an understanding of management development as possible. In practice, a single study may combine (more or less reflexively) elements drawn from two or more of the Discourses and this is particularly the case when it comes to the critical and the dialogic. Our own view is that no particular Discourse is, on its own, particularly satisfactory when it comes to analysing management development. And while there may be aspects of any one Discourse which are epistemologically incommensurable with the others, we believe that fruitful dialogue can nonetheless take place between them.

Summary

- The critical Discourse to management development is concerned with exposing, overturning and replacing situations of injustice, inequality and repression.
- It is dissensual and analytically (as opposed to ontologically) dualist in approach.
- It regards the very notion of management (as a separate category of person) as an unnecessary social division.
- As such it is suspicious of attempts to develop the manager either because it sees management development as:

  — a carrier of exploitative ideology *vis-à-vis* the non-manager; and/or
  — an ideological means to subjugate managers themselves in the service of 'capital', thus obscuring their own 'real' interests.

- The critical Discourse does not, however, abandon all hope towards the emergence of more critically-informed forms of development, such as critical action learning.
- Such forms of development need, however, to be capable of transcending individual experience in order to tackle wider structural forms of injustice and inequality.

Part III

Meso-discourses of management development

Part two of the book was concerned with four Grand Discourses of management development: functionalist, constructivist, dialogic and critical. We now turn our attention to three meso-discourses of management development: best-practice, institutionalist and diversity. We have chosen these three from many that might have been selected, because we believe them to have particular currency at this time (others would include: talent management, life-long learning, social capital, continuing professional development, intangible assets). Also, they are illustrative of different types of meso-discourse. Best-practice discourse, by definition, is driven by a practitioner concern with competitive performance which has subsequently attracted scholarly attention and respectability. Institutionalist discourse has a more theoretical origin, arising from debates about the influence of socio-cultural context on firm behaviour. Diversity discourse is also fuelled by theoretical debate, but the focus here is arguably more ethical than economic, less about how corporate beliefs and values are explained and more about how they are expressed.

Now is perhaps an appropriate time to recap on the distinctions that can be made between Grand Discourse and meso-discourse. Recall that in Chapter 1, we drew on Alvesson and Kärreman (2000) in describing the former as: an assembly of discourses, ordered and presented as an integrated frame which may refer to/constitute organizational reality. Take functionalism as an example. There is a whole host of texts (e.g. academic books, papers, organizational documents and conversations) that without much controversy can be characterized as functionalist. Such texts are liable in one way or another to interact, however partially and randomly, as a myriad of social actors draw upon them to inform their thoughts, words and deeds and hence their very subjectivities. Gradually, functionalism (even though people don't necessarily refer to it as such) comes to be so pervasive as to form a shared sense of reality. It is in this respect that it can be considered a Grand Discourse.

Consider now the notion of meso-discourse. We described this in Chapter 1 as: language and social practice whose meaning is more context-specific than Grand Discourse but which nevertheless transcends the particular text in question, thus forming broader patterns of meaning that can be generalized to similar local contexts. The meso-discourse of diversity is an example. When a group of (even disparate) HR managers invoke the term 'diversity management', the chances are that they each know roughly what kinds of practices the others are referring to and they can each employ broadly the same vocabulary to discuss those practices. Meaning is thus shared at a level that permits it to form patterns that can be generalized to similar local contexts (i.e. as per our definition of meso-discourse above). However, such meaning and the vocabulary/social practices to which it relates, are not so generalizable as to provide the basis for effective communication within other contexts. It is unlikely (though not inconceivable), for example, that a large contract for the sale of military equipment would be negotiated using the language of diversity management. In contrast, it *is* entirely plausible that the separate conversations within the group of HR managers, on the one hand, and within the group of military sales negotiators on the other *will* both be conducted using the language of functionalism. Here lies the difference between Grand Discourse and meso-discourse (or to use our shorthand 'Discourse' and 'discourse').

A further point to note is that meso-discourse cannot be seen as merely a subordinated subset of Grand Discourse. For example, it is far from inevitable that diversity (or any meso-level) discourse will be constructed in purely functionalist terms. As we shall see in Chapter 9, we ourselves employ a combination of the dialogic and critical Discourses as we engage in our own diversity discourse of management development. Indeed, throughout Chapters 7–9, the perspectives from which we speak will be informed by any one of the four Grand Discourses, depending on the particular point we are making at the time. We will not always be explicit about this but would encourage you to look out for these switches of perspective or Discourse.

7

Management development and best-practice

Mandalay is one of the few place names in Burma that have not been changed by the Burmese military government. … The generals were rewriting history. When a place is renamed, the old name disappears from maps, and eventually, from human memory. By renaming cities, towns, and streets, the regime seized control of the very space within which people lived. (Emma Larkin, Secret Histories, *2005: 11)*

After reading this chapter you will be able to:

- **Describe how management development strategies and interventions come to be part of a best-practice discourse**
- **Explain how the systemic nature of organizations can often frustrate the strategic aspirations of management development**
- **Discuss and assess three best-practice approaches to developing managers and leaders**
- **Provide a critical assessment of a competency-based approach to management development**
- **Describe and evaluate the contribution of 360-degree feedback and executive coaching to the effective development of managers**
- **Identify some of the opportunities and pitfalls provided by a best-practice discourse of management development**

Introduction

For many firms the training and development of managers and leaders is seen as a luxury, for others it is a necessary way of life. For some it is synonymous with expensive, formalized programmes, for others it is woven seamlessly into daily routines. Some argue that the best way to create management capability is via astute recruitment, reward and recognition policies, while others maintain that management training and development is the cornerstone of an organization's HR strategy, the real litmus test of how highly it values its staff. There is probably some validity in all these views. However, for all the divergence of opinion, there is undoubtedly a growing recognition by both governments and organizations that the development of managerial talent cannot be left to others or to chance. There is a compelling belief that to engage in management development is somehow emblematic of being a progressive employer, that it will enhance market-place reputation and improve competitive performance. In short, a 'best-practice' management development discourse has emerged.

As it happens, the best-practice management development discourse, with its concern for emulation and performativity, aligns itself very much with the functionalist Discourse although the other Discourses are helpful in highlighting difficulties with the notion of best-practices on the one hand and their application in organizations on the other. We explore the best-practice management development discourse in two ways. First, we examine how 'best-practice' is appropriated as a rationale for launching strategic management development initiatives. Second, new techniques, leading-edge programmes, fresh approaches are regularly paraded as the latest means to enhance management talent. We look more closely at three such initiatives that figure prominently in organizations at present. In so doing, we assess not only the appeal of best-practice but also some of the pitfalls associated with this management development discourse.

Best-practice as a strategic rationale for management development

Most organizations have got to the point of recognizing that management development is more than a tactical or knee-jerk response to a skills gap. Obviously there is a legitimate place for sending individual managers on a course to update their knowledge or improve their competency, but increasingly organizations are using management development as part of a wider strategy to achieve their longer-term aspirations. Three strands to this best-practice thinking can be detected: facilitating strategic change, building learning organizations and creating intercultural competency.

Facilitating strategic change

Underlying many management training initiatives is the belief that such activities will help organizations achieve competitive edge. And this is not just the case for private companies. Because public and not-for-profit enterprises cannot register success simply in terms of profit and market share, the way their management teams acquire resources and deliver services is increasingly becoming a driver for sustainable growth. It is difficult to pinpoint the source of such ebullient belief. In part, it is promoted by HR professional networks comprising professional bodies, training agencies, consultants, academics, the forums and conferences they attend and the literature they produce. The motivation for management development, the diffusion of new management practices and the relevance of different forms of training to individual managers is strongly associated with and influenced by the networks and communities of practice that both firms and individual managers are involved in. An example is the 'Investors in People' (IiP) initiative, a nationally recognized training accreditation scheme that has been widely adopted in the UK and with growing international importance in Germany, France, Holland, South Africa and Australia (Hoque et al., 2002) (see page 121 for more detail). In their post-structuralist study of six UK organizations involved in the IiP process, Bell et al. (2002a: 1077) found that much of the attraction lay in the prestige of association with other high-status organizations who had successfully achieved IiP accreditation: 'The prospect of becoming part of the external IiP "club"'. It is easy to see, how under such conditions a best-practice belief arises which serves to legitimize the use of management development.

Symbolically and politically motivated decisions to invest in training are not confined to the level of the organization. Government rhetoric also plays its part. In the UK, the causal connection between management development and GDP is often enunciated and rarely questioned: 'Management and leadership have long been known as key factors in driving performance of individual organizations and the wider UK economy, and in narrowing the gap with our international competitors' (DfES/DTI, 2002). And yet national training policies inevitably incorporate mixed motives. For instance, in the USA, Lafer (1999: 146) notes that the Job Training Partnership Act was 'essentially political strategy aimed at containing the response to economic hardship rather than addressing its root causes'.

Despite the logical appeal of creating and harnessing individual skills and competency around business strategies, this can be problematic for a number of reasons. First, we know that the formulation and implementation of strategy at any level is an uncertain, emergent and iterative process. Even if the strategic intent can be clearly articulated, in some cases it can take four to five years before the first fruits of concerted management development appear at corporate level. This presents the distinct possibility that the original strategy has now shifted in focus and/or some of the design features have become outmoded. Furthermore, the evolution of corporate strategy, and by implication management development strategy is likely to be messy and overtaken by unpredictable events. At best, it gives those responsible for deriving such strategies 'some sense of control and direction in the midst of chaotic and unpredictable reality' (Pattison, 1997: 30–1). Even where organizational objectives are stated, these may bear little resemblance to the actual intentions and values of those initiating and sponsoring the development (Lees, 1992). More pragmatically, it seems that linking corporate and management development strategy is an unfulfilled aspiration for most organizations (see Box 7.1).

Box 7.1   Learning in organizations: not so leading edge?

An investigation into management development in the UK was carried out by the Chartered Institute of Personnel and Development (CIPD, 2002). This involved a survey of 433 organizations, seven consultation groups and a senior executive seminar with 60 participants, 25 interviews with HR/D Directors and leading business schools and five case studies. Among the findings were:

(Continued)

(Continued)

- 85 per cent of senior managers see integrating management development with the implementation of organizational goals as a top priority. Yet only 16 per cent of the survey respondents believe their organizations are very effective at developing business plans that specify the management capabilities required, while 30 per cent of organizations do not even have business plans.
- In terms of learning processes, project and action learning, internal management courses and coaching were seen as most effective; least effective were external seminars, conferences, distance learning and internet packages, visiting speakers and courses for a management qualification.
- Only a minority of organizations adopt a business-like approach to evaluating the performance of management development. Nearly 80 per cent rely on assessment from 'happy sheets'.

In some organizations, management development is conscripted not just to build skills to support strategy but also to change attitudes, as part of a wider attempt to shift culture. Given that culture is a central, all-pervasive reality of organizational life, encompassing the spectrum of attitudes, values and norms that make up the distinctive feel of an enterprise, this is indeed a bold aspiration. In the same ways that nations rewrite their history, as in the opening quotation, organizations frequently enlist best-practice approaches like management development to re-oriente their corporate 'maps'. Bate (1995) elaborates four different strategies adopted by organizations seeking to change their cultures. One of these, the so-called 'indoctrinative approach', relies heavily upon training and development. This kind of intervention, with its reliance on democracy and consultation, is softer and more communal than the prescription of the 'aggressive approach' and the subterfuge of the 'corrosive approach'. Nevertheless it is still a socialization programme where the aim is to fit the participating individuals into a pre-defined mould: 'They are therefore "taught" courses … and do not presuppose the existence of any kind of reciprocal interaction or mutual learning' (Bate, 1995: 194). With some irony, Bate refers to the contention that cultural learning can only occur in routine, continuous, experiential and interactive settings, and notes that, almost by definition, indoctrinative programmes are non-routine, discontinuous, non-experiential and conducted in a non-interactive setting (see Box 7.2).

Box 7.2   Manager development as a tool of culture change

In the mid 1990s a leading food retailing organization in the UK introduced a company-wide change effort to tackle specific and far-reaching strategic issues (Ogbonna and Harris, 1998). As part of this, 8,000 managers were

(Continued)

(Continued)

sent on workshops run by an external consultancy comprising whole days away from regional/central offices. Mixed groups of employees from diverse backgrounds were encouraged to understand why things had changed, why the company had restructured as well as being told of the work-style which the company saw as ideal. Participants were encouraged to criticize past attitudes and behaviours (which the consultants labelled as 'old world') while praising currently espoused attitudes (which became known as 'new world'). Company documents provided to employees at such workshops emphasize the focus of the campaign as one of re-energizing wherein individuals were encouraged to develop ideas rather than the company telling the workforce of the changes they should make. Responses to the change effort were reported as varying from re-orientation (apparent adoption of new value sets), re-interpretation (partial acceptance), re-invention (recycling of existing values so that they are presented as in alignment with the newly espoused values) and outright rejection. The researchers conclude that while managements have become more sophisticated in their attempts to change cultures, it is clear that employees have become equally shrewd in their tactics of resistance and have developed better ways of coping. Indeed, instrumental values-compliance implies that some employees have cognitively accepted espoused values in order to further their careers.

This example illustrates that it is too simplistic to view management development as a lever to facilitate attitudinal change, as a neutral process where the only resistance trainees have to absorbing new knowledge or acquiring new skills is their individual capacity or learning style. Because to do so neglects the nature of learning as 'a politicized process where new knowledge, systems and techniques are viewed suspiciously, even rejected because they are seen to represent the priorities of others whose priorities are distinct and possibly opposed, or to result in a re-allocation of organizational resources, or a weakening of a section's traditional power-base' (Salaman and Butler, 1990: 187).

Building learning organizations

Partly in recognition of the difficulties noted above, there has been a concerted effort by many employers to focus less on instrumental issues of organizational performance improvement and more on the learning potential of groups and the untapped talent of individuals. Here the creation of a learning climate lies at the very core of their management development strategy. Accordingly, the trend is away from structured, didactic courses and towards enhanced opportunities for self-development through such methods as on-the-job training, e-learning, strategic secondments and participation in communities of practice. The idea of 'the learning organization' flourished in the 1990s as one way of summing up the sorts of organizational quality called for and valued in today's changing environment. There is no 'right model' of a learning organization. Developing a learning organization is not a matter of adopting policies and procedures used successfully elsewhere because such 'copying' inevitably runs contrary to the spirit of knowledge management as discussed above. It has been argued however that a learning organization has a recognizable and distinctive 'feel'. Box 7.3 offers one such early description (Dale, 1993).

Box 7.3   What does a learning organization look like?

A learning organization:

- will work to create values, practices and procedures in which 'learning' and 'working' are synonymous throughout the organization
- is inextricably bound up with organizational change and will seek to move beyond the learning associated with 'first-order change' – learning to improve current performance and do the same things differently and more effectively – to the learning associated with 'second-order change' – learning how to learn and develop the capacity to continuously generate new ideas and insights in order to do different things
- will involve the discomfort of living with the uncertainties and ambiguities associated with iterative processes of change. It also involves acknowledging the risk associated with dynamic conservatism and consensus, working through and recognizing the positive value of – rather than just overcoming – the conflicts arising from multiple agendas and diverging perceptions
- will require its managers to redefine their roles and responsibilities – rather than being isolated individuals, they are members of a professional community of co-learners
- will provide a safe environment for the risks and openness required for reflective practice in which questioning and self-doubt are as important as certainty and control.

It is not difficult to see the attraction of the learning organization as part of the best-practice management development discourse. Many top teams yearn, as part of their rhetoric at least, for dismantling conservative mindsets, spotting dysfunctional patterns of behaviour and galvanizing energy around the exploration of a new purpose and core values. However, for all its appeal, is the learning organization more than an ideal-type and is it practically attainable? Critics argue that the rhetoric too often assumes or implies a unitarist framework of relationships, the pursuit of shared goals in a climate of collaborative high trust and a rational approach to the resolution of differences (Coopey, 1996). In other words, it becomes a convenient metaphor, attractive and widely prized, but actually masking the fact that it reinforces managerial pressures to conform, aiding and abetting managerial control. Paradoxically, the climate of open questioning and non-defensive argument can be the very opposite of what is produced.

Creating intercultural competence

The simultaneous pursuit of global coordination and multinational responsiveness creates a natural learning agenda for many organizations. This involves the sharing of information and the joint implementation of strategy through an integrated network where resources, products, information and people flow freely between units. International productive capabilities may be assigned to different national subsidiaries according to their strengths. One example is the Swedish–Swiss electrical engineering group ABB, which along one dimension is a dispersed global network while along another dimension is a collection of national companies serving local markets. The managers running the 50 business areas have both global and local roles. One manager may have global responsibility for one product while also having local responsibilities for many projects. This requires senior managers who are not only internationally mobile but who are mentally versatile and culturally sensitive.

In this context, it is not surprising that management and leadership development have also entered best-practice discourse in recent years. What are the sources of this discourse? From a practitioner perspective, multinational corporations (MNCs) undoubtedly play a major role in the dissemination of HR practices, with parent companies often using management development as 'corporate glue' (Gratton, 1996). Much of the theoretical influence arises from the growing field of knowledge transfer. The possibility of intra-corporate knowledge transfer is one of the guiding hallmarks of the so-called 'transnational' firm (Bartlett and Ghoshal, 1989). But the successful diffusion of knowledge in such a firm is by no means automatic and requires concerted effort and significant internal coordination. This is especially the case for tacit knowledge, which is, by definition, non-procedural, experiential, subjective, like the local 'know-how' relating to marketing and distribution, management systems and product design. It is here that a firm's intangible assets lie, rather than in more explicit, declarative types of knowledge, such as the reporting of monthly financial data (Gupta and Govindarajan, 2000).

Nahapiet and Ghoshal (1998) refer to three dimensions of social capital.

1 The structural dimension refers to the presence or absence of specific networks or social interaction ties across and between organizations. There is a good deal of evidence to suggest that HRM generally, and management development in particular, can help create all three forms of social capital and effective knowledge transfer (Gooderham, 2006).
2 The cognitive dimension refers to shared interpretations and systems of meaning, and shared language and codes to enable communication. This is possibly what Gertsen (1990) describes as the ability of successful managers to be 'cognitively complex': not relying on crude stereotypes or narrow categorizations, but dividing up the world in more subtle ways.
3 The relational dimension refers to the creation of networks, trust, reciprocity, obligations, respect and friendship which facilitate the sharing of this tacit knowledge.

Structural capital: mechanisms to build structural capital might include: intranet communities as sources of knowledge-sharing where high degrees of reciprocity and identity can be established despite the absence of face-to-face contact

(Teigland, 2000); inter-unit taskforces and global forums set up to solicit a wide range of ideas and deliberately counter business ethno-centric solutions and international assignments for individual and organizational development. For example, case studies of Singapore-owned subsidiaries in China indicate the importance of Chinese managers not only spending time at corporate headquarters but also in other parts of the MNC (Tsang, 2001).

Cognitive capital: this may entail self-development, especially raising awareness of one's cultural assumptions and how they interact with host-country values and behaviour. To create this *cognitive* capital, such methods as cross-cultural sensitivity workshops, diversity training with multicultural teams, field trips aided by tools for ethnographic orientation, action learning with a multicultural set, job rotation involving international assignments and multicultural team-building exercises might be used.

Relational capital: similarly, the strategy of holding training in different countries alongside international action learning programmes to facilitate both formal and informal interaction, might be a means to building *relational* capital. In effect, such networks can facilitate the transfer of knowledge. However, this needs to be qualified in two ways. First, the socio-institutional heritage of different countries will exert a strong influence on the way such networks operate, as illustrated in Box 7.4.

Box 7.4   Chinese conceptions of management development

The Chinese enterprise has been described as a political coalition and a socio-political community, and the Confucian principle of hierarchy implies that individuals need to be conscious of their position in the social system and abide by it. This means managers need to cultivate vertical relationships with superiors as well as non-market exchange relationships with other enterprises (Walder, 1989). A study of managers in 100 firms in Henan province (with relatively limited exposure to the West) confirmed this, concluding that the Chinese enterprise is not merely influenced by its environment, but is a vehicle through which the institutional order is super-imposed:

> The Chinese manager must hence fulfil a dual and often contradictory role: to compete for the scarce resources that are critical for the enterprise's survival, and to satisfy an environment that views organizational processes as equally important to organizational performance. Personal relationships with key stakeholders act as the boundary scanning mechanisms that enable the manager to fulfil this dual role. (Shenkar et al., 1998: 59)

A Western manager, concerned primarily to build a network for business purposes, might miss or not appreciate these wider concerns of her/his Chinese counterpart.

Second, inclusion in, or exclusion from, networks and participation in management development initiatives can 'cut both ways'. It has been found that women in UK organizations are disproportionately less likely to benefit from personal and professional development afforded by overseas assignments due to gender bias arising from the predominant use of 'closed, informal selection processes' (Harris, 2002). This is despite evidence that European women are more effective than men as leaders in regions like Asia because they frequently utilize intuitive and empathetic skills that are highly valued in such host cultures (van der Boon, 2003). Many of the international management development activities within the best-practice management development discourse are designed to foster heterogeneity, where individuals can 'retain their dimensions of diversity while at the same time avoiding such damaging processes as dysfunctional interpersonal conflict, miscommunication, higher levels of stress, slower decision-making and problems with group cohesiveness' (Kyriakidou, 2005: 112). However, there is always a danger that international management development programmes, far from legitimizing, celebrating and benefiting from the diversity inherent to effective knowledge diffusion, can have the opposite effect of reinforcing inequality, homogenizing corporate behaviour and perpetuating cultural conformity (Kamoche, 2000). Certainly, the postcolonial critique of management theory and practice which we encountered in Chapter 2, alerts us to the possibility of such hegemony (see Box 7.5).

Box 7.5   Western bias in international management development

... Theories that define the desired worker or manager in terms of his [*sic.*] identification with the central values of Western culture directly influence the ethnic and racial global division of labour. Armed with assumptions that define management as Western, managers do not easily allow the promotion of 'others' into management positions in industrialized, so-called multi-cultural countries, and in multi-nationals in developing countries. Positions filled by members of 'other' countries within this framework of the global division of labour are defined as requiring inferior skills, and so they are poorly paid in rational considerations of job evaluations.

[...] The international management literature addresses the Western manager as he [*sic.*] sets off to manage 'local' workers, and who needs to be aware of their irrational peculiarities. An equivalent literature for managers from developing countries is virtually non-existent, and has certainly not been canonized. This asymmetry represents the 'Western' person as the natural candidate for management. (Frenkel and Shenhav, 2006: 872)

In this section we have noted how three strands of best practice discourse have served to energize and legitimize management development as a means to achieve strategic intent. Now we turn to an assessment of three management development interventions, each illustrative of best-practice.

Best-practice management development interventions

There is no doubt that approaches to training and development have become more sophisticated in recent years, along with a sharper appreciation of how true learning can be cultivated. This is not the place for an extensive review of methods used to enhance management and leadership; other books do this well (e.g. Woodall and Winstanley, 1998; Raelin, 2000; McCauley and Van Elsor, 2004). However, in this section we examine three approaches that have become almost synonymous with progressive management and leadership development in recent years. Each utilizes sophisticated methodologies first to identify, diagnose and then guide management development as an ongoing process.

Competency frameworks

Competency-based management development has been a major and growing organizational activity over the past decade and a half. It was reported in the USA that businesses spent $100 million per year over recent years implementing competency models (Athey and Orth, 1999). An estimate put the number of UK employees covered by such schemes at over 3.2 million (Rankin, 2001). A longitudinal study of nearly 100 UK firms found a significant increase in the adoption of competency-based development from 2000 to 2004 (Mabey, 2005: 44), and using organizationally devised skills or competency frameworks is an approach to management development which is widely favoured across Europe (Mabey and Ramirez, 2004). Undeniably, a competency-based approach is almost synonymous with progressive or best-practice management development.

What is a competency-based approach to management development?
Usage of the term *competency* can be traced back to the late 1970s in the USA, where it was popularized as a result of research carried out by the McBer consultancy (Iles, 1993). Since then, the term has been defined in a number of different ways although Woodruffe's (1993) widely quoted definition sees it as 'the set of behaviour patterns that the incumbent needs to bring to a position in order to perform its tasks and functions with competence'. The turn to competency can be seen as an attempt to capture the nature of management in taxonomic form via behavioural statements. These might typically allude to knowledge, skills and/or ability in areas such as leadership, problem-solving, dealing with pressure, decision-making, creativity, teamwork, entrepreneurship and so on (Townley, 1999). Such behavioural statements purport to identify those key characteristics associated with superior job performance. As such, they often form the basis for an integrated and structured approach to the

recruitment, appraisal, training and development of managers (du Gay et al., 1996). The emphasis on deriving behavioural repertoires that are organization- ally meaningful and specific would seem, at least in part, to answer the early criticisms of generic competency definition levelled by Reed and Anthony (1992). They saw the rigid application of technical and functional competen- cies as an unhelpful retreat into narrow vocationalism which crowds out any sustained concern with the social, moral, political and ideological ingredients of managerial work.

There are good reasons as to why competency frameworks have been swiftly incorporated into the best-practice discourse. Arriving at a recognizable compe- tency profile for particular management positions/career paths in a given organi- zation helps provide a common language and observable behaviours for different standards of performance. This removes ambiguity and addresses the often-heard complaint of shifting 'corporate goalposts'. Competencies also serve to translate organizational strategies into individual priorities, enabling managers to fine-tune their development around a few skill areas which have high salience for their own and the organization's success. Providing sufficient cultural latitude is given to def- initions, it has been demonstrated that this can even be achieved across interna- tional business units (Sparrow and Bognanno, 1993). A further advantage is that a common set of competencies introduces the possibility of horizontal integration across all HRM policies. If the criteria for recruitment, performance manage- ment, promotion, reward and recognition are consistent with the goals of man- agement development, there is at least the possibility of tracking their combined impact on the strategic objectives in a way that is far less likely when such HR initiatives are piecemeal and uncoordinated.

Some difficulties and possibilities

Despite this, there remain serious concerns about the basis for many of the prac- tices or indeed the very purpose of competency-based management development (Clarke, 1999). Based on research conducted in four UK case study organizations which had implemented management competencies, Salaman (2004) makes sev- eral observations which represent the 'downside' of the advantages referred to above. First, competency frameworks reflect a shift in definition from the tradi- tional notion of management (seniority, privilege, status, as someone who is 'in charge') to that of the manager as entrepreneur, as someone responsible for com- mercial targets, budgets, costs. In short, managers (and as we explore at some length in Chapter 5) become responsible for ensuring their own compliance with the new competencies via self-regulation. Second, competencies can be used as a senior management tool to remove undesirable sectional affiliations and to replace them with organizational commitment. Some managers feel this undermines their professional identity. Third, while the scientific nature of competency frameworks appears to promote equal opportunities, the competency method has been shown to be far from gender neutral. This is something we give detailed attention to in Chapters 5 and 9. But what are the functionalist consequences of competency discourse (see Box 7.6)?

Box 7.6   The importance of contextual leadership

In an essay addressing the question: 'Can leadership be taught?', Mole (2004) critiques conventional leadership development programmes which rely on self-insight questionnaires, interpersonal skills training and well-worn models from the world of organization development. Far better, he argues, is an approach which specifies the expectations of managers and leaders within a given organizational context: 'where the leadership role is defined in terms of content, outcomes, and the knowledge structure, skills and attitudes which are most strongly predicted, on the basis of empirical evidence, to be associated with successful performance in this role' (2004: 130). This is exactly what a well-derived competency framework amounts to. For Mole, the problem is not with the concept of competencies, but their implementation. Furthermore, competency-based leadership development offers three distinct advantages over more traditional approaches: (1) the focus on real jobs and a real organizational context obviates the time and expense of using off-site residential training; (2) the content can be delivered in short bursts of one day or less, possibly spaced out to allow on-the-job practice of new skills; and (3) the possibility of meaningful evaluation is enhanced due to the contextually specific nature of leader performance.

This has resonance with those who advocate work-based learning, where training and development has become a natural and ongoing part of normal work relations: well *internalized* but less visible to the casual observer. This might represent a company where line managers are highly skilled in coaching and developing their staff, able to 'construct' everyday occurrences as learning opportunities for themselves and their staff and where the prevailing ethos of people development militates against departmental talent-hoarding. In proposing a resource-based view of HRM, Kamoche (1996) also notes the value of skill formation arising from tacit knowledge, action-centred learning, learning from mistakes, learning-by-doing and as a by-product of other activities. It is the very embeddedness of these activities into daily work routines (as compared with isolated, formalized training programmes) which makes them 'resource mobility barriers' because competitors will find them difficult to imitate.

It would appear then that practitioners remain largely committed to the approach, with any perceived 'failure' being put down to issues of refinement, as opposed to any fundamental questioning of the concept of competency-based management development itself (du Gay et al., 1996; Grugulis, 2000).

360-degree feedback

Effective leader and manager development is usually catalysed by accurate feedback on work performance. Rather than relying on the performance feedback from a single, usually senior source, 360-degree feedback (or multi-source, multi–rater feedback, as it is sometimes referred to) solicits the views of several colleagues at senior, peer and junior levels in the workplace. In 1995, nearly all Fortune 500 companies used or intended to use some form of 360-degree feedback (London and Smithers, 1995). A decade later it was estimated that over one-third of US companies used some type of 360-degree feedback process for managers (Ostroff et al., 2004). The technique is also used widely in UK organizations (Bailey and Fletcher, 2002) and regarded as best-practice, certainly in Western organizations.

The growing popularity of 360-degree feedback as best-practice might be attributed to a number of changes in the way organizations operate. It is particularly relevant to areas of job performance where objective outcome criteria are difficult to measure, such as in the development of management and leadership capabilities (Day, 2001). The approach is predicated upon a competency framework (which has enjoyed rapid uptake, as discussed in the previous section) and also fits those organizations pursuing a culture of work-based learning and continuous improvement. The increased trend towards remote-working, geographically dispersed workforces and matrix management also lends itself to managers in different locations/functions (rather than the line manager alone) giving and receiving quality feedback on fellow team members. What is more, although open to misuse by senior management, 360-degree feedback programmes are *potentially* distinguishable from most other human resource interventions in that they offer individuals a process which is voluntary, confidential, self-determining and designed to assist learning rather than as a tool for assessment (Mabey, 2001).

Evidence for the benefits of 360-degree feedback

Reflecting the functionalist Discourse, many attempts have been made to investigate the impact of 360-degree feedback in the workplace, although we should be careful to note that slightly different outcomes have been measured. For instance, based on a seven-year study of 60 managers, McEvoy and Beatty (1989) concluded that: 'if an organisation is looking for a prediction approach for up to seven years into the future, subordinate ratings may be as effective as assessment centres and certainly less expensive' (1989: 50–1, cited in Mole, 2000: 67). In a study of over 1,500 staff involved in providing upward and peer feedback in one organization, positive outcomes were identified, providing three climate factors were perceived to be in place: perceived freedom from constraints and competing time demands, perceived availability of development resources to enhance skills and perceived social support for development and improvement (Maurer and Tarulli, 1996; Maurer et al., 2002).

Two design features are salient when making such claims: tracking performance over time to allow for opportunities for skill development, and using control groups to ensure any changes are attributable to 360-degree feedback-related development. In a longitudinal study of 48 participants, the efficacy of 360-degree feedback as a development tool was established, in terms of advancement, effort made and training activities undertaken, when reported by 150 raters two years after the first 360-degree feedback (Hazucha et al., 1993). Similar results were found by Bailey and Fletcher (2002) in their study of 104 managers: two years after initial 360-degree feedback, significant increases in managers' competency was perceived by the managers themselves and by their subordinates; also development needs were seen to reduce and self and co-worker ratings were seen to become more congruent. These results appear to confirm the finding of effective learning transfer for leadership behaviours when diagnosed by 360-degree feedback (Bass et al., 1996).

Creating control groups in a field setting is not easy. Two studies that have achieved this report encouraging results. In their study of 17 managers in a savings bank, Siefert et al. (2001) investigated the effects of multi-rater feedback and subsequent training on a specific example of managerial behaviour, namely 'influencing tactics'. Eight managers in an experimental group, which had received relevant training following their 360-degree feedback, were rated as significantly better in the use of these core tactics to influence subordinates than a control group which had received their 360-degree feedback, but no subsequent training. In a study in a UK university, 200 middle and senior managers who had participated in 360-degree feedback rated almost all aspects of their training and development as significantly better than a matched sample of non-participants. Furthermore, this led them to assess their employer more positively (Mabey, 2001).

Caveats concerning 360-degree feedback

Questions remain, however. Increasing numbers of employers, especially in the USA, are using 360-degree feedback as part of a performance management process. This is likely to remove some of its distinctive benefits: namely, that it is voluntary and developmental in focus. Quite apart from abrogating the principle of confidentiality, Fletcher and Baldry (1999) note that the reliability and consistency of feedback is seriously compromised when the purpose of ratings is evaluative rather than developmental. Related to this is the issue of anonymity. Some organizations insist on anonymous and confidential ratings. This is primarily to reassure participant raters that there will be no repercussions as a result of their feedback, thus encouraging them to be more honest. It may also be less threatening to participants to receive their feedback on an anonymous basis. Other users of 360-degree feedback argue that named feedback is more useful because it allows the feedback to be contextualized and related to specific situations and relationships, and it can reduce the scope for unconstructive personal comments.

Questions might also be asked about the extent to which 360-degree feedback aids diversity. A study of an MNC using the 360-degree feedback found the process was generally effective across subsidiaries in five countries (Shipper et al., 2004). However, country comparisons revealed differences in the subsequent changes in employee affective reactions, managers' self-awareness, the use of interactive and controlling skills and managerial effectiveness. This led the researchers to conclude that low power distance and high individualism are important cultural prerequisites for 360-degree feedback to yield positive changes. Given that 360-degree feedback is based on organizationally derived competency frameworks, there is always the danger of conservative bias which favours the dominant groups (see Box 7.7).

Box 7.7   Inbuilt bias of 360-degree feedback

Given the continued inequality of men and women in leadership positions, it is important that 360-degree feedback does not become a vehicle for indirect discrimination. As individuals are increasingly being given greater responsibility for their own career management, their self-perceptions have become particularly critical to their advancement. Leaders who perceive themselves to be lacking in required competencies for higher-level positions may be reluctant to apply for these jobs. The Multifactor Leader Questionnaire (MLQ) has been used in a number of studies of self-perceptions of leadership style, and the findings have consistently shown that women are significantly more likely to be perceived as transformational than are male managers, irrespective of the sex of the subordinates rating them (Alimo-Metcalfe, 1998). Given that on traditional measures of transactional leadership men have consistently been rated more highly, and on new measures of transformational leadership women tend to be rated more highly, it seems likely that gender stereotyped measures influence subordinates ratings of leadership effectiveness. (Robinson, 2004)

When designing their competency frameworks and 360-degree questionnaires, HR departments need to be wary of inadvertent reinforcement of gender, ethnic, cultural or other stereotypes. Despite these caveats, 360-degree feedback remains firmly part of the best-practice management development discourse.

Executive coaching

The use of coaching to develop managers, especially senior executives, has also become extremely popular in recent years. Some estimate that executive coaching is growing at 40 per cent per year (*The Economist*, 8 March 2002). A further arresting statistic reveals that 60 per cent of coaching clients say they confide in their coach almost as much as they do in their best friend, spouse or therapist (Withers, 2001). A few years back, it was estimated that there were more than 15,000 full- or part-time coaching practitioners world-wide, according to the International Coaching Federation, which after just five years' existence boasted 3,500 members (Arnaud, 2004). These were working either as independent consultants or for larger training and development agencies.

There is no commonly agreed definition for coaching. The boundaries between what is a coach, a counsellor, a mentor or an organization development expert are often blurred and there is little clarity about how to measure the impact or value of coaching (Sparrow and Arnott, 2004). Some definitions highlight the performance-enhancing aspects of coaching (reflecting a functionalist Discourse). Others focus on the experiential aspects, in sympathy with the constructivist Discourse, which may or may not directly enhance performance in the workplace. A brief definition is offered in Box 7.8.

Box 7.8   Executive coaching as management development

The key ingredients of this type of management development can be identified as follows:

- Generally a one-to-one learning intervention through which coachees establish their own criteria for improvement and development, with the assistance of their coach.
- A relationship is formed between the coachee, who has managerial authority and responsibility in an organization, and a consultant, who uses a wide variety of behavioral techniques and methods to help the client.
- The intention is to achieve a mutually identified set of goals to improve the coachee's professional performance and personal satisfaction and, consequently, to improve the effectiveness of the client's organization within a formally defined coaching agreement.

As with the other best-practice interventions reviewed above, the rapid adoption of executive coaching appears to be driven as much by imitation as by empirical support. The amount of *practitioner* literature published in recent years on executive coaching has mushroomed as the profession itself has grown, but in contrast, the availability of refereed academic literature and research on the topic remains small (Grant, 2003).

In a comprehensive review of the phenomenon, Kampa-Kokesch and Anderson (2001) call for more rigorous research into the impact and outcomes of executive coaching; they were only able to identify seven empirical studies in the literature, all of which had design flaws which minimized the generalizability of their findings. Indeed, some studies suggest that public sector management practices such as executive coaching, which began in the province of the private sector, are actually having a destabilizing effect on the culture of government organizations into which they are introduced (Newman, 2000). There has since been very little critical analysis of these changes in the public sector from an organizational behaviour perspective (Schofield, 2002).

Reflection point

To what do you attribute the explosion of interest in and use of executive coaching?

One factor may be disappointment with more conventional approaches to manager and leader development. A frequent criticism of conventional management development programmes, whether 'open' or designed in a more tailor-made manner, is that the transfer of learning to the workplace is seen to be poor. More individualized methods, like mentoring, seem to hold more promise because of the higher intensity and personal relevance. But mentoring relationships can be variable, with some working well for a time whereas others, especially where the mentor is assigned rather than chosen informally, rarely seem to achieve their developmental potential.

Another aspect of collective management development activities is that they often expose weakness and highlight unconscious incompetence, as a precursor to building new skills, confidence and competence. Not surprisingly perhaps, senior managers tend to shy away from this kind of feedback and exposure in a relatively public arena. To have the services of a personal coach, operating within a contract of confidentiality, is far more acceptable. Feedback from, say, 360-degree questionnaires (and the growth of coaching alongside the rapid uptake 360-degree feedback in organizations is probably no coincidence) is more palatable when mediated via a coach who is then available to help generate personal strategies for addressing weaknesses.

In the past 15 years, there has been a significant shift towards more informal, on-the-job, action learning approaches to management development. A number of reasons are cited for this shift, including the delayering of organizations, the withdrawal of centralized HR career management, cost-cutting, more entrepreneurial styles of management and the advent of more transactional psychological contracts between employer and employee. As a consequence, organizations are increasingly conferring coaching interventions on their high-flying senior managers in recognition of the need for individualized support at a time of major change in organizations. This is by way of an acknowledgement that managers are increasingly isolated (Hirsch and Carter, 2002), with heavier workloads and staff responsibility. Managers need to be able to self-develop as HR departments shrink. In these circumstances, organizations may use executive coaching as a kind of palliative to overstretched and stressed members of their senior team. Executive coaches can also provide a convenient substitute for hard-pressed line managers. However, there are dependence risks of replacing one authority figure with another in this way (Mabey, 2003). Additionally, instability can be created in the direct report layer when coaches are withdrawn after a finite intervention (Jackson, 2005).

As with other management development activities, coaching can be regarded as an effective acculturation device. Some theorists, notably those writing within the critical Discourse, cite this form of development as an instrument of organizational control, as a means to create corporate elites. Such culturally-sanctioned management development activities can elicit the compliance of managers, especially when intangible incentives (like the vague suggestion of promotion) are promised in return. In contrast, Arnaud's (2004: 1135) polemic makes an important point about the value of coaching interventions in providing a symbolic locus and space for potentially counter-cultural 'individual utterances' and the expression of 'otherness' inside organizations. Certainly, it would seem undeniable that coachees generally find the opportunity to voice their struggles and to explore alternative solutions to be emancipatory.

Conclusion

In this chapter we have explored the best-practice discourse of management development and the way this influences both the strategic rationale for management development in organizations and the choice of specific training/development interventions. For the most part the best-practice discourse reflects the priorities of the functionalist Discourse. However, you may have noted how the other Grand Discourses help us to identify flaws and shortcomings in the best-practice approach. For example, it is not always easy to identify how and why particular policies and practices come to be subsumed within the best-practice discourse (various actors, including government, professional bodies, informal networks and consultants all appear to play their part), but as the constructivist Discourse might predict, once a discourse has become established, it can become highly resilient and influential.

We have found that the alignment of management development with strategic priorities is highly appealing but beset with difficulties. Critical Discourse would question whether such alignment is indeed desirable in the first place, since the added value of management learning, enshrined in the concept of the learning organization, is innovation rather than conformity, constructive critique rather than control. Indeed, one promising contribution of functionalist thinking is to consider management development as catalyst for counter-cultural reform and proactively shaping, rather than passively aligning with, wider strategic intent. And on the other hand, dialogic Discourses would point to the ever-shifting and chimerical nature of strategic priorities. Even if they can be clearly articulated, the time taken to create apposite management competencies is likely to render at least some of the targeted skills and mindsets obsolete. This represents both a shortcoming and a virtue of competency frameworks. At worst, they homogenize, de-humanize and simply add to the apparatus of senior management performance-scrutiny. At best they provide a contextualized, consistent and consensual means to identify and nurture leadership capabilities over a sustained period. Likewise, 360-degree feedback and executive coaching are open to abuse and misuse on a number of levels. But a growing body of evidence, much of it generated by organizational psychologists, suggests that, if well designed and implemented, these are techniques that have the possibility of catalysing and guiding effective development in the workplace. A further potential strategic contribution of management development is in the arena of creating intercultural competence, with particular reference to knowledge transfer in international organizations.

However, viewing management development through the discourse of best-practice urges caution. There are several reasons for this. First is expedience. Given the relentless pace, fragmented, discontinuous and largely unreflective nature of much managerial work, it is not unreasonable to find HRD managers, when faced with the need to develop their leaders, turning to 'off-the-shelf solutions' which are readily available and promoted by the best-practice discourse. The attraction is that such approaches and products appear to address universally pre-existent problems. And they do so without the hard work of tailoring and lengthy lead times described.

Second, and linked, is mis-diagnosis. In describing the shortcomings of so-called genre training which seeks a choice of solution from a limited range of pre-scribed options, Mole (1996) quotes Katz and Kahn: 'Attempts to change organisations by changing individuals have a long history of theoretical inade-quacy and practical failure. Both stem from a disregard of the systemic properties of organisations and from the confusion of individual changes with modification in organisational variables' (1978: 658). The result is a poor matching of training provision to actual learning requirements and a failure to understand the situa-tional factors that shape behaviour.

Third is the very notion of discourse. As discussed in the opening chapter, the nature of discourse is that it constructs and maintains (linguistically and by other artefacts) its subject matter such that it becomes beyond question. So a given man-agement development strategy or technique gains cogency by arriving with an internal consistency, for instance, and gains credibility via a respected accreditation scheme or by association with other 'successful' companies ('benchmarking' is a close ally to best-practice discourse). This obviously makes the initiator's task eas-ier, but more difficult for critics, who may be concerned about issues of relevance, ethics, contextualization, timing and so on. The critical and dialogic Discourses allow us to problematize the very notion of 'best' within best-practice discourse: best for whom? best for what?

Fourth, European research has found that the mere existence of best-practices in the form of management development systems and infrastructure makes little difference to a firm's performance (see page 66). Of far more consequence is the longer-term ethos an organization creates with regard to developing its manage-ment cadre and the credence given to this by line managers (Mabey and Ramirez, 2004; Mabey and Gooderham, 2005).

Finally, by definition, best-practices have a limited shelf life. Earlier we referred to the study of a national accreditation scheme by Bell et al. (2002a). The authors wryly observe that, as quality badges (in this case, membership of the IiP network) become ever more effectively produced and consumed, they become somewhat devalued for the possessor, such that new prestige indicators and networks need to be found.

Summary

- The need to align management development with organizational strat-egy has become a best-practice truism, yet, in practice, this proves very difficult to achieve.
- Even less ambitious attempts to use management development to facil-itate organization change can falter because systemic resistance and repercussions are underestimated.

- Competency frameworks, 360-degree feedback and coaching have become part of the best-practice discourse; if well designed and contextualized they have potential to enhance the effectiveness of management development interventions.
- The knowledge management literature is beginning to highlight the contribution of management development more generally for organizations operating in an international arena.
- Viewing management development as a best-practice discourse helps alert us to a number of pitfalls when choosing and implementing policies and practices.

8

Management development and institutionalism

[Analysing management development] is like trying to find out the rules of a particular game across cultures when the existence of the game itself in some cultures is in doubt. (Tayeb, 2000: 12)

After reading this chapter you will be able to:

- Describe what is meant by the institutionalist discourse of management development
- Critically appraise the institutionalist discourse in its account of the way managers and leaders are trained and developed
- Link different approaches to developing managers and leaders to national culture
- Cite empirical work which supports the differential impact of international strategy, size and sector in shaping management development
- Explain how all the above factors combine to influence management development discourse in different contexts
- Defend your own conclusion as to which factors have most influence in the way managers and leaders are developed in different circumstances

Introduction

In the previous chapter we analysed the best-practice discourse of management development. For some writers, this particular construction of management development, driven and shaped by free agents and/or coalitions of influential players, is problematic. In the view of such critics, it is untenable on two grounds: first, morally, because it attributes power to such players, including top teams in organizations, that they do not have (even though they'd like to think they do!). Second, the free-agent thesis underestimates the structuring influence of socio-institutional context. By contrast, institutionalist accounts of management development focus attention on the relations between the individual manager and/or groups of managers and their employing organization; these relations will be mediated or constituted by such factors as education systems, sectoral labour markets, occupational ladders, career paths and corporate development opportunities. However, these do not exist as neutral and objective entities with equal appeal, access and value to all managers. Rather, it is argued, they are encountered and taken up according to the institutions which are specific to the regional/cultural context.

This is an interesting counterpoint, then, to best-practice discourse, although they do have commonalities. Both point to the constraining and constituting nature of discourse. In one instance, the compulsion and kudos of being seen to adopt management development that accords with best-practice. In the other, the way cultural and institutional heritage leads to the privileging of some notions, methods and approaches of management development and the relegation of others.

We are not suggesting that the studies referred to in this chapter adopt discursive methodologies. For the most part they do not. Rather, we propose that, collectively, the writing on management development assembled here comprises want we might call an institutionalist discourse of management development. Again, we use the term 'discourse' because we believe it 'works as a structuring, constituting force, directly implying or tightly framing subjectivity, practice and meaning' (Alvesson and Kärreman, 2000: 1145). In so doing we hope this chapter will shed an additional shaft of light on the practice of management development in different country settings.

We have already noted in this book that views about management development vary considerably, even on preliminary issues of definition and interpretation. This may, in part, be due to differing understanding and acceptance of management development as a concept in the first place (see opening quote). Certainly national culture plays an important role in understanding management development and we shall discuss this more fully later. Interwoven with culture, however, are themes arising from institutional labour market literatures which suggest that there are durable and consistent national differences in the styles and methods by which firms develop their managers. Linked to this are the sector, the size and the international strategy adopted by a firm. Each of these factors comprise interlocking facets of the institutional discourse of management development and in this chapter we analyse them in turn.

Understanding management development through the lens of institutions

Institutional discourse has the potential to enrich our understanding of different country systems of management development. Such discourse is both formed and informed by theories which argue that social and institutional arrangements are critical in shaping the social structures in a given country/region. These define, for example, how firms are constituted and how labour markets are structured. Furthermore, once firms are constituted and labour markets are in place, they have long-lasting consequences that influence norms and values, serve vested interests, foster expectations and generate societal effects (Rubery and Grimshaw, 2003). Also influential are informal institutional factors, such as customs and practices

(Brown, 1972), social norms (Wootton, 1955), traditions and unwritten rules. Collectively, this institutional context serves to regulate the relations between interest groups and helps to mediate conflicts. In so doing, it reduces uncertainty and risk and creates clear 'rules of the game' for firms to operate in a reasonably stable manner. Those institutions which relate to training in a given country play a crucial role in ensuring that both employers and employees have the incentives to invest in and engage in skills development. However, the debate over cross-national convergence or divergence in human resource practices, and specifically management development practices, has been running for some time.

Convergence

Over the past decade, a strand of literature, particularly from the USA, has forcefully proposed that, as a result of globalization and institutional change, businesses that grew in isolation from the world economy are being superseded by universally applicable techniques. Whereas early convergence discourse invoked structural aspects such as technology and economic change, current debates stress the impact of globalization, incorporating cultures, institutions and firm-level practices as a force of convergence (Geppert et al., 2002). This argument is reinforced by research that suggests that the growing focus on shareholder value and the erosion of corporatist relationships, particularly in Northern and Central Europe, underlines the growing dominance of the Anglo-Saxon societal system (Hunt, 2000). Furthermore, the influence of the multinationals (MNCs) in the world economy, serving to weaken national societal institutions and internationalize 'best-practice' through the diffusion of benchmarking, are also seen as key powerful agents in the process (Geppert et al., 2002).

How might this apply to management development? It might be argued that although governments in different countries pursue quite different goals in their early education systems (Geppert et al., 2002) and adopt varying levels of corporate intervention at a policy level (Noble, 1997; Tsui-Auch et al., 2004), there is some evidence of a general trend towards regarding management development as market-driven. The globalization of the market place and the increasing reach of multinationals tend to create common expectations of managers across the world, and corporate cultures are arguably becoming more influential than national cultures. For example, having noted the particular historical emphases of management models in five countries, Thomson et al. (2001: 61) note that:

> the general trends are similar. All the models expect something from the individual manager in terms of self-development over and above what might be done by the organisation. All five countries favour development beyond the initial education and induction; in Germany and Japan it is more formalised, especially in the large companies, than in France, the United States, and Britain. All the countries have problems with management development in small businesses.

But this idea of convergence in the realm of HRM, fuelled by the inexorable diffusion of best-practices, has been questioned (Marchington and Grugulis, 2000), particularly where it is assumed that global HR practices are inevitably converging on a US model (Gooderham and Brewster, 2003). Based on extensive survey data gathered over the last decade, Brewster et al. (2004) reach a more nuanced conclusion. They point to *directional* convergence of HR practices in Europe, with increasing training and development as one example of a generic trend. However, they differentiate this from *final* convergence, noting that there is very little evidence that countries are becoming more alike in the way they manage their human resources. Similar conclusions were reached by Ralston et al. (2006) in their longitudinal analysis of managerial work values in China, Hong Kong and the USA.

Divergence

Other authors point out that the different practices adopted by firms in different countries in dealing with issues such as training and development represent more than deviations that will disappear as nations advance along a 'best-practice' trajectory (Hall and Soskice, 2001). Rather, these idiosyncratic practices reflect the existence of different industrial infrastructures and sets of interlocking institutions that shape the paths firms take towards both skill formation and the types of product market in which they compete (Dore, 1986; Boyer, 1990). The formal content and labelling of management and leadership skills development between countries may appear similar, but the process and definitions behind common terms can diverge significantly. As Lane (1989: 34) comments: 'Although organizational goals may not differ significantly across organizations, courses of action towards reaching these goals do, because action is socially constructed and hence shaped by culture as manifested in societal institutions.'

Whitley's (1992) analysis of cross-country business systems also relies heavily on institutional factors and labour market analysis to explain significant differences in how countries coordinate their economic decision-making processes (see Box 8.1).

Box 8.1   A business systems analysis

Whitley's (1992) framework emphasizes three critical features of business systems: first, how the autonomy of managers is exercised *vis-à-vis* the owners; second, the extent of long-term cooperative relations between firms and business sectors; and, thirdly, questions of authoritative coordination and control systems, including decentralization. This last component is highly relevant to how management training is perceived and conducted. It encompasses issues such as the separation of the technical knowledge of line managers from production, the distance between managers and subordinates and how the authority of the former is conceived. Such matters are closely interlinked and interdependent. For example, the reliance on formal rules and procedures in many Western countries means that cooperation beyond contractual obligations may be less easy to obtain than, for example, in East Asian societies.

Thus, the sorts of skill firms want their managers to develop, the discretion managers have to subsequently use these skills and how managers themselves view their training are all likely to be strongly influenced by the societal system in which managers live and work.

This approach, which encompasses the working of labour markets, may help to explain why certain traits in the behaviours of both managers and firms have roots in national systems and stubbornly refuse to disappear in spite of the growing global integration of production and ownership structures. Crucially, it may also explain why, although national systems often appear to borrow or learn from the successes of other societies, they do so in ways that are in tune with their own particular historical path of development. Future developments are conditioned by past arrangements.

For example, a key finding of recent cross-country institutional studies is that the degree of interdependence, cohesion and integration of institutions and business organizations in the Anglo-Saxon countries is much lower than in other capitalist countries such as Germany and Japan (Geppert et al., 2002). Thus, businesses in the Anglo-Saxon countries may be in a position to integrate global best-practices more easily than businesses in, say, Germany or Japan.

Identifying national approaches to management development

The debate around cross-country comparisons of human resource management therefore suggests that the extent of isomorphic tendencies in management practices, arising from the pressures of global integration, will vary in different national contexts. This will be driven by the extent to which these practices are at odds with institutions such as industrial relations, professional associations and state regulations. It will also be affected by the degree of interdependence between business strategies and the wider societal institutions.

How might all this influence the patterns of management development in different countries or regions? With some notable exceptions (Dore, 1986), most analyses which have fully or partially utilized an institutional approach have been conducted in Europe (e.g. Lane, 1989; Tregaskis, 1997; Thomson et al., 2001). Drawing on this and related work, Table 8.1 compares different approaches to management training within six European countries, using five separate categories (Ramirez, 2004). The first column refers to the dominant skill type of managers in each country. In this regard, Estevez-Abe et al. (2001) suggest that national labour markets will tend to specialize in one type of skill. These may be *firm-specific* skills, paid for by the employer and linked to promotion structures within firms; *occupational or industry* skills, usually associated with vocational and educational training (VET) and transferable jobs within specific industries; and *generalist skills*, more common where there is little employment security and often financed by employees. Therefore, skills types are quite closely associated with promotion structures (column 2), who finances training (column 3), recognition of qualifications for mobility and employment security.

TABLE 8.1 *European management development systems* (adapted from Ramirez, 2004: 438–40)

	Skills type	Career paths	Who pays for training?	Agents driving training and status of training institutions	Distinguishing national characteristics of managers
UK	Managers can maintain skills when moving jobs.	Less emphasis on firm-level career development (Bournois et al., 1994). Managers exposed to losing jobs in hostile takeovers.	Growing general business education financed by employee (Bennett, 1997).	High status of chartered institutions. Low status of vocational training (Tregaskis, 1997).	High premium on the 'gifted amateur' (Bennett, 1997). Managers are 'specialist coordinators' (Lam, 1994).
Germany	VET for managers and employees' technical/scientific skills prior to becoming managers (Streeck, 1993). Formal management education emphasizes scientific, theoretical principles.	Strong emphasis on succession planning (Bournois et al., 1994). Low mobility between firms (Lane, 1989).	Hands-on managerial training funded by firms (Lane, 1989).	High status of VET for managers (Streeck, 1993). Formal management training routes lie in the *Diplom Kaufman* and *BWL* in the university system (Shenton, 1996). High-level CEOs would have PhDs.	Managers are subject to intense monitoring. Managers are 'players' (Lam, 1994). High consensus between managers and workers.
France	*Grandes Ecoles* vocational origins and proximity to business world (Shenton, 1996).	More likely to lose skill status when moving jobs (Eyraud et al., (1990). Job hierarchies and seniority. Internal labour markets (Maurice et al., 1986). Promotion into *cadre* status is rare (Tregaskis, 1997).	Law requires firms to spend at least 1.5% of wage bill on training.	*Grandes Ecoles* technocratic elite (Shenton, 1996). 75% of senior executives in large firms have *Grandes Ecoles* qualification (Bennett, 1997).	Managers are 'coordinators' (Lam, 1994). Comparatively weak retention and short-term training plans.

(Continued)

TABLE 8.1 *(Continued)*

	Skills type	Career paths	Who pays for training?	Agents driving training and status of training institutions	Distinguishing national characteristics of managers
Spain	Traditional focus on internal training (Baruel, 1996).	Foreign assignments play an important role in career (Bournois et al., 1994). Careers paths offered to high proportion of managers.	Training and development concentrated within large firms (Paralleda et al., 2002).	Successful MBAs because of weakness of other managers (Shenton, 1996).	Few apprenticeships (Paralleda et al., 2002). Weak retention and comparatively short-term training plans.
Norway	Emphasis on company and VET training.	Strong long-term commitment, though increasing mobility.	Norwegian private sector firms finance their management development programme.	Larger firms recruit from the elite engineering and/or business education schools. Thereafter these firms will employ both national and international consultancies and business schools to assist with firm-specific programmes.	Managerial autonomy, functional responsibilities and task variation enshrined in legislation.
Denmark	Combination of experiential firm-specific learning with formal education and VET.	Strong promotion and internal labour market opportunities.	State offers affordable post graduate managerial training.	Combines VET and formal MBA education (Brewster, 1995). High degree of social capital. Cooperative and consensual system between State, employers, trade unions and individual managers.	Managers willing and encouraged to take risks is supported by safety net.

Another important category compares the principal agents or institutions driving training and the status of these (column 4). As discussed earlier, the Northern European countries have traditionally had rigorous VET systems, and potential managers as well as skilled employees may have similar vocational qualifications. In Germany, the rigorous training means that in manufacturing sectors, in particular, managers gain their authority as 'players' (Lam, 1994). In the UK, VET and apprenticeships were common until the 1970s, but were associated with craft manual jobs rather than managerial tasks. This negatively affected their status in the past and still does today.

A third category, which has been given less prominence in cross-national comparisons of management training, lies in the different perceptions of the role of managers and what managers do (column 5). Reliable up-to-date comparative data on issues such as management style (authoritarian or allowing autonomy), values, attitude towards risk and its relation to training and development still largely remains fragmented. We revisit some of these issues in relation to culture later in the chapter.

The influence of international strategy, sector and size

In contrast to comparative HRM, which compares HRM practices across different cultures or nations, international HRM (IHRM) focuses on how different organizations manage their people across national borders (Boxall, 1996). Although these have been parallel fields of enquiry, an increasing degree of convergence between the two has been noted (Budhwar and Sparrow, 2002). IHRM research has been dominated by examination of the link between strategy–structure configuration in the internationalizing firm and the competing demands for globalization on the one hand and the need for local responsiveness on the other (Sparrow et al., 2004). Other studies have taken sector and size as their reference point. Taken together, these threads of literature might also be considered to be an important part of the institutional management development discourse.

International strategy

We know that the potential influence of multinational parent companies over host country management practices is likely to be powerful (see Box 8.2). This is especially the case in the arena of management development because this is typically seen as a way of exerting control and/or inculcating cultural expectations (Kamoche, 2000) and building internationally skilled, high-potential managers who have been identified as vital to the company's future and survival (Scullion and Starkey, 2000). Second, it has been established that there is a tendency for MNC subsidiaries to adopt parent or 'best-practice' norms particularly in more macro-HRD practices like training needs analysis, management development delivery and evaluation procedures, while allowing their subsidiaries considerably greater autonomy in the local implementation of training (Noble, 1997; Tregaskis, 2001). Third, there is empirical evidence that US-based MNCs diverge from their host country counterparts by attempting to apply their parent company HRM practices to their subsidiaries in Western Europe (Gooderham et al., 2004). Finally, it is well known that the economies of scale associated with MNCs permit access to a richer vein of resources for management development than is possible for many indigenous companies.

Box 8.2   Strategic variations on management development

It is clear that a firm's chosen international strategy will directly affect its patterns of management development. Using terms first coined by Adler (1991) we can differentiate:

- domestic organizations which are located in a single country and characterized by a centralized structure and a focus on functional divisions. Here management development will be devised and delivered locally and targeted at local staff.
- multinational organizations with a centralized hub and international affiliates taking degrees of responsibility for business lines, sourcing, production and marketing. Here management development is typically originated in the home country and delivered in a fairly prescriptive and uniform manner (perhaps using common management competencies) with the deliberate intent of achieving cultural coherence across affiliates.
- global organizations, typified by a mix of control from the centre and 'push back' from local centres of excellence. The development of managers is far more respectful of cultural diversity, both in design and delivery.

An interesting variation on this is to view manager and leader development through the prism of expatriation and repatriation. Baruch and Altman (2002) propose five different models for organizations, based on values, time, global versus local orientation, individual versus company criteria, and the nature of the psychological contract. However, even this more recent analysis may soon be eclipsed. Given that international assignments are costly, lacking in consistency and often disappointing in their impact (Harris and Brewster, 1999), companies are increasingly turning to global education by means of partnerships with leading business schools, drawing upon multinational faculty, a variety of distance and virtual learning opportunities and validation/qualifications often jointly awarded by several institutions.

Size and sector effects on management development

International strategy and its implied structure explain much but not everything. Patterns of management development can be moderated by the influence of size and sector.

Size of firm

Indeed, average firm size can be connected closely to the institutional context within which it operates. For instance, we know that the total population of all EU firms with 20 or more employees is around 1.5 million, of which 80 per cent have 20–100 employees (European Commission, 2002a). However, within these average figures, institutional environments across Europe vary markedly. OECD data reveal that firms with more than 20 employees range from 11 per cent of all firms in Denmark to 22 per cent in Germany, accounting for 71 per cent of employees in Denmark to 85 per cent in Britain and France (OECD, 2003). The number of staff employed by an organization will inevitably shape the concept and expectations of the manager's role and therefore the nature of management development. The marginality, resource constraints and isolation of many of these smaller firms means that their strategic choices are limited and formal strategies and formal training and development practices are rare (Curran et al., 1998). Likewise, sector will probably place differing demands on managerial and leadership capability. On average, one-third of European firms with 20 or more employees in the private sector are in the manufacturing and production industries, roughly one-third in distribution and transport industries, and a little under one-third in business and personal services.

Not surprisingly, small firms tend to rely on informal management development activities and those running small businesses focus on survival and performance improvement in the short term and prefer informal learning, such as mentoring, shadowing and networking (Curran et al., 1998; CEML, 2002). Smaller firms have higher rates of 'churn' (new entrants and early exits) and can ill afford to release precious staff for development activities because of time and skills pressures. Indeed, finding and retaining skilled staff is a major, and growing, management problem for SMEs in Europe (European Commission, 2002b, 2003).

In addition to size-related resource and time constraints, in many cases, a self-employed and microfirm culture of individualism and anti-participation limits the economic role of many very small firms (see Box 8.3). The desire for personal independence is consistently the most commonly cited career-choice motive reported by small firm owners. This can have the effect of inhibiting cooperation with other firms, failing to utilize external support effectively and inefficient delegation of responsibilities. It is perhaps not surprising that the smallest firms have been shown consistently over time to be generally growth-averse and resistant to training, staff development and other support initiatives.

Box 8.3   Developing managers in micro-enterprises

O'Dwyer and Ryan (2000), in a study of micro-enterprises in Ireland (where 90 per cent of firms are micro), looked at firms with ten or fewer employees. Owner managers were found to be cautious about training and felt that they would not understand it and would not be able to identify with the issues or content. They wanted to listen to someone who knew about running a small

(Continued)

(Continued)

business, not someone from a large company or a consultant. They had the same doubts about business coaching and mentoring as about more formal courses. Their main reason for not participating in coaching and mentoring programmes was that they doubted that the mentor would have the right kind of small business experience. Their doubts about courses were that they would be too academic or too general. These owner managers were only interested in topics related to their immediate business concerns. They saw themselves as business people rather than as professional managers. The research concluded that short workshop-format sessions, specifically focused on particular subject areas of interest, would be the most likely kind of initiative to be welcomed (Burgoyne et al., 2004: 72).

Table 8.2 shows the size effects on formal and informal management development activities in European micro (less than ten employees), small (10–49 employees) and medium (50–249 employees) firms (European Commission, 2003).

Data from the European Commission (2003) shows that micro-firms engage in proportionately fewer development activities whether they be formal or informal. However, there is evidence to suggest a strong association between smaller firms which are anticipating and pursuing a growth strategy and a greater emphasis upon training and development activities (Patton and Marlow, 2002; Wong et al., 1997). This is borne out in a European study comparing 392 large and small firms (Gray and Mabey, 2005). It was found that an active minority of smaller firms (20–100 employees) which adopted structured management development policies and practices also reported significantly higher growth than those with little or no formal development of their managers. It may be that the owners and top managers of such small firms are more aware of the organizational need to create a strong 'family' or 'learning organization' culture in their firms to counteract the external career aspirations of key line managers.

For all this, some, like Bartlett and Ghoshal (1997), believe that size is not necessarily the key issue. They argue that organizations face difficulties in developing their managers when they remain wedded to the idea of a generic management role. They call this a 'Russian-doll model of management', where managers at each level are expected to play similar roles and have similar responsibilities, only for a different size and scope of activities. From a study of 20 organizations, they argue that managers at different levels play distinctly different roles and add value in fundamentally different ways which cannot be captured by a single set of competencies and call for quite different development strategies.

Sector

Sector is a related part of the institutional landscape. To take the case of Germany, firms pursuing a technological leadership strategy in hi-tech areas such as pharmaceuticals and aerospace tend to spend large sums on research and development

TABLE 8.2   *Management development activities in EU SMEs (n = 7750)*

Informal	Micro	Small	Medium	All
Visits to expos/trade fairs	57	70	78	58
Consultants/advisers	21	32	39	22
Reading: professional literature	36	39	58	37
Internal mentors	10	20	27	11
Job rotation	8	17	29	9
Formal	39	56	70	41
No development activities	20	9	4	19

Source: ENSR Observatory (EC, 2003). Column percentages, multiple mentions.

(R&D). They also tend to encourage staff to spend their careers within R&D and try to attract, retain and develop staff with high professional, less managerial orientations (Geppert et al., 2002). Other German companies, pursuing strategies emphasizing reliability, quality and efficiency in capital-intensive industries with standardized technologies, employ R&D staff with more managerial orientations. Their human resource practices place a premium on the identification and development of managerial potential, job rotation within R&D and assignment to other functions. In contrast, technological leadership strategies are integrated with human resource practices supporting this stance: selection on the basis of technical expertise, promotion within the R&D unit rather than out of it, and the granting of time and budgets to attend conferences, to work on professionally challenging projects and to contribute to scientific and professional journals.

This contrasts with Spanish organizations, where it has been argued that the primary factors influencing training and development are structural (Paradella et al., 2002). Provision is more likely in larger organizations, in those that belong to a holding company, and in those that have a training department exclusively involved with staff development functions (see Table 8.1). Greater training activity is also associated with firms located in non-manufacturing and chemical industries, financial concerns and business services, the sectors which are most influenced by a combination of technical innovations and organizational changes.

A similar conclusion about sectoral bias was reached by Storey et al. (1997). In-depth case analysis of the processes and methods used to develop managers in eight matched Japanese and UK organizations revealed many differences that conformed to national stereotype, but some differences between companies were due to the sector in which they were located and not to national characteristics. A study of 482 European organizations operating in Spain, Denmark, Germany and the UK found that those in the manufacturing sector were neglecting qualifications-based development for their managers when compared to firms in the transport/distribution and service sectors (Tamkin et al., 2006). The authors conclude that given the growing importance of accreditation and continuing professional development, relying on inherent ability and work experience could constitute a serious weakness for manufacturing firms.

Public and not-for-profit sectors

In many countries, the public sector has been responding to political thinking which actively promotes the adoption of private sector management practices as a means of increasing efficiency and effectiveness. In the UK, for example, the parentage of this so-called new public management (NPM) lies in the field of institutional economics with its emphasis on user choice, transparency and incentives and in the rise of business type managerialism incorporating ideas of professional management, the freedom to manage and a focus on outputs. We might anticipate that approaches to management development in public sector organizations would increasingly emulate those in private firms. However, this can be countered on several levels.

First, the role of a manager in public services (and, for that matter, in not-for-profit organizations) continues to have distinctive dimensions, such as: accountability to multiple stakeholders, partnership working, the vagaries of dealing with political clients and the need to develop frameworks which put users and citizens at the heart of their change agendas. Second, case studies reveal the difficulties encountered when attempting to transfer organization/management development principles and policies from the private to the public sector, whether this be in the health sector (Currie, 1999; Bate, 2000; Boyett and Currie, 2001) or government organizations (Newman, 2000). Third, there is concern that the traditional and valuable characteristics associated with public administration, such as detachment, honesty, equity and fairness, will be eroded (Richards and Rodrigues, 1993). Meanwhile, reports indicate that the lack of up-to-date and effective leadership development, skills to deal with the political dimension and capacity to generate creativity and innovation, continue to be lamented by managers working for public sector organizations (Charlesworth et al., 2003).

A cultural take on management development

Our institutional discourse of management development so far has alluded to national culture in several places. This is not surprising. The institutional context of a firm, its international strategy, its sector and size are all closely connected to its geographical and cultural location. In this section we explore more fully how local culture serves to constitute management development. Authors tend to approach this issue from two opposite directions. Some take an inductive approach by determining what management development is taking place across different countries via field research, then attempt to explain these differences in terms of, among other things, culture. Others are more deductive: they begin with generic models of cultural difference and from this anticipate the kinds of development activities that might be favoured or predicted in different socio-cultural settings.

Inductive approaches

What empirical evidence do we have to support the notion of regional or national differences in the way managers are trained and developed? Although comparative studies of international HRM have demonstrated country differences in relation to a range of practices like selection and promotion (Laurent, 1986), hiring strategies (Segalla et al., 2001b), early socialization (Budhwar and Sparrow, 1998), perceptions of career management (Derr and Laurent, 1989) and terminations (Segalla et al., 2001a). However, surprisingly little comparative research has been published in the specific arena of the way organizations train and develop their managers.

One exploratory study set out to compare training and development practices (for all employees, not just managers) within and across nine countries and one region (Drost et al., 2002). They found evidence of similar practices within country clusters, which they attributed to cultural values and industry trends. For instance, they linked the relatively high commitment to training in Korea, China and Taiwan to the collectivist nature of these societies, whereby training reinforces the individual's dependence on the organization and completion confers higher status, social mobility and acceptance. They go on to point out that this is expressed in quite different ways. In Japan, training and development tends to be planned and executed in a diligent, disciplined manner, with systematic job changes as part of a long-term relationship with staff at every level. In Korea, training and development is seen as a primary means to mould future managers to fit the corporate culture. In China, there is a high degree of government involvement compelling companies to train and re-train their staff at every level. In Taiwan both the government and local companies work together in developing the workforce. However, Taiwanese organizations seem to have a greater interest in managerial, rather than technical, training.

A study of management training in 12 European countries adopted a slightly more sophisticated approach and identified five distinct typologies of management development (Bournois et al., 1994). In their study the authors selected three practices: the level at which management training decisions were made, the nature of management training procedures and approaches to career management. Using these criteria, cluster analysis revealed five distinct typologies of management development in Europe: Germany, on its own; an 'English-speaking' group of Ireland, the Netherlands and the UK; a Latin group of Spain and Portugal; a nordic group consisting of Norway and its neighbour Sweden; and a fifth hybrid group of France, Finland and Denmark.

To some extent, these corresponded with the typologies of management development described by Evans et al. (1989) and later elaborated by Evans et al. (2002) (see Box 8.4).

Box 8.4 Typologies of management development

Researching potential identification and development of managers at major European corporations, four types of management development were identified by Evans and his colleagues (2002):

- The 'Latin' or elite political with a propensity for senior managers to privilege 'political games' over bureaucratic rules when it comes to promoting

(Continued)

(Continued)

managers to top positions; an emphasis on hiring high-potentials rather than developing an internal pool of managers with the help of various training and development tools.

- The 'Germanic' or functional model characterized by the internalization of the competency-building process and an internal labour market perspective.
- The 'Anglo-Dutch' MNC model characterized by the market-like nature of managerial job opportunities (typified by the USA and the UK).
- The Japanese or elite cohort model which relies on heavily filtered recruitment of potential managers from the top universities.

Despite the high face validity of these four 'types' and some confirmation of most, though not all, aspects of the three European cultural models (Klarsfeld and Mabey, 2004), their derivation appears to be based on limited case study and interview evidence. More problematic is that the original study involved interviews with just 60 large companies, many of which were MNCs (including subsidiaries of Japanese multinational enterprises), and all of which were employing 2,000–350,000 employees (Derr, 1987). Such a sample, apart from being skewed to larger companies, is likely to be heavily influenced by foreign parent HRM policies, and this makes it difficult to disentangle the differential effects arising from MNC status on the one hand and country of operation on the other.

Also, in the spirit of post-colonial critique, we should be wary of such generalizations and stereotypes (see Box 2.3). For example, in Germany, as in Japan, there is the small to medium-sized company sector as well as the voluntary and public sectors, both of which often appeal to people with more entrepreneurial, creative and technical orientations. Considerable sectoral differences also exist *within* a society. In some respects, the way a Japanese and a British bank train their managers is more similar than retail businesses within their respective countries (Storey et al., 1997). Although in general Japanese managers are more highly educated than British ones, they do not necessarily receive more off-the-job training; more emphasis is given to on-the-job training, role models and mentors and `voluntary' self-development activities. Training, development and job rotation are also more likely to be internally integrated with other human resource systems in Japan, more likely to be continuous and life-long, and less likely to be confined only to management.

For all this, there appear to be some grounds for asserting that the peculiar cultural heritage (as well as the market context, as dicussed earlier) of a given firm will predispose its HRD specialists to favour one or more of these approaches for developing their management cadres (Stiles et al., 1997; Delamere et al., 2003; Louart, 2003).

Deductive approaches

Given the very different cultural conceptions of what a manager is and does in the first place (as illustrated by the final column of Table 8.1), it should come as no surprise that nationally distinctive approaches to management development exist. For example, in a paper which seeks to penetrate the national psyche with regard to managers and their development, Lawrence (1993: 17) notes that: 'Management development is less salient in France because in that country management is regarded more as a state of being than as the result of fashioned development processes within the company. It is or connotes an identity, more than an activity or set of capabilities.' This contrasts with the conception of management in Britain, where it is seen as essentially an interpersonal task, focused on getting things done (Sparrow, 1996). In this context, personal experience is prized and management development is pre-occupied with 'soft' skills, especially the ability to motivate, lead and get the best from teams, and elitism codified in national culture is eschewed. However, this perception that management is generalizable from one function and industrial sector to another is quite different again from the German conviction that specialist knowledge (especially technical) and experience is all important. Lawrence (1993) notes that this prevalent view, together with a variety of historical factors, militates against a flourishing management development activity in Germany, with the result that it is less widespread, salient and more restrained by the personnel function.

By contrast, it has been argued that the practice of management development is seen as a science by many Asian governments and thus that it can be taught and applied like any systematic operation. This is reflected in how managers learn in countries such as China, Hong Kong and Singapore (Borgonion and Vanhonacker, 1992; Warner, 1992). In countries like China, the result can be that when personnel managers work on a problem in their business, they invariably seek a 'systematic' approach to training (Branine, 1996). In turn, Asian managers typically appreciate lectures and more of a structured type of learning delivered by 'experts'. Furthermore, while they may look to Western management to provide the science, there is caution among Chinese officials and administrators concerning the full adoption of Western principles. In efforts to reinforce traditional values that include preserving the doctrine of present leadership while introducing Western management values to suit the needs of society, the result can be an interesting collage of desired leadership attributes (Fu and Tsui, 2003). Within this, the underlying cultural traits remain resistant to change (see Box 8.5).

Box 8.5   Chinese models of management development

The management of human resources in China is deeply rooted in the country's history, and reinforced by tacit social norms of solidarity, equality, mutual assistance and obedience to the law. Such cultural norms and values have continued to influence aspects of work behaviour and employment relationships despite the consolidation of increasing economic reforms. The main features of uniquely adapted Chinese models of management development and training are teacher-centred, culturally bound and politically oriented, making it fundamentally different from the learner-centred approach of western countries. (Branine, 2005: 468)

All this suggests that a culturalist perspective, best associated with the work of Hofstede (1980), might be a promising source of explaining management development. Through a study of the actions of a multinational corporation, Hofstede focused on the range of norms, beliefs and values that together can constitute a culture. He identified four dimensions – power–distance, uncertainty avoidance, individualism versus uncertainty avoidance, masculinity versus femininity – to which he subsequently added a fifth, Confucian dynamism (Hofstede and Bond, 1988). He found significant differences between what he described as 'national cultures' on these dimensions. Despite being widely cited, this simplistic dimensionalization of culture has been criticized (Tayeb, 2000), as has the underlying factor validity (Bond, 1988). The reliance upon a heavily socialized sample of IBM employees, the assumption of a common, world-wide, occupational IBM culture incorporating all staff and numerous aspects of his research methodology are among other flaws (McSweeney, 2002; also see Gooderham and Nordhaug, 2002, together with Hofstede's trenchant riposte, 2002).

For our purposes of understanding management development in different cultural contexts, Hofstede's typology falls short in other ways. Critically, it fails to explain why differences in values and norms have developed and why a particular constellation by countries is detected (Rubery and Grimshaw, 2003). Specifically, we are left to speculate as to the implications of this cultural perspective towards management development. Fortunately, some studies have investigated this. For instance, Sparrow (1996) found that national values, such as individualism–collectivism, influence the social cues that managers use to decode information in their psychological contract. This is highly pertinent because the way an organization sets up and runs its management development activities conveys potent signals about what is important, what behaviours will be rewarded, which mindsets are in vogue and so on. Sparrow's point is that such perceptions are socially constructed and heavily filtered through aspects of national culture like power–distance. Other authors explore the role of culture in both the way management development is diagnosed and delivered.

Investing in and diagnosing training and development

In Box 8.6 an attempt is made to predict how firms in different national cultures might approach training and development, in terms of initial investment and the way needs assessment might be conducted. Although the author is referring to training generally, similar observations might be made about management development.

Box 8.6   Cultural influences on training decisions

Investing in development

In cultures where there is a heavy emphasis on performance excellence and quality, there is a large budgetary allocation to and widespread application of training and development activities. Examples include China (Tsang, 1994)

(Continued)

(Continued)

and the United Arab Emirates (Wilkins, 2001). The importance of training and development, however, is undermined in fatalistic cultures where managers assume that employees, by nature, have limited capacity that cannot be improved (Aycan et al., 2000). In performance-oriented cultural contexts, training and development are primarily geared towards improving individual or team performance. However, in collectivistic cultures, such activities serve an additional purpose and that is to increase loyalty and commitment to the organization. Wong et al. (2001) reported that by providing training, Chinese organizations instilled the perception that the organization treated employees well. This perception, in turn, stimulated the need to reciprocate the favour (the indigenous concept of '*pao*' – paying back those who treat you well) by working hard and staying committed to the firm. In such contexts, training and development is used as a tool to motivate employees and reward loyalty and commitment, a phenomenon observed in India (Sinha, 1997) and China (Tsang, 1994).

Training needs diagnosis

Training needs are determined on the basis of performance outcomes, especially in performance-oriented or universalistic cultures. In low performance-oriented and high power–distance contexts, decisions on who will participate in training are based on criteria other than job performance. Employees who maintain good relations with higher management are selected for attractive training programmes (i.e. training overseas or in resorts) as a reward for their loyalty (Sinha, 1997). There is also in-group favouritism based on kinship or tribal ties in collectivist cultures (Wilkins, 2001). In low power–distance cultures, training needs are usually determined jointly by the employee and his/her superior. In collectivistic and high power–distance cultures, training needs of the work group are determined by the paternalistic manager in an authoritarian or consultative way (Wilkins, 2001). However, this may not be resented because superiors are assumed to know what is best for the employees.

Based on Aycan (2005: 1097).

This leads Aycan to offer two propositions. First, that cultural fatalism or a low performance orientation will correlate negatively with the level of investment in training and development activities. Second, that in low power–distance, high performance-oriented or universalistic cultures, training and development needs will be determined based on performance evaluation outcomes, and the needs assessment will be conducted participatively. In high power–distance, collectivistic or paternalistic cultures, selection for training will not be based primarily on performance, but on group membership (i.e.

in-group favouritism), and needs assessment will not be conducted in a participatory manner.

Designing and delivering development

Attempts have also been made to apply Hofstede's cultural values to the design and delivery of training. The various training and development techniques used by organizations can be arranged on a spectrum from didactic (trainer-centred, low-risk, content-oriented) to experiential (learner-centred, high-risk, process-oriented). In Hofstede's terms, didactic methods can be considered to have high power–distance/strong uncertainty avoidance and experiential methods are suggestive of low power–distance/weak uncertainty avoidance. Building on an original framework by Pfeiffer and Jones (1983), Francis (2001) provides a guideline for predicting the relative appropriateness of a range of development methods in different cultural groups. Naturally, this is idealized and will not always apply strictly as predicted, and poses difficulties for those training multicultural groups, which are increasingly commonplace. Francis (2001: 194) defines appropriate methods as: 'those that most effectively challenge the participants without eliciting a high level of resistance'. She gives the example of a fishbowl exercise which meets resistance and with-drawal in a Latin culture and a lecture in Denmark which quickly turns into a discussion with participants readily challenging the lecturer.

Some empirical support can be found for this kind of framework. For exam-ple, managers in economically developing countries are found to be most analyt-ical and seek certainty while Anglo, Northern and Latin Europeans are found to be the most intuitive and more likely to question norms and assumptions and hence undermine the power–distance between trainer and trainee (Hayes and Allison, 1998). To instil trust in the development activity, organizations in such cultures prefer high-level managers as instructors, rather than hiring external con-sultants or trainers (Wright et al., 2002).

In a study contrasting leadership styles in the USA, Japan and Taiwan, Von Glinow et al. (1999) conclude that, in comparison with many other political and economic factors, culture is probably the most stable factor that drives manage-ment thinking. In particular, they find that the more a culture assumes human potential to be uneven across organizational members (as against 'talent' being uniformly distributed), the more likely leader training will emphasize specialized expertise rather than general management skills. An important caveat made by these authors – and one which applies to this whole discussion – is that national boundaries may not always coincide with cultural boundaries. In their research, Von Glinow et al. found cultural heterogeneity (internal dissimilarities) to be highest in the USA and lowest in Japan.

Cultural complexity in the realm of management development comes in other forms. As more organizations form cross-national joint ventures and collaborative alliances, managerial style can jar, as can cultural differences (Iles and Yolles, 2003). A further level of complexity is the globalization of organizations, markets and competition (see Box 8.7).

Box 8.7   Competition between corporate and national cultures

In Sri Lanka, some companies operating in the capital (Colombo) have orga-nizational cultures similar to those of developed countries. However, this type of culture would be significantly different from companies operating in rural districts. Although cultural diversity within a nation can have more complex implications for the implementation of HR systems, it can also be viewed positively. Companies in developed countries have outsourced some of their knowledge-based business processes to Sri Lanka, taking advan-tage of its cheap labour. Although Sri Lanka is viewed to be a high power–distance nation, such companies have found little difficulty in recruiting employees to an organizational culture more similar to that of low power–distance nations. This is mostly due to the type of individuals they seek to employ. They are often young, foreign-educated individuals with much exposure and experience to cultural diversity and who in fact prefer to work in such cultural environments. Our own culture is more apparent to ourselves when we come in contact with other cultures. Exposure allows us the opportunity to select the values and norms we want to retain while enabling us to adopt other (foreign) values we perceive are more appropri-ate (in different contexts and situations). A foreign company may have a ready supply of labour in a local country provided that the individual's cul-tural values (as opposed to the national culture) match the desired organi-zational culture. However, if such a supply is not present, creating that common mindset is much harder to achieve. (Yasangi Wijesingh, personal communication)

This example shows cultural diversity between certain groups of cultures across different nations reducing while cultural diversity within a nation increases.

So, how helpful is the cultural explanation of management development? Certainly, cultural context plays an important part in the priority given to man-agement development, assuming it is seen as necessary in the first place, as well as how strategic or tactical it is considered to be. An understanding of cultural pref-erences also sensitizes us to the style of such training and development (formal or informal, elitist or democratic, programmed or opportunistic, and so on) which might be favoured in different countries. It also allows a degree of comparative cross-cultural analysis, which may in turn lead to learning about and the transfer of effective approaches to management development from one country to another. However, the cultural dimension of the institutionalist discourse also has limitations. The tendency is to classify rather than explain. So typologies of man-agement development may be identified (inductive) or preferred methods of development allocated to countries or country groupings (deductive). But this fails to actually explain a great deal. Invariably, we need to dig deeper into insti-tutional arrangements, historical precedents in a given cultural setting, or look for wider pan-regional dimensions like gender (see Gooderham and Nordhaug,

2002) to uncover why managers are developed in the way they are. There are the dangers of treating culture and country as the same thing and, related to this, of over-simplifying national culture and glossing over exceptions and contradictions (see Tayeb, 2000, for several examples of this) and underestimating the variety of responses from individuals located in the same culture (Triandis et al., 1985). Furthermore, cultural analyses often suffer from ethnocentric bias. This is because researchers or observers, especially those operating deductively, naturally impose their own predetermined dimensions of culture (Hofstede, 1980, and Trompenaars, 1994, are cases in point) when examining and comparing practices across countries. Few studies have the luxury of multicultural teams, with each researcher located within and investigating their own culture from the inside. And even here, blind-spots and perceptual distortion are not eliminated (Mayrhofer and Brewster, 2005).

Conclusion

In this chapter we have sought to deepen our understanding of management development by invoking a meso-level institutionalist discourse. To do this we have examined accounts of management development which elevate socio-institutional and cultural factors as determining the nature, style, emphasis and extent of training and development that are undertaken in different countries. This literature, and the assumptions upon which it is based, have a structuring effect on both the researchers and their subject matter. Whether conscious or not, the institutionalist discourse frames their action (the types of variable, the choice of research sites, methods and presentation of findings). A further feature of this form of discourse is the underlying normative ideal that management development is a 'good thing' (much like 'best-practice'), for building social capital, facilitating knowledge transfer, developing individual talent, and the like. This, in turn, gets translated into practice. So the implicit or explicit intention of much of this writing is to identify factors which facilitate or forestall the development of managers in the country/company settings being examined.

We have seen that, within the institutionalist discourse, there are many factors which might shape the design, delivery and impact of management development in different countries. Among these are the vocational and educational systems, the extent of government involvement in skill formation, the dominant patterns of employment relations and career systems, and the demand and supply of key managerial staff in the labour market (Tregaskis, 1997). In addition, and intertwined with these factors, are the important issues of sector, size and national culture: what do organizations expect of their managers and leaders? How is performance rewarded? How much emphasis is given to formal systems as against informal patronage? To what extent is hierarchy respected? And so on (see Sparrow, 1996). Again such priorities are an amalgam of national, occupational and organizational cultures.

The institutionalist discourse also highlights both generic and country-specific features in the way managers are developed. In relation to Europe, for example, in-house training is the most common type of management development method *used* in all countries, while on-the-job experience and in-house training are considered the most *effective* methods for the development of managers (Ramirez, 2004). Most learning for managers is embedded in diverse organizational systems and applied in the context of specific cultures, routines and shared norms that define individual firms (Penrose, 1959). This suggests that an explanation of the key external factors shaping management development at firm level should rely on neither the agency-driven best-practice discourse, nor the more macro-institutionalist discourse alone. An interplay of both at the meso-level would appear more adequate.

Summary

- Among the key external factors shaping management development at firm level are institutional context, international strategy, size, sector and national culture.
- The management development literature that analyses these factors might collectively be referred to as an institutionalist discourse: this has a structuring effect on both researchers and their subject matter.
- Accounts within the institutionalist discourse reveal much about the local construction of management development, including the feelings and norms towards these activities as expressed in different national/organizational settings.
- The normative ideals implicit within institutionalist discourse translate into different management development emphases, priorities and practices, depending on the local setting.
- Organizations do not organize and implement training and development in a vacuum: an analysis of management development which fails to take account of institutional factors, and their interrelationships, is likely to be incomplete and misleading.

9

Management development and diversity

How modern can we claim to be when our three main [political] parties appear to think that 'leader' is a masculine noun. (Joan Smith, The Independent, 17 January 2006)

After reading this chapter you will be able to:

- **Develop your own views as to how important it might be to consider issues of diversity when seeking to understand management development**
- **Describe and critique different approaches to managing diversity**
- **Explain and critique management development's relationship to each of these approaches**
- **Form your own judgements on the extent to which (and the circumstances under which) management development might work either for or against the interests of diversity**
- **Reflexively examine your own motivations for either engaging with or objecting to the content and spirit of this chapter**
- **Identify relevant literature sources should you wish to further develop your knowledge in the area of management development's relationship to diversity**

Introduction

The third meso-discourse of management development we examine in this part of the book is that of diversity. Diversity can mean different things to different people but as a business buzzword it forms an almost universal aspiration when it comes to drafting the corporate mission statement. Look at any corporate website or annual report these days and it will almost inevitably contain the ubiquitous eulogy to the benefits of diversity and the steps being taken to actively 'celebrate' or 'embrace' it. Why then, a cynic may ask, do the ranks of management in many Western/multicultural economies remain overwhelmingly white, male, able-bodied and ostensibly heterosexual, especially at the higher echelons of the corporate hierarchy? And this despite sex, race and other forms of discrimination being long since outlawed in many of these societies. Why is it, for example, that 30 years after the UK's Sex Discrimination Act, women constitute less than 4 per cent of executive directors in the UK's top 100 quoted companies? And why is there only one female CEO (Rees, 2004)? Why are women in the

UK private sector paid on average 22 per cent less than men for full-time work, rising to 41 per cent less in the financial services sector (EOC, 2006)? Why is it that part-time work is still valued hour-for-hour significantly less than full-time work (EOC, 2006)? Why is it that the gender pay gap is even higher when it comes to ethnic minorities, reaching almost 30 per cent on average for women of Pakistani descent (Platt, 2006)? Why is it that white women and ethnic minority men and women are particularly likely to be concentrated in low-paid jobs, with many men of Chinese and Bangladeshi origin working as cooks or waiters, and with care assistant being one of the most common jobs for white, Pakistani, black Caribbean and black African women (EOC, 2006)?

Of course, potential answers to these questions are many, varied and hotly disputed. And we are not proposing that reasons for the relative lack of diversity within management lie exclusively at the door of management development. What we *are* suggesting, however, is that a book of this nature should at least be challenging the currency of management development when it comes to issues of diversity. We will commence the chapter with an examination of four distinct approaches to managing diversity, namely those of resistance, discrimination and fairness, access and legitimacy and, finally, the learning approach. The vocabulary and social practices associated with each of the four approaches can be considered constituent elements of a meso-discourse of diversity. Having critically explored these, we go on to examine management development's relationship to each, arguing that much management development remains consistent with the resistance perspective to diversity. We will examine the implications of this argument and then finish the chapter by suggesting a few ways in which management development might usefully be shifted towards being more consistent with the learning perspective to managing diversity.

Four approaches to managing diversity

Although the literature on organizational *diversity* can be traced back to the early 1980s (Janssens and Steyaert, 2003), it is the Workforce 2000 report, authored in the USA by Johnston and Packer (1987), that is widely identified as catalysing the entry of the term *diversity management* into Western managerial parlance. This was a report predicting that, by 2000, the majority of the workforce in the USA would comprise members of groups traditionally referred to as having minority status (e.g. blacks, Hispanics, women, etc.). Although 'diversity management' is defined in different ways by different authors, the definition offered by Prasad and Mills (1997: 4) appears fairly representative in stating that it 'refers to the systematic and planned commitment on the part of organizations to recruit and retain employees from diverse demographic backgrounds'.

Since its relatively recent inception, the field of diversity management has risen quite rapidly to form a prominent part of HRM policy, certainly within Anglo-Saxon countries and increasingly elsewhere. Indeed, it would, today, be unusual for any large European and/or Anglo-Saxon organization not to have explicit diversity objectives enshrined within its policy statements. Despite such widespread adoption of the term, there are a number of different ways in which organizations can be understood to respond to diversity. A useful framework for mapping these responses has been put forward by Dass and Parker (1999), drawing on earlier work by Thomas and Ely (1996). They identify four different approaches to the management of diversity, namely

- The *resistance* approach
- The *discrimination and fairness* approach
- The *access and legitimacy* approach
- The *learning* approach.

The authors apply a rough chronology to the approaches, but only in the sense that more recent ones can be characterized as being progressively more sophisticated or enlightened than their predecessors. In practice, however, the picture is less neatly organized with some organizations still aligned with early approaches and with any one organization potentially adopting different approaches simultaneously in different policy areas and/or parts of the business. Before examining such dynamics in relation to management development we set out below a brief synopsis of each approach in turn.

The resistance approach to diversity management

Dass and Parker (1999) chronologically locate the roots of the resistance approach to diversity within the pre-civil rights era in the USA and the post-colonial era in Europe when there were few legal or societal pressures against discrimination in the workplace. However, as pressures for minority rights grew during the 1960s, so did resistance towards them from the established majority, with such resistance being predominantly reactive and characterized by denial, avoidance, defiance and/or manipulation. The authors are careful to make the point that the resistance approach can be seen to be still alive and well today, giving high-profile examples of organizations which have been successfully sued for discrimination despite their protestations to the contrary. While we would agree with this, some organizations, characterized at least in part by the resistance approach, may well at the same time be struggling, more or less sincerely, to implement what they regard as enlightened diversity policy (see Box 9.1).

Box 9.1   Sexism and the City

In many countries, banking organizations are notorious for their propensity to attract discrimination lawsuits. Despite this, there always seems to be the website declaration, of which the following real example is typical:

We employ many women and view diversity as a strength which is reflected in our workforce. We are constantly reviewing our compensation

(Continued)

(Continued)

process and looking to improve its transparency without compromising our business.

While such declarations may sincerely represent organizational aspirations at one level, it seems one never has to look too far to glean a different image. The organization expressing the above commitment was also the subject of press reports concerning a female employee claiming to have been treated in a 'humiliating and offensive' way on revealing she was pregnant. Part of this treatment was the cutting of her bonus by 80 per cent, resulting in her male colleagues receiving nine times more than her. An employment tribunal found the company guilty of sex discrimination, awarding the employee substantial damages.

Another organization declares:

At [our company], diversity is more than just a word or a single program — it is part of an environment in which employees are recognized and rewarded based on their accomplishments. Rooted in one of the company's five guiding principles — Respect for the Individual — the [company's] culture promotes mutual respect, acceptance, cooperation, and productivity among people from varying backgrounds.

The same organization was also reported in the press as having paid multi-million dollar damages to one of its female employees. This was part of an ongoing series of claims which saw more than 1,000 female brokers alleging systematic sexism within its ranks.

The discrimination and fairness approach to diversity management

Writing in 1996, Thomas and Ely described the discrimination and fairness approach as the dominant way of understanding diversity and in many respects this still holds true today. The approach can be characterized as one which is driven by an overall concern to be compliant with the legislation when it comes to issues of discrimination. It is frequently coupled with more intrinsic ethical and moral concerns for equality of opportunity, social justice and fairness of treatment. An expressed concern of organizations pursuing such an approach is that of aspiring towards a demographic profile that is broadly reflective of the wider society. Typical initiatives within such an approach include the diagnosis of direct and indirect sources of discrimination, along with interventions aimed at palliating historical imbalances in access to opportunity (Lorbiecki, 2001).

In terms of management development, interventions may include mentoring and career development programmes directed at minority groups, combined with diversity compliance training for the whole workforce (Thomas and Ely, 1996). Numerical targets for the recruitment and retention of minorities will typically be a key element to this approach, with 'success' being defined by the degree to which such targets are achieved. While the discrimination and fairness approach may be well intentioned, it can be criticized for paying too much attention to 'body counting' (Alvesson and Due Billing, 2000). This can result in insufficient consideration of the degree to which employees are allowed to actually express their 'difference' within the workplace. The end result is one in which the organization may well become more diverse (temporarily at least) in terms of its demographics, but the actual work that gets done and the way it gets done remain broadly unchanged. In this way, the approach favours a philosophy where difference is assumed to be irrelevant to how the organization should function. According to Thomas and Ely (1996: 83), this can give rise to unresolved tensions as organizations struggle over 'what to do with [their] diversity', thus undermining the organization's capacity to learn, evolve and improve. Dass and Parker (1999) make the point that the approach is prone to take a rather superficial view of diversity and difference. So, for example, progress is seen as appointing members of a minority group to certain key positions notwithstanding the fact that such appointees (apart from their obvious superficial differences of, for example, colour, gender or ethnicity) may be culturally indistinguishable from those of the dominant (i.e. typically white, male) majority. Lorbiecki (2001) supports this view by making the point that the approach is one where 'difference' is typically regarded as a liability. It is assimilationist in that it follows a 'deficit model' whereby the diverse individual is 'helped' to fit into existing organizational norms. While such norms may appear eminently rational and neutral, the diverse 'other' can often end up being implicitly 'judged against a norm of male characteristics and behaviour' (Liff and Wajcman, 1996: 81).

The access and legitimacy approach to diversity management

Thomas and Ely (1996) contrast the conformism and assimilationism of the discrimination and fairness approach to the way in which the access and legitimacy approach to diversity not only accepts but actively celebrates difference, primarily as a route towards competitive advantage. This approach derives its label from the way in which organizations adopt it primarily out of a desire to seek *legitimacy* with the public at large and gain *access* to a more diverse consumer base and labour pool. Internal legitimacy is also secured via the approach's emphasis on the 'business case', which claims that diversity and effective performance go hand in hand. As a consequence, 'success' under this approach tends to be defined in terms of the extent to which bottom-line benefits do materialize, albeit with such assessments being notoriously difficult to carry out (Acosta, 2004).

A common and most basic form of management development within this approach is diversity awareness training premised on the business case for diversity (Litvin, 2002). Companies adopting the approach may, for example, be faced with difficulties recruiting sufficient numbers of staff from traditional sources and therefore turn towards minority groups to fill the gap. What is more, once recruited to the organization, members of such groups may be actively encouraged to bring their specific expertise and insights to the fore in helping tap previously unconsidered market segments. Both Dass and Parker (1999) and Lorbiecki (2001) see the approach as being broader in scope than this in the sense that almost any dimension of difference (legally protected or not) might be valued or 'celebrated', so long as it can be rationalized as a source of competitive advantage. Although it is generally seen as more progressive and sophisticated than the discrimination and fairness approach, it can be criticized on a number of fronts (see Box 9.2).

> ### Box 9.2   Criticisms of the discrimination and fairness approach
>
> One danger is that minority groups may be pigeon-holed into specialist or niche roles, creating the risk that opportunities for progression within other parts of the organization will be restricted (Thomas and Ely, 1996; Kersten, 2000). This can result in resentment from minority populations who, for all the rhetoric around them being valued for their diversity, may feel they are merely being exploited to serve the ultimate interests of the dominant elite (Dass and Parker, 1999). A related critique is that in many ways the approach may lead to conformity or assimilation as much as its discrimination and fairness predecessor, since it typically does not involve any deep or meaningful challenge to dominant power structures, values, cultures or ways of working within the organization (Acosta, 2004). Furthermore, the sheer range of differences that the approach can cover has attracted much criticism for the way in which it detracts from and therefore dilutes the experiences of genuinely oppressed groups. It does this by conflating deep sources of structural inequity towards historically marginalized groups with differences of minor discomfort among the dominant majority (Kersten, 2000; Smithson and Stokoe, 2005).

Litvin (2002) mounts a strident and somewhat ironic critique of the approach, claiming that the 'business case' on which it so heavily relies amounts to little more than a rhetorical tool to legitimate ritualistic practices such as diversity mission statements and universal or 'sheep-dip' (our term) forms of awareness training. This, in her view, serves the elite defenders of the status quo by masking their failure to implement the kind of holistic transformations that might deal with deep-seated structural and systemic causes of workplace inequalities.

The learning approach to diversity management

This last approach to diversity management that we present here has been variously referred to under the label of 'learning and effectiveness' (Thomas and Ely, 1996) and more recently 'integration and learning' (Ely and Thomas, 2001). However, like Dass and Parker (1999), we refer to it merely as the 'learning' approach in order to emphasize its inherently open-ended and recursive features. It is open-ended and recursive in the sense that it considers diversity as a source of learning which, in turn, has the potential to impact our very understanding of the concept of diversity. This takes the approach into the kind of critical/reflexive territory that was perhaps not envisaged by Ely and Thomas but which certainly *has* been the subject of calls by authors such as Acosta (2004), Lorbiecki (2001) and (more implicitly) by Kersten (2000).

Put simply, the learning approach to diversity management is driven by the belief that diversity ought to involve more than just a change to the demographic profile of an organization, whether such change be motivated by moral, legislative or indeed bottom-line concerns. It is an approach that seeks to transcend the assimilationist tendencies of its predecessors by considering that the increasing diversity of individuals comprising the organization might be expected to fundamentally impact the nature *of* the organization. Changes to the organization could extend to its systems, structures, networks, cultures, values, expectations, internal power bases, and indeed its very mission or purpose.

Interventions within such an approach would be less episodic or freestanding (Dass and Parker, 1999) than with the previous approaches, which tend to rely on isolated bouts of diversity training coupled perhaps with development programmes aimed specifically at minority groups. Typical examples of the latter would be coaching or mentoring schemes directed at women or ethnic minorities. Instead, a learning approach to diversity would encourage open, participative and democratic dialogue reminiscent of critical action learning (Willmott, 1997), where the voices and perspectives of all demographic groups would be accorded equal credence. Furthermore, people would begin to be seen and see themselves less in terms of their diversity-group membership and more in terms of their unique, fragmented and multiple identities. Importantly, this goes beyond the kind of 'turning a blind eye to difference' philosophy of the discrimination and fairness approach because it is coupled with a shared appreciation of how discriminatory advantage or disadvantage can be deeply embedded within organizational structures (Acker, 1990). Under this approach, therefore, the notion of 'difference' extends to the inherent power differentials that exist within an organization (and society more generally) by dint of one's attributed demographic group membership (Lorbiecki, 2001). It is only by recognizing, exploring and challenging such differentials that meaningful change might occur. Crucially, this applies as much to the (usually) white, male, heterosexual, able-bodied majority as it does to any other demographic grouping within the organization (Kersten, 2000; Sinclair, 2000; Acosta, 2004).

This substantially concludes our exploration of the four different approaches to diversity management. Before moving on to examine the relationship of management development to each, we close this section with a couple of caveats or critiques. The first of these relates to the fact that they are 'ideal types', calling into question the degree to which they can be separately identified in the real world. In practice, it is possible or even likely that more than one approach could be operating within any single organization at any one point in time. The most obvious example of such a dynamic relates to the resistance approach. It is unlikely that any diversity initiative would be entirely free of resistance from some quarters, either conscious or otherwise (recall Box 9.1). Our second point relates to the fact that there are other ways in which the field can be categorized. We have chosen the above, first, because the four approaches are quite widely referred to in the academic and practitioner literature but also because they provide a useful heuristic against which to compare management development practices. And it is to this that we now turn our attention.

Management development and its relationship to diversity management

> If the literature of management that produces management rules which apply to management practice are normatively male, then women's practice of management will always be perceived as different, 'not male' and 'not management'. (Hall-Taylor, 1997: 259)

Although there is a growing body of literature that tackles management development in specific relation to diversity, especially from a feminist perspective (e.g. women-only management development), the bulk of the literature on management development tends to treat the managerial subject as an abstract, asexual, non-raced and somehow disembodied individual (Acker, 1990; Nkomo, 1992; Acosta, 2004). This is something that we hope to at least partially remedy in this section. We do so by examining management development in relation to each of the four approaches to diversity as set out above, commencing with the resistance approach. In mounting our critique we draw mainly on the feminist literature since this is where the majority of the diversity-related critiques of management development can be found. As a result, our analysis centres mainly around issues of gender, although we believe that many of the issues raised can be extended to other dimensions of difference. See Box 9.3 for our theoretical position with regard to gender.

Box 9.3   Theorizing gender

There are various ways in which the notion of gender can be conceptualized (Meyerson and Kolb, 2000). At one extreme is the view that gender is synonymous with biological sex and that women and men are fundamentally, inherently and irreconcilably different, not just in terms of their reproductive functioning, but in all sorts of other ways that form the 'essence' of what it is to be either male or female (hence the 'essentialist' label that is given to this approach). At the other extreme is the strong social constructionist view that gender is nothing more than an empty linguistic category that has no meaning other than that which is applied to it and that has served to divide and rule for generations. Somewhere in the middle is the view which

(Continued)

(Continued)

accepts the social constructionist view but without wishing to take it to its logical and somewhat paradoxical conclusion. This conclusion would be one where the very notion of gender, along with its dualisms (such as 'man' and 'woman', 'feminine' and 'masculine') must be abandoned for there to be any hope of true 'gender' equality. The paradox lies in that the avoidance of gendered categorizations removes the possibilities for debating gender inequality in the first place. The middle ground of which we speak (and which we adopt for the purposes of this chapter) is one of pragmatism, where distinctions between 'woman' and 'man' based on anatomy (and without discounting androgyny) are accepted as, to all intents and purposes, socially unavoidable and in many instances socially useful. All other aspects of gender are considered ontologically fluid in the sense that we consider there to be nothing 'essential' in the make up of men or women that dictates that the former be principal breadwinners, competitive, macho, understand the offside rule in football, etc. or that the latter be principal carers in the home, soft, gentle, nurturing, enjoy coffee mornings, etc. As such, femininity comes to be defined as qualities that are socially, culturally and historically (but not inherently or 'essentially') associated with women and vice versa for masculinity. This acknowledges that different eras, societies and cultures construct both masculinity and femininity in different ways. It also draws an epistemological separation between the analytical dualism of sex (i.e. male/female) and the duality of gender (i.e. masculinities/femininities).

The corollary of Box 9.3 is that both masculinity and femininity (collectively 'gender') become notions that are multiple, fragmented, potentially overlapping, context-specific and in theory (if not in practice due to social structural and cultural constraints) accessible to both men and women. So, to be clear, wherever we refer to *sex differences* (i.e. men/women, male/female) throughout this chapter, we do so in an 'analytically dualist' sense and wherever we refer to *gender differences* (i.e. masculinity/femininity) we do so according to the dialogic notion of duality. As such we do not wish to infer any essentialist conceptualization of the sexes beyond, to all intents and purposes, the anatomical.

Reflection point

Recall our discussion of analytical dualism in our chapter on the critical Discourse (Chapter 6, p. 127 and p. 134). Contrast this with our discussion of *duality* within our chapter on the dialogic Discourse (Chapter 5, pp. 102–3 and 110). Note how we now adopt the former in our approach to sex differences but the latter in our approach to gender differences. As you read through this chapter, try to reach your own judgement as to how this partial combining of the two Discourses facilitates discussion and whether you find it useful.

Management development and the resistance approach to diversity management

Much of what goes on in the name of management development can, in our view, be understood to be aligned with the resistance approach to diversity. Typically, this would involve the kind of management development that is, on the surface at least, considered to be diversity-neutral. On closer inspection, however, the types of practice involved can be understood to merely perpetuate the status quo in terms of an organization's patriarchal cultures and power structures (see Box 9.4).

Box 9.4   Patriarchy

Calas and Smircich (1993) use the term 'patriarchy' in referring to sex–gender relations that naturalize and universalize social practices wherein men and/or masculine values dominate over women and/or feminine values. They go on to state that patriarchal domination is particularly pervasive when women uncritically assume stereotypical feminine patterns within traditional structural relations. One example of such relations might be the traditional organizational structure that relies on hierarchical principles underpinned by linear, ladder-like notions of career (Acker, 1990) that are typically less accessible to women (for a discussion of this see Chapter 6).

Much (if not all) of the time, this will constitute unknowing resistance, since it is simply a question of perpetuating deeply engrained and taken-for-granted forms of managerial subjectivity (see Box 5.6). Before going into some specific examples of management development's resistant functioning when it comes to diversity, we draw on a number of authors to examine some theoretical reasoning for such functioning.

Management theory: have minorities been airbrushed out?

Betters-Reed and Moore (1995) highlight how early business organizations, certainly within the clerical and managerial ranks, were essentially devoid of women and people of colour, something which has set the scene for a remarkably enduring image of organizational normality. Part of this image is constituted by the early stages of management theory, which omit any consideration of women as members of the management profession. Bartram (2005) develops the point further by citing examples of how even *recent* management theory is written from an exclusively male perspective. She draws attention to how, for example, Kolb's (1984) learning cycle and Belbin's team roles owe much to the legacy of Mintzberg's (1975) ten manager roles, namely figurehead, leader, liaison, monitor, disseminator, spokesman, entrepreneur, disturbance handler, resource allocator, negotiator. Not only was the research on which Mintzberg based his findings conducted exclusively with men, but his subsequent use of the generic 'he' throughout his writing effectively airbrushes women out of the managerial picture. Nkomo (1992), albeit writing from an explicitly US perspective, makes a similar argument with regard to race. She coins the term 'faulty generalization' in referring to the way in which management and organizational studies have amassed so much knowledge from researching just one group (i.e. white males) and then generalizing the resulting theories and concepts to all groups. Most theorizing has therefore tended to regard organizations as homogeneous entities in which distinctions of race or ethnicity are either left unstated or considered irrelevant. She regards this as a form of subterfuge given the way that race in the USA remains a profound determinant of one's political rights, social privileges and sense of identity. It is also a means by which the division of labour even today occurs in many organizations, however intentional or inadvertent such dynamics might be.

In broad sympathy with this, Cooke (2003) traces the origins of US management practice back to the pre-Civil War era of slavery. He argues that there is a dynamic of collective denial within the management and organizational literature surrounding slavery's role in both the rise of modern capitalism and its related practices of management. He argues for a post-colonialist understanding of management which seeks to critique the universalizing knowledge claims of Western civilization. Such a view is further developed by Frenkel and Shenhav (2006), who also view the field of management and organizational studies as rooted in theoretical and empirical traditions that are overwhelmingly 'Orientalist' (i.e. white/Western).[1] They cite the influential human relations theorist Elton Mayo as an example of work that relies on a strong Orientalist epistemology and assumptions. For them, theories that define the model manager in terms of his/her identification with core values of Western culture directly influence the ethnic and racial division of labour: 'Armed with assumptions that define management as western, managers do not easily allow the promotion of "others" into management positions in industrialized, so-called multicultural countries, and in multinationals in developing countries' (Frenkel and Shenhav, 2006: 871). They later draw on Acker (1990) to extend their theorizing to the field of gender in combination with those of race and ethnicity: 'Not only are the abstract managers formulated in canonical management and organization studies men ... but they are also white' (Frenkel and Shenhav, 2006: 872).

So, a number of authors have sought to foreground the socially, historically, geographically and politically situated nature of management theory which, despite its sectional origins, has come to be regarded as the very epitome of scientific neutrality and universal applicability (Alvesson and Deetz, 2000). This raises some thorny questions: if the *development of management theory* can be regarded as anything but neutral when it comes to issues such as race, gender and ethnicity (or

---

1   Said explains Orientalism as 'the corporate institution for dealing with the Orient – dealing with it by making statements about it, authorizing views of it, describing it, by teaching it, settling it, ruling it: in short, Orientalism as a western style for dominating, restructuring, and having authority over the Orient.' (1978: 3)

indeed any other dimension of diversity), then should we really expect the *development of managers* to be any less sectional when it draws on such theory? We now present a number of examples to illustrate how and why we should not.

Management development and the resistance approach: a case of gender blindness?

In sympathy with the theoretical arguments above, Mavin et al. (2004) claim that mainstream management theory might more accurately be described as 'male stream' because of the way in which it fails to recognize the relationship between management and gender. This they refer to as a form of 'gender blindness' (see Box 9.5).

Box 9.5   Gender blindness in management education

Mavin et al. (2004) mount a strident critique of the way in which UK business and management schools tend to apply a gender-blind approach to the education and development of managers. By ignoring the notion of gender, such institutions, in their view, can be understood to collude with the status quo by simply repeating rather than calling into question established management theory and practice. They go on to cite a number of influential theorists, including Maslow, Weber and Taylor, whose theories have relied on male-centred assumptions. Most starkly, they cite McGregor (1967) (best known for his X and Y theories of management behaviour) as the epitome of the 'management as male' paradigm in as much as he 'commented that the model of a successful manager was aggressive, competitive, firm and just, and argued that he is not feminine or intuitive in a womanly sense' (Mavin et al., 2004: 295). In sum, for Mavin et al., the very concept of management revolves around social constructions of 'competence' that involve characteristics typically associated with men.

Others have been even more explicit when it comes to examining the gendered status of management development. Rees and Garnsey (2003) used a Foucauldian post-structuralist analysis to critique competency-based management development within six organizations. Despite widespread claims concerning the objectivity of such frameworks, they found the processes surrounding their elaboration to be characterized by negotiation and subjective experience. Almost inevitably, the resulting frameworks merely ended up reflecting traditional (i.e. masculine) perceptions of what a 'competent manager' should resemble. They concluded that competency-based management development frequently acts as a disciplinary technique of control whereby both male and female managers are encouraged to identify with (and judge themselves against) these broadly masculine norms of behaviour. However, they also found that women are faced with a double bind. Not only are they required to emulate masculine behaviour as a condition for accomplishing their managerial self, but these emulations are never evaluated as positively as are identical ones exhibited by male managers. Bartram (2005) also picks up and further develops this point. Writing from a feminist post-structuralist perspective, she argues that mainstream management development can be a 'dangerous place' for women because it is typically a site of activity that reinforces and maintains masculine ways of acting. Faced with this, women are confronted with little option but to adopt a masculine style, but with little prospect of such a style being granted the same kind of legitimacy when adopted by a woman as it is by a man. Even a woman who chooses to play the management game (Bryans and Mavin, 2003) according to prevailing masculine norms will inevitably be cast as the lesser other, no matter how successful she is at adopting such a style. Meanwhile, Bartram also alludes to a kind of 'triple bind' (our term) in the sense that apparent trends towards the feminization of management roles in recent times (see, for example, Fondas, 1997; Hatcher, 2003) has not led to any improvement in the lot of women managers for precisely the same reason, that is that 'the appropriation of feminine attributes by men … brings a legitimacy to these that is not possible when they are associated with women…' (Bartram, 2005: 114).

A number of authors have examined the gendered impact of socialization experiences of management trainees within organizations. This is an especially fruitful area for research since experiences shortly after entry into an organization can be extremely influential for managers (Eriksson–Zetterquist, 2002). A notable example of such a programme comes from the Kamoche (2000) study within 'IP' (a UK multinational) that we briefly explored in Chapter 6. In our view, the study provides a prime example of both a gender-blind form of management development combined with an equally gender blind way of researching it.[2] The development initiative covered a group of international managers on secondment at IP's UK headquarters involving a programme of education (resembling a mini-MBA) at the company's prestigious training institute. The initiative was seen as a means of socialization and enculturation for the managers in the sometimes mysterious social and corporate workings of IP. From an anthropological perspective (as adopted by Kamoche), it could also be understood as a crucial 'rite of passage' for any manager seeking to transit from the 'profane' world of middle management to the 'sacred' terrain of the senior ranks. Despite this being, in our view, a well-executed and intriguing study in many respects, it does beg a number of questions from a gender perspective. For example, it would have been interesting to know whether reactions to and experiences of the programme differed along gender lines and the extent to which the 'success' of the socialization and enculturation aspects differed between the genders. Unfortunately (from our perspective) none of these questions is addressed in the paper and the reader is not even informed as to the gender split of the programme and/or research participants. Given the notoriously low participation rate of women in international management (Haines and Saba, 1999; van der Boon, 2003), however, it is highly likely that

---

2   This last comment is meant more in terms of a simple observation of the Kamoche study as opposed to a critical condemnation of it. On the contrary, the Kamoche study we feel is intriguing in many ways. Our argument is not that researchers (of whatever hue) should always be on the lookout for gender issues within their analysis, but a more general lament that there is so little attention to gender and diversity issues within mainstream analyses of management development.

female managers would, at best, have formed only a small minority of participants in both the programme and the research study. Yet the paper on which the study is based makes a number of apparently gender-neutral findings upon which a number of theoretical generalizations are made. We are told, for example:

- that managers on the programme were expected to be highly and competitively ambitious and to actively pursue high-profile careers
- that they were offered the opportunity for such outcomes in return for committing to the company values
- that manager turnover was 'close to nil' (Kamoche, 2000: 757) as a result of this retention/control strategy
- that effective networking was considered essential to career advancement, enabling the IP manager 'to acquire the social knowledge necessary to be an "insider" and to be accepted...' (2000: 761)
- that the ability to engineer effective mentoring from top managers (widely referred to as 'Senators' due to the political nature of such encounters) was considered equally important
- that decisions on who gets to 'join the club' (2000: 762) of programme participants depends as much on the lobbying of one's superiors as it does on job performance.

On such issues Kamoche concludes that:

[The development] process is politically charged: through networking and socialization. By lobbying powerful executives, individuals seek to influence the circumstances that determine their career. These circumstances constitute and define organization structures, rules of behaviour, forms of language and cultural manifestations which are reproduced in structurationist fashion. (2000: 763)

He goes on to suggest that such dynamics re-legitimate the way things were done in the past, provide a medium for the present and set the stage for future interactions. So while Kamoche *does* allude to the way in which development practices such as those at IP can act as a conservative force, preventing change and producing 'ideological homogeneity', he does so in only very general and certainly non-gendered terms. As such, we need to look elsewhere for theoretical insights as to how and why development programmes of this nature might be complicit in actively resisting gender diversity within the ranks of managers, international or otherwise.

A striking feature of the IP development programme is the way in which it is closely linked to a very traditional, linear, lifetime and hierarchical notion of career:

Managers reported that IP offered the prospects of a very rewarding career, they felt 'valued', and in turn developed an obligation to 'make the operation work' in the words of one manager. As such the firm made a promise of success to those who were prepared to internalize its values. (Kamoche, 2000: 759–60)

One cannot advance [in IP] from grade C to B, or B to A without MTD [management training and development]. (2000: 767)

This 'promise of success' in return for ideological conformity bears uncanny resemblance to McKinlay's archival genealogy of early career forms within nineteenth-century Scottish banking: 'In essence the word "career" speaks of a promise, the vow that an organization makes to the individual that merit, diligence and self-discipline would be rewarded by steady progress through a pyramid of grades' (McKinlay, 2002: 596).

What is notable for our purposes, is that this kind of career model originated during an era when the managerial and clerical grades to which they applied were exclusively the preserve of men (see also Savage, 1998, and his study of early career forms in the UK's 'Great Western Railway'). As such, it takes scant account of contemporary demographics where predominantly women (but increasingly men) cannot be expected to conform to the linear model of unbroken service that it assumes (Halford et al., 1997). But as we have seen, this same model appears to be operating largely unchanged more than a century after its 'birth' (McKinlay, 2002) in companies such as IP, where it is underpinned in no small part by management development. This alone ought therefore to provide some fairly large clues as to how and why the participation of women in the ranks of management remains so lamentably low.

In this regard, Eriksson–Zetterquist's (2002) study of a two-year graduate development and socialization programme in a Swedish firm is illuminative. Like Kamoche, she applied an anthropological perspective in order to analyse the programme as a 'rite of passage' from a lower to a higher status (Trice and Beyer, 1993). Unlike Kamoche, however, she very much focused on the gendering effects of such functioning, with close attention paid to the way in which the notion of career contributed to such effects. She found that a paradox was operating whereby the company appeared sincere in wishing to use the programme in order to expedite the progression of more women through to its senior ranks. It even went so far as to favour the recruitment of what they regarded as 'normal women' (Eriksson–Zetterquist, 2002: 101), that is those who were open about their wishes to start a family. However, this did not prevent the notion of 'family' subsequently serving as a discursive resource (at various levels throughout the company) for the marginalization of women and their career prospects within the organization (see Box 9.6).

Box 9.6   Discursive resource

In Chapters 1 and 5 we explored at length the notion of discourse. Discourses both depend upon and make available certain resources for those wishing to adopt, perpetuate and even resist them. These relate predominantly to the context-specific use of language but they can extend to non-linguistic forms, such as body language, dress codes and in fact any social practice that transmits meaning. So, depending on the context of its use, the word 'family' can be used as a resource in the construction or maintenance of many different discourses. This is what we mean when we refer to it as a discursive resource. In the case, we explore here, it was used in such a context as to contribute to a discourse around management being an essentially masculine activity.

While having a family was discursively constructed as a source of balance and harmony for male graduates, it came to be constructed as a problematic source of distraction for female ones. The net effect was that a high-flying career came to be regarded as impossible for all but the 'deviant' woman with no family responsibilities, who, paradoxically, was not the type of woman that the company approved of in any event: 'A woman who wanted to have a career had to deviate – at least from a picture of "normal femininity" that assumed having a family – but a woman accepted by the company had to be a "normal woman"…' (Eriksson–Zetterquist, 2002: 101). The author goes on to make the point that such dynamics introduce not just a gendered aspect to the development of managers but one of sexual orientation as well: 'During the programme men learned that they needed to have a family in order to fit in with the normality of a career. … The norm was not just being a normal masculine man: it was also being a normal heterosexual man' (2002: 101).

But returning to the specific case of IP's development and career model in the Kamoche (2000) study, we find that gender intervenes in other aspects of it too. As we have already alluded to, the model very much emphasizes the importance of lobbying for inclusion in the programme, of networking with peers once on it and of seeking patronage (in the guise of mentoring) from top managers in order to secure the programme's full careerist benefits. Insights into the gendered nature of these dynamics can be gleaned from Anderson-Gough et al. (2005). These authors studied the interplay of both formal and informal development and socialization practices among a sample of trainee and qualified auditors within two large UK accounting firms. As in the case of IP, the ability to 'fit in' and to effectively network with colleagues was considered important to career development within both firms. This was enshrined within the competencies upon which managers were formally evaluated, with heavy use of 'team'-based metaphors. But, as the authors point out, the gender composition of the organizations dictated that such networking almost inevitably took place within a largely male environment. The gendered possibilities of actually meeting such competency requirements are vividly elucidated by the following quote from a female trainee:

> … You don't go and enter into a boyish laddy chat at half past eight in the morning on a Friday, so you end up going to speak to the Secretaries, I'm not saying that's bad, but you can't be, I don't feel that I'll ever be wholly part of the team to that extent. (Anderson-Gough et al., 2005: 480)

This was echoed by the response of another female trainee who was encouraged by her male mentor to 'walk the floors' of her department every now and then in order to 'increase her profile':

> … You think 'God do I really need to be thinking about something like that, is that a real big point' and I also in terms of increasing my profile in the Department I find that very hard simply because I'm the only professional woman. (2005: 481)

The authors link this to the 'double-bind' effect that we alluded to earlier in that socially constructed conventions dictating what is deemed acceptable behaviour differ according to gender. The social norms associated with a female manager 'walking the floor' to network with male colleagues are not the same as for a male doing exactly the same thing. Indeed, Anderson-Gough et al. are joined by an array of other authors (e.g. Brown, 2000; Simpson, 2000; Fernandes and Cabral-Cardoso, 2003) in drawing attention to how male networks can function to exclude or marginalize female managers. In particular, Simpson's (2000) comparative study of male and female MBA graduates found that the 'men's club' was cited by over a quarter of her female respondents as the single largest barrier to their advancement within organizations. This included informal networks where much valuable business information was exchanged, such as impromptu lunches, trips to the pub, golf sessions and attendance at various other sporting events (see Box 9.7).

Box 9.7   The exclusionary potential of informal networks

Example 1: Augusta National Golf Club

The 'Hall of Hypocrisy' is a project of the National Council of Women's Organizations (NCWO), the USA's oldest and largest coalition of women's groups. Their website (http://www.augustadiscriminates.org/index.cfm) 'names and shames' a plethora of firms whose top executives, board members, and CEOs belong to Augusta National Golf Club, an organization that, in their words 'publicly and proudly discriminates' by barring all women from membership. The NCWO argues that the example set by corporate leaders who maintain membership of and sponsor events at the club, trickles all the way down their organizations, legitimating a culture in which women are regarded as second-class citizens.

Example 2: Discriminatory 'bonding' sessions

In July 2004, an international bank was forced to pay out $54 million to settle a sex discrimination case involving hundreds of its female employees. One of the plaintiffs commented on the masculine culture which involved frequent company 'bonding' trips to strip clubs and casinos. Despite being a keen golfer, she claimed never to have been invited to company golf events attended by male colleagues. She claimed her boss had no serious professional relationships with women beyond 'cute banter' and thought women were 'snippy' while men were 'aggressive'. The result, she alleged, was that she was denied the chance to bond with colleagues and was passed over for promotion. The company insisted it fired the plaintiff for 'insubordination, inappropriate behaviour and verbal abuse' and continued to deny discrimination even after the settlement. (Source: *Evening Standard*, 13 July 2004)

As we also saw in the IP case, outward demonstrations of competitive ambition, allied to the lobbying of one's seniors, formed an important part of the decision as to who got to be selected for development in the first place. Once again, we turn to the Anderson-Gough et al. (2005) study where a quote from a female manager illustrates how such behavioural expectations can themselves be gendered:

> ... a lot of women aren't very good at blowing their own trumpet. ... You can see the lads ... really every opportunity and it's flagged up. I'm being very stereotypical but this is just how it is. And the women just can't be arsed, they just get on with their job. (Anderson-Gough et al., 2005: 481)

In summary, we have sought within this section to overlay insights from studies by Eriksson-Zetterquist (2002) and Anderson-Gough et al. (2005) in order to cast light on how a seemingly gender-neutral programme of development (i.e. Kamoche, 2000) can be analysed as anything but gender-neutral. One conclusion supported by the former authors is that the price for pursuing 'development' as a manager can often involve in part a denial of female or feminine identity with the consequent adoption of male or masculine characteristics. It is in this respect that we put our argument that much activity taking place in the name of management development can be located within the resistance approach to diversity, gender-related or otherwise. We now turn our attention to examples of management development aligned with the discrimination-and-fairness and the access-and-legitimacy approaches to see whether these fare any better.

The discrimination and fairness approach: becoming 'one of the boys' through management development?

As set out on pages 202–3, this approach to diversity is driven by concerns for equality of opportunity, social justice and fairness, and includes interventions aimed at correcting historical imbalances when it comes to such concerns. Typical examples of management development located within this approach would involve programmes aimed directly at minority groups in the hope of increasing the representation of such groups within the ranks of management, especially at the more senior levels. Classic examples of this type of development are explored by Brown (2000), who describes a number of 'women-only' initiatives aimed at female managers within the higher education sector in the UK. The programmes are designed to help women become more strategic in the management of their careers, develop and exploit their networking skills and in general to increase their personal effectiveness. Benefits reported by participants include those of becoming more confident and assertive in pushing for promotion, having their achievements recognized and developing enhanced relationship skills with seniors and peers. Despite these reported benefits at the personal level, however, Brown was unable to report any perceptible change in the numbers of women moving into more senior positions. Perhaps we should not be surprised by this. A number of authors (e.g. Betters-Reed and Moore, 1995; Meyerson and Kolb, 2000) have criticized this kind of approach for following a deficit or deficiency model of difference. This is an assimilationist model that encourages the absorption of minority groups into the dominant culture (Nkomo, 1992). The assumption is that such minorities might succeed if only they could become more adept at displaying the behaviours of the white male majority. It is to deal with this critique that Anderson (2004) suggests that development programmes aimed at minority groups need to be accompanied by initiatives aimed at changing structures and cultures at the organizational level of analysis. However, structural and cultural change can be notoriously difficult to bring about. This leaves minority groups with a big dilemma when it comes to their development as managers. Do they try to become 'one of the boys' or something else as a result of their development experiences? This was a key question faced by a group of female managers in a study by Bryans and Mavin (2003). All of them, to one degree or another, felt that the price of being included as managers was to collude in 'a game that was not theirs' (2003: 129). In summary, the discrimination and fairness approach to diversity presents no real answers to such dilemmas and neither do the types of management development that are consistent with this approach.

The access and legitimacy approach: management development's role in the gendered division of labour

In contrast to the deficit or deficiency model of difference implicitly assumed by the discrimination and fairness approach to diversity, the access and legitimacy approach purports, on the surface at least, to value and celebrate difference. But as we mentioned in our earlier section, it does so only from an economically instrumental viewpoint, concentrating on the 'business case' for diversity and the ways in which a diverse workforce can contribute towards competitive advantage. Continuing with our theme of gender diversity, Box 9.8 sets out a management development-related example of the approach.

Box 9.8   The Australian Industry Task Force on Leadership and Management Skills

The task force was set up in the early 1990s to suggest ways of improving Australian business performance. One of its conclusions was that Australian enterprises, training providers and educational institutions were not addressing a new, more feminized, paradigm of management. It called for a move away from an apparently outdated 'hard' or masculine/military model of management and a shift towards 'soft' skills of management associated with a more relational, nurturing, affiliative and cooperative model. The report gave rise to a management development course (designed as an MBA module)

(Continued)

(Continued)

called Gender Issues in Management (Edith Cowan University, 1996). The course material refers to women as Australia's 'largest untapped labour market resource' (1996: 4) and implores educational institutions to play their role in 'ensuring that the issue of women in management is placed high on their business agenda' (1996: 2) (cited in Hatcher, 2003: 403). The course is divided into three modules. The first module sets the overall context with respect to changing workforce demographics and the legislative environment. The second describes and distinguishes between the traditional, 'masculine' model of organization and the desired, 'feminine' model. The third deals with strategies designed to bring about change in the desired direction.

Adapted from Hall-Taylor (1997) and Hatcher (2003).

While the kind of approach we see in Box 9.8 may sound very enlightened, progressive and encouraging, certainly for the prospects of increased female participation in the management ranks, it has come in for some severe criticism. Hatcher (2003) takes a Foucauldian post-structuralist angle to her critique, claiming that the approach amounts to little more than a new way to induce self-regulation among both men and women. Furthermore, she sees it as a formula that invites all managers to adopt the prescribed behaviours and as such may be of little advantage to women. This concern is echoed by Mavin et al. (2004), who see this kind of approach more as a call for men to 'feminize' their own styles rather than encouraging the inclusion of more women into management. And, as alluded to earlier, the appropriation of feminine attributes by men brings a legitimacy to these that does not exist in the context of their association with women (Bartram, 2005). Hall-Taylor (1997) is particularly critical of the very notion that there is some kind of essentialist distinction between women's and men's styles of management. She regards the propagation of such stereotypes as a potential trap for women in as much as: 'To claim that females have different qualities to males, rather than qualities that are human qualities, may serve to justify the status quo in organizations, to excuse males for not demonstrating these human qualities and avoid challenging the constructs of masculinity' (Hall-Taylor, 1997: 258). She fears that for as long as women are considered to be innately different from men, even in terms of some supposedly superior or desirable 'soft' skills, they will continue to be pigeon-holed into the kinds of jobs that are associated with soft skills, thus limiting their overall potential. Encouraging women to focus on these supposed qualities therefore detracts from any focus on how they might instead challenge patriarchal power structures. It also detracts from a consideration of how it is that women have come to be associated with certain qualities (such as caring, nurturing, etc.) in the first place, since 'a caring attitude could represent the behaviour of those who are forced into subordinate positions [organizationally/domestically] and have to placate those on whom they depend' (Hall-Taylor, 1997: 259).

Perhaps the most intriguing critique of the approach comes from Calas and Smircich (1993), who draw upon a labour process perspective. Similar to Hall-Taylor,

FIGURE 9.1   *Rosie the Riveter*

they are sceptical of the apparent valuing of some 'essential women's' qualities when it comes to management because this maintains an illusion of opportunity while obstructing a deeper examination of the structural causes of inequality. But they also criticize the approach for being just one more episode in a long history of masculine reasoning that ends up valuing women out of instrumental and economic necessity. They trace the evolution of such reasoning (in the USA) from the need for women's labour in the mills of the 1800s through to the 'Rosie the Riveter' icon of the Second World War (see Figure 9.1). They attribute the current rhetoric of female advantage to the contemporary discourse of globalization, which necessitates a certain feminization of the domestic economy. For them, this amounts to little more than an extension of the patriarchal family's female role from the private to the public domain in which 'a whole army of "organizational wives" (Huff, 1990) play their patriotic roles in sustaining the heroic "boys" who serve abroad' (Calas and Smircich,1993: 75). And as the authors also point out, occupations that become feminized, including managerial ones, also tend to become both socially and economically devalued. As such, the 'the feminine-in-management rhetoric provides precisely the low-cost answer [required] for national restructuring toward global competitiveness' (1993: 75).

Meanwhile the fields of international business and global/strategic decision-making remain the preserve of a largely masculine elite. Importantly, however, Calas and Smircich also point out that plenty of men will also be occupying these 'feminized' jobs and so it is far from being a question of just men exploiting just women. Rather, their point revolves around the forces of patriarchal capitalism adopting the feminization discourse to exploit both (some) men and (some) women. The authors finish off their essay by examining the role that management education plays in fomenting the conditions for this gendered division of labour in the age of globalization. It does so by encouraging the masses to turn towards practical forms of vocational training under the guise of 'better education'. Rarely, they observe, has the feminine-in-management rhetoric made a case for women's superior intellectual capabilities. Instead, the feminine side of management is turned to in order to humanize the workplace. An example is the feminized HRM role of pacifying the majority of workers having to adjust downwards their material expectations in the age of globalization, allowing the truly educated few to 'reap the fruits of this situation from the distance of their own very well paid, cosmopolitan spaces' (Calas and Smircich, 1993: 77). This brings us to the aspect that we find most intriguing in Calas and Smircich's exposé, being its implicit links to the Kamoche (2000) study that we explored and critiqued earlier in this chapter. Compare the following quotes from each paper:

> Unfortunately … education for globalization translates into higher education for a few elite thinkers … while the rest would require no more than a basic 'doer' training. (Calas and Smircich, 1993: 76)

> There's scope to develop more people but they [IP] don't do it. They simply ignore the benefits because they can't see them now and they think it's too costly in the short term. So they focus on the high-fliers and ignore the other 95 per cent. … So what happens to them? There's a lot of wasted potential. (Interview extract from Kamoche, 2000: 760)

For all its vaguely conspiratorial tone, Calas and Smircich's theorizing does, in our view, provide a perceptive means not just for making sense of the field of international management as a persistently and overwhelmingly male environment, but also the role that management education and development can play in keeping it so. We now turn our attention to the learning approach to diversity management.

The learning approach: management development and structural change

In stark contrast to previous approaches, the learning approach to diversity management is one which holds out the promise of diversifying the very nature of organizations and the way work gets done within them. This goes a lot further than just diversifying the people that do the work. The focus moves away from minority groups being expected to learn from the organization in terms of how to 'get on' or 'fit in' or 'perform' as a manager. Instead, the organization as a collective opens itself up to learning from the diversity of its members (Nkomo, 1992) and then undergoing systemic change as a result of that learning. This implies a forum for management development that is very different from the classic model that involves a transfer of knowledge from an authoritative source to the novice trainee. Critical forms of action research or action learning (as more fully outlined in Chapter 6) would appear to fit particularly well within the approach. This is often referred to as a democratic and inclusive form of learning and participants may extend well beyond the ranks of those formally designated as managers. See Box 9.9 for an illustration of this type of approach.

Box: 9.9   Action learning in action!

Meyerson and Fletcher (2000) facilitated action learning sets with groups of women in several organizations. The aim was to identify and address (via experimentation) a number of systemic barriers to gender equality. These barriers had hitherto remained largely invisible even to the women themselves. In many cases, the women found that the very act of giving a name to a particular dynamic helped bring it to everybody's attention and engender its resolution. One such example comes from a European retail company where there was an undisciplined time culture of meeting overload, meeting overruns, late-night meetings, last-minute schedule changes and general tardiness. It became clear during discussions that the culture was disadvantageous to everybody within the organization but was particularly damaging to women. The term 'unbounded time' was coined to describe the dynamic and this sparked a new narrative throughout the company that proved the catalyst for overall culture change. The authors describe such outcomes as 'small wins' that can eventually add up to larger-scale organizational change at the structural/systemic level.

Despite the successes reported by Meyerson and Fletcher (2000) above, a related paper is rather more circumspect on the implementation issues involved with such an approach. Meyerson and Kolb (2000) describe the difficulties they faced as action researchers in maintaining a dual focus comprising improved gender equity and improved organizational effectiveness. Their main problem was one of gender either getting subordinated to the effectiveness imperative or indeed getting 'lost' from the action learning project altogether, largely as a result of resistance from the learning set members. This chimes with others who have critiqued the learning approach to diversity for a certain 'naïvety'. Lorbiecki (2001), for example, points out that those in powerful positions are likely to resist either directly or indirectly any intervention that threatens their perceived interests. Introducing diversity into core work processes and strategic decision-making is likely to do just that. Acosta (2004: 19) makes the point that 'if unconventional thinking runs the risk of being perceived as insubordination under the best of circumstances, then how much more so when it is expressed by an individual with tenuous social capital in the organization (i.e. women and people of color)?'

There is also the argument that change at the organizational level of analysis (especially of the 'small wins' type) may be insufficient when many of the root causes of inequality lie at the broader societal level (Martin, 1990). Changing an organizational norm away from late-night meetings, while laudable, does little to transform a societal norm which considers a woman's real place to be in the home. Even more fundamental is the possibility that capitalism, especially in an age of globalization, might actually rely on a gender pay gap to maintain domestic, let alone international, competitiveness. Perhaps this lies behind the kind of double-speak emanating from a UK government that legislates against unequal pay yet refuses to mandate statutory pay audits. It is difficult to see how a learning approach within individual organizations can address these broader societal issues. But perhaps we can expect them to be tackled within the field of public management education instead? A number of academics have recounted their less than encouraging experiences of trying to do this: Cavanaugh (2000) tells of the difficulties he has encountered in getting his students to engage with issues of structural inequality; Fournier (2006) laments her students' reluctance to engage with non-capitalocentric forms of organizing; Sinclair (2000) is equally discouraged at her male students' reluctance to examine their own relationship to notions of masculinity.

This largely concludes our brief exploration of the learning approach to diversity, along with management development's relationship to it. Although it could be considered more sophisticated and enlightened than its predecessors, the learning approach is far from unproblematic in its philosophy and implementation. Nevertheless, we do not wish to come across as over-pessimistic. However imperfect, the learning approach does, in our view, provide a promising platform, not least for reconciling the sometimes opposed imperatives of diversity and management development. No doubt over time other approaches will supersede it in true dialectical fashion.

Conclusion

In the first part of this chapter we explored four different approaches to diversity management and then in the second part we examined management development's relationship to each. We suggested that much management development remains consistent with a resistance approach to diversity management. But we also suggested that less obvious forms of resistance to diversity can be discerned within the other three approaches, along with their associated forms of management development. As such, we have yet to encounter an approach to management development that is completely problem-free when it comes to issues of equity and inclusion. Perhaps that is an unreasonable aspiration in any event. As such, some form of integration between management development and the learning approach currently seems to present the most promising way forward.

We now turn to some caveats to our diversity discourse of management development and some reflexive self-critique. We have focused mainly on issues of gender, primarily because the bulk of existing critiques of diversity management emanate from the feminist literature. Also, in a chapter of limited length it would have been difficult to do full empirical and theoretical justice to a fuller range of diversity dimensions. While we feel that many of the theoretical arguments surrounding gender can arguably be extended to other dimensions of difference, we are acutely aware of the arbitrariness and reductionism of focusing on just one such dimension. This presents the danger that when we refer to the category 'man or woman', we may implicitly assume 'white, Western, heterosexual, able-bodied man or woman', thus doing an injustice to the multiple, fragmented and shifting subjectivities of organizational members. We are also aware of the injustice we do to readers from non–Western economies, whose organizations will not be numerically dominated by the 'whiteness' or even perhaps the masculinity of which we speak. As such we are, at least in part, guilty of adopting the kind of orientalist assumptions that we critique herein. Finally, as white males, we are acutely aware of our inability to speak from a position of having been systematically discriminated against during our own managerial careers. As such, we do not profess to speak on behalf of those who have experienced such things. We merely seek to present our own, very personal, subjective and inevitably 'outsider' views on the topic.

Despite these caveats and critiques, we hope nevertheless to have given a flavour of some of the different ways in which diversity management has been conceptualized and of management development's somewhat complex and often-times uneasy relationship to each.

This concludes part three of the book, in which we have invoked three meso-discourses of management development: best-practice, institutionalist and diversity. As we said in the introduction to this part of the book, these are just three of the many meso-discourses with which we could have chosen to engage. Apart from their salience to current debates, one of our main reasons for invoking best-practice and institutionalist discourses was to highlight the contrast between agency and structure, respectively. However, as you will have noted, they are expressed very much in functionalist terms (albeit not immune from critique inspired by our other three Grand Discourses). One reason for invoking a diversity discourse to management development was to show how a contrasting (i.e. less functionalist, more critical/dialogic) approach can provide a contrasting understanding. We also believe that far too little attention has hitherto been paid in the literature to problematizing the relationship between management development and diversity. It remains the case, however, that there are other compelling discourses in relation to management development that we have not been able to cover. Examples would include those of ethics, social responsibility and sustainability.

Summary

- Diversity management can be conceptualized according to four approaches or ideal types: (1) resistance; (2) discrimination and fairness; (3) access and legitimacy; and (4) learning.
- Management development is often consistent with the resistance approach.
- Integrating management development with the learning approach currently appears to represent the most promising avenue for the promotion of organizational inclusion and equity.
- But even this presents problems of overall philosophy and implementation.

10

Conclusion: making sense of management development

Management theories ... often present themselves as homogeneous and incontrovertibly true, a kind of universal panacea. It would be extremely useful if such faith systems were to be subject to serious criticism from inside as to their limitations, self-delusions and partial distortions ... Becoming critical of faith, while not abandoning it, is emancipatory, empowering work. (Stephen Pattison, The Faith of Managers, *1997: 52, 54)*

Introduction

On several fronts, there are indications to show that organizations, irrespective of country, sector and size, are taking management development ever more seriously. This can be seen in terms of financial investment, the sheer amount of training undertaken, the incidence of policy statements and the range of methods used to achieve that elusive goal of management and leadership capability. Collectively, these measures amount to a step-change in raising the profile and formalizing the delivery of management development. It could be argued that they amount to an attitudinal and operational shift across the corporate world. Less clear, however, is why management and leadership development should be enjoying such a renaissance. Certainly, attempts to demonstrate the worth of such activities in tangible terms have progressed only modestly in recent years; indeed, there is even evidence that 'developmental training tends to be associated with *lower* shareholder value ... it increases the value of the individual but does not necessarily increase the value of the firm' (Watson Wyatt, 2002: 17, our emphasis). In short, something significant appears to be happening which cannot be explained solely in functionalist terms. The quest of this book has been to tease out other interpretations in order to provide a broader, more insightful and, ultimately, a more practically useful understanding of management development. Let's retrace our steps:

- We commenced by suggesting five overarching reasons for considering the study of management development to be important for both practitioners and researchers. The first two are economic and financial. A third relates to the diverse array of contested and often obscured meanings invested in the activity. Such meanings frequently transcend the economic and financial. A fourth reason relates to the often neglected moral and ethical implications of management development. Our fifth reason relates to the capacity of management development to provide the very foundations for the establishment of managerial identity or 'subjectivity'.

- We investigated different options for doing justice to the above issues. We considered the notions of frames, paradigms and discourse. We built a case on both ontological and epistemological grounds for the latter, while stressing the importance of reflexivity in its application.
- On the basis of this, we devoted Part II of the book to an investigation of management development according to four theoretical or Grand Discourses: the functionalist, the constructivist, the dialogic and the critical.
- We followed this up in Part III by invoking three practice-oriented, meso-discourses: best-practice, institutionalist and diversity.
- At all times we have endeavoured to remain consistent with four guiding principles: an international orientation, a focus on both individual and contextual factors (agency and structure), attention to issues of diversity, and empirical substantiation.

So what can a reflexive, multi-discourse approach tell us about management development that might be different from what other, more conventional approaches might leave uncovered? Common-sense logic tells us that the careful development of managers is likely to have a positive influence upon individual capability and organizational performance. Work within the *functionalist Discourse* has begun to identify those variables which facilitate and those which frustrate such impact. Employing both quantitative and qualitative research designs, positivist research therefore has value in delineating more carefully the linkages between activities and outcomes with the intent of creating a coherent, robust model of management development. Alongside this, there are other, equally compelling stories to tell.

The *constructivist Discourse* is well suited to gaining insights concerning the more perplexing, local and emergent processes associated with management development interventions. The approach allows us to privilege participant responses and reflections by attending to the feelings, intuitions and meanings ascribed to development activities they have experienced. This Discourse also provides a valuable counterbalance to the implicit unitarism and rationalism of functionalism. It reminds us that management development will be invested with different meanings by different organizational stakeholders, many of which may collide and conflict.

The *dialogic Discourse* draws attention to the multiple voices, the local politics and the metaphorical language that surround management development activities. For example, this perspective problematizes 'self-evident' notions of performance improvement by pointing out that ways of conceptualizing success will be highly contested, fragmented and fragile. And at a time when organization leaders often enlist management development programmes to transmit cultural values and convey corporate 'messages', it is instructive to note from the dialogic that the discursive practices associated with this can be instrumental in the very construction (and hence the regulation) of managerial identity.

Meanwhile the *critical Discourse* brings yet another perspective. For instance, it shows how management development provides a means of maintaining order, predictability and control. Its concern with the way corporate orthodoxy prevails helps draw attention to the way the interests of minority groups may be marginalized.

As a domain, management development is concerned with knowledge and power; as an activity, it is usually tied closely to the decision-making nexus of the organization; as a tool, it remains a potent means for regulating employees and preserving the status quo when it comes to power structures. Alternatively, and less commonly, management development can serve to bring about emancipatory structural change by challenging orthodoxy. As Pattison (1997), a former theologian reminds us at the opening of this chapter, this requires an openness towards critiquing (if not necessarily abandoning) the faith assumptions underpinning such orthodoxy, assumptions which often masquerade as fact.

Applying a multi-Discourse approach: the case of competency

Examining the notion of management competency, a theme that runs throughout the book, provides a good way of illustrating the different understandings enabled by our four Grand Discourses. Functionalist Discourse tends to conceptualize competency as separable from the manager while also being an integral part of the manager. An analogy would be that of the motor engine in relation to the car. The engine is separable from the car while forming a central component of it, its driving force in fact. The engine can be diagnosed, tinkered with, de- and reassembled and then tuned, all without affecting the other parts of the car. Similarly, functionalism sees competencies as providing a means by which the human manager can be dismantled, analysed, improved and then reassembled. Just as a car mechanic is guided by an operator's manual, those responsible for developing the competencies of managers are equipped with graduated and context-free lists of such competencies, along with an array of tools and techniques for their 'development'. By contrast, constructivist Discourse sees competency not as an objective property of the individual manager but as a fluid consequence of interpretative interaction between the manager, his/her job, the organizational context and the social environment. A constructivist understanding therefore shifts competency development away from functionalism's exclusive focus on the individual and towards an equal focus on social and organizational factors. All of these in concert become implicated in the notion of competency and hence in its 'development'. In sum, a manager's development arises from a subjective inter-social framing of experience at work. One can see from this how a constructivist understanding of competency makes the developer's task infinitely more messy, complex and unpredictable. This is not least because competency is constituted by the meaning work takes on for the manager in his/her lived experience of it. As such, it is not reducible to a set of objective standards and this may go a long way to explaining why the functionalist view continues to predominate.

Dialogic Discourse takes the constructivist understanding of competency even further by highlighting the fragmented, fragile and contested nature of all meaning. As such, managers themselves cannot be expected to subscribe to constantly stable interpretations of their own lived experiences. What is more, such fluctuating interpretations will also be recursively affected by those of bosses, subordinates and peers.

If the situation appears messy within the constructivist perspective, then it is infinitely more so within the dialogic. Is it any wonder, then, that the temptation for developers, clients and managers alike is to seek refuge in the comfortably predictable world of the functionalist? The dialogic reaction to such temptations is not to dismiss them but to reflexively critique them. Within such critique, functionalist forms of competency development constitute little more than a means by which to eliminate existential angst. It does so by providing a vocabulary and set of practices by which we come to conceive the managerial self in knowable, calculable, controllable and predictable terms. If these terms can at the same time be linked 'strategically' to outcomes considered desirable at both the individual and organizational levels of analysis (as they often are with the notion of competency), then so much the better.

Reflection point

Consider how the dialogic Discourse might 'handle' the statement in Box 10.1.

Box 10.1   The potential impact of development

The hard-edged outcomes, the tangible benefits of management development can no more be guaranteed than can memories be contrived or manufactured. Yet the catalytic effects of developmental experiences, orchestrated or spontaneous, can, for individuals and groups, remain vivid for a lifetime. We all as managers can probably point to learning experiences, where new insights were gained, fresh wisdom was assimilated and personal competency was enhanced. Likewise, organizations have a collective memory of key moments and landmark learning. What is more, the effects of such catalytic episodes endure and shape subsequent learning.

The paradox here is that, on the one hand, the dialogic considers there to be nothing more than 'discourse' underpinning the dynamics expressed in Box 10.1, discounting any essential or ontological substance to competency. On the other hand, not even the dialogic would deny that individuals require some means to construct a sense of self. But by dint of its own relativism, the dialogic ultimately denies itself the epistemological basis on which to express any moral judgement as to the merits of 'competency' versus any other means.

In contrast, critical Discourse is all about making judgements as to the moral or ethical currency of organizational phenomena, with that of competency being no exception. While there may be nothing inherently immoral in the notion of competency, it is the way it is typically deployed within management development that renders it ethically suspect from a critical perspective. Instead of being the outcome of a democratic process wherein each member of the organization has an equal opportunity to be heard on the matter, competencies frequently reflect the sectional views of a dominant few as to what its managers should be aspiring to (whether in terms of character, attitude, personality, culture, behaviour, etc.). The fact that such competencies and associated development processes are often communicated using the self-assured language of science renders them all the more suspect. If they comprise such a universally 'good thing' for the organization and its members, then why not acknowledge them in all their splendid subjectivity, rather than dressing them up as pseudo-science? But here we turn full circle because the answer is obvious. Organizations in an age of modernity owe their very functioning to (functionalist!) notions of objective neutrality. And this applies as much to external stakeholders as it does to internal ones such as employees and managers. Imagine a company going to its shareholders or bank manager looking for the finance required to keep it in business or fund a growth strategy. It is hardly likely to admit that it develops its managers according to notions that remain unproven at best and work as a repressive control mechanism at worst. And it would arguably be doing its employees a disservice were it to do so. Because subjective judgements in the contemporary world of business are to be avoided whenever and wherever possible, using discourse we socially construct competencies as objective and desirable properties of an essential and developing self. While this may be considered an ontological fallacy, it is difficult, even from a critical perspective, to condemn it out of hand. The exception of course is when critique within critical Discourse extends to the very system of capitalism that gives rise to such objectivist dynamics in the first place. But that may be of little comfort to the 'developing' manager caught up and obliged to live out his/her corporate life within such a system.

The aim of this section has been to illustrate, via the notion of competency, the radically different understandings of management development, depending on which Grand Discourse is invoked at any particular time. To this might be added: the way best-practice discourse peddles and packages competency-based management development; the way institutional discourse provides cultural legitimacy to local formulations of competencies; and the way diversity discourse variously endorses or questions attempts to encapsulate managerial behaviours in gender-blind competency frameworks. The temptation is for us to follow this up with a set of recommendations as to how these understandings might 'inform practice'. But this is highly problematical. It is problematical because any recommendation will most likely be motivated by one of the four Discourses. We could, for example, seek insights that might permit competency development to be rendered more 'productive' for both the individual and the organization. But the very term 'productive' can mean different things within the different Discourses. Within functionalism it is likely to denote the degree to which the manager adds value both to the organization's bottom line as well as to his/her own economic or social 'capital'. Within the dialogic perspective it is likely to denote the production of managerial identity or subjectivity. But from this perspective, competency development is irremediably productive anyway and so hardly amenable to prescription. From the critical perspective, functionalist notions of productivity are seen as deeply suspect given their theorized role in perpetuating a capitalist system which is also 'productive' of social division and inequity.

Given the structural constraints of, for example, capitalism, in our view the best we can do is to draw from each Grand Discourse to equip ourselves to 'see through' the dominant Discourse/discourses to which we are exposed (such as the functionalist Discourse of competency). We might then be able to reflexively form a personal and subjective judgement as to where we stand on the issues this raises. This would include forming our own judgements as to how our own practice of, or participation in, management development might be 'better informed'. It may be that we choose to go along with, or even champion, the dominant Discourse/discourse. We may choose to challenge it either individually or collectively. Or we may remain ambivalent. With this in mind, we now return our attention to some of the questions we posed in Chapter 1. These have all been addressed in one way or another as we have moved through the book. What follows below is no more than a summary of how each Discourse might attempt (if not reach) an answer.

A pragmatic approach to multi-Discourse analysis

We do not approach this section out of any meta-theoretical motivation to imply the superiority of one Discourse above another. Indeed, as co-authors, we each tend to intuitively favour different Discourses. And like others, we have both found ourselves ontologically and epistemologically oscillating across several of them in the course of our academic careers and sometimes within a single piece of research. Our concern here is primarily one of *pragmatism*: irrespective of the meta-theoretical arguments concerning the commensurability of the different Discourses, how can multi-Discourse analysis contribute 'usefully' to an overall understanding of management development (or any other phenomenon for that matter)? As set out in the previous section, we think that only you can be the judge of this, depending on the 'uses' to which you wish to put your knowledge. We now turn to a few of the questions posed in Chapter 1:

- Why is management development typically preoccupied with programmes and events rather than the developmental space between them?
- Why is there so little in the way of serious attempts to evaluate management development?
- Why does so much management development stress the importance of collective collaboration, yet employ methods that focus uniquely on the individual?
- Why does there continue to be so much investment in management development when its promise remains so often unfulfilled?

Why is management development typically preoccupied with programmes and events rather than the developmental space between them?

We might turn to the meso-discourses to shed some light on this question. Research reviewed in this book shows growing sensitivity to socio-cultural, institutional and diversity issues, albeit painfully slow in some quarters. It also suggests that employer approaches to developing their managers are a good deal more contingent and cogent than they used to be. Partly this has been forced upon them. The managerial world has changed radically and, as a result, the style, content and mode of management development has also re-invented itself. For example, in the West:

> the increased participation of women in the workforce, the information revolution, the emergence of the boundary-less organization together with the time-stressed, fragmented nature of the manager's job, are making ever more clear precisely why it is that organizations are paying their managers. They are paid for doing the tasks that computers cannot yet do. They are paid for their social skills in building up trust networks and for their intuition and gut feel. (Paauwe and Williams, 2001: 94)

This begins to redefine management development. Some firms continue to invest heavily in structured and systematic training of all their managers, conceived and designed at the centre, but this assumes a relatively predictable labour and commercial market. An increasing proportion are looking to more flexible, informal, on-the-job developmental opportunities and expecting managers to take responsibility for their own learning and development. Indeed, the notions of 'blended learning' and 'communities of practice' have become discourses in themselves, under the umbrella of *best-practice*.

The salience of co-learning has been consistently apparent in preceding chapters and from quite different sources. *Institutionalist discourse* sees managers as a type of network (Chapter 8). This approach to describe group relations fits in closely with a meso-level approach because it analyses individuals in the context of a wider web of relationships. So, for example, we have noted the importance of the educational system in France to identify status and training priorities of managers, and highlighted, on the other hand, quite specific attitudes to authority, leadership and social status for managers in Japan. Here the role of culture through 'Japanese Confucianism' creates a sense of community and strongly influences patterns of labour turnover, which in turn influences training decisions.

In our discussion of international and multinational firms, we noted the opportunities, not always taken, to build social capital by building good informal relations and communities of practice across diverse subsidiary businesses, together with an emphasis on tapping into local, host-country know-how through regional networks. Similar conclusions are reached by a study of learning and development in a construction project environment. Here the key ingredients were found to be project autonomy, knowledge integration and intra-project learning: 'The physical relocation of the project team and the severing of links with head office were associated with a significant increase in knowledge integration activities exemplified by "making their own rules", "openness" and greater "exchange of information"' (Scarborough et al., 2004).

Further corroboration for the power of informal learning and development comes from the literature on virtual work environments. Sparrow and Daniels (1999) refer to a qualitative study of 16 participants during the middle weeks of the production of a UK–US feature film, in which several telling observations are made concerning learning and development (De Fillippi and Arthur, 1998). We report a selection of these in Box 10.2.

Box 10.2   The power of informal learning and development

- Human capital (knowing one's trade) and social capital (each knowing one another) become inextricably linked. Inter-project employment is highly dependent on the career competencies of participants. Network processes and skills become critical and reputation is a key asset. Reputation and knowledge are owned, managed by and distributed across a loose network of project participants.
- The formation of some stability in social relationships is not an automatic prerequisite of success. Moderate levels of experience of working together are helpful, but too much prior experience is harmful and can be replaced by good corporate governance and team management techniques.
- Organizational learning does not reside in the standard operating procedures, systems and structures. It resides in a process of episodic learning and the creation of a collective memory of what works and what does not, shared across project participants.
- The value of idleness is characterized as learning by watching others during one's own downtime. Master–apprentice relationships and craft-based learning techniques become important in virtual organizations and form the basis of socialization into shared values and tacit knowledge. This learning is particular to participants' roles and the unfolding of their careers.

This kind of analysis places the process of management development firmly within the context of group practices (selective observation, shifting networks, temporary projects, moments of productive idleness) and, not incidentally, beyond the realm of deliberate orchestration by the employer. It also begins to expose the poverty of normative methods for researching such learning and development episodes. To access and understand the lived experience of the realities of the workaday world, in this case the way managers learn, interact, develop their skills and progress their careers, requires participant observation and engagement with participants' sense-making of their own actions and reactions. Yanow (2000) eloquently describes this in relation to flute-making.

To focus less on events and more on the space between them would appear, then, to increase the chances that management development will be directed towards learning opportunities; will be more timely, more flexible (from a lifestyle perspective), more relevant and more holistic than traditional management training. We know from research on coaching and mentoring, for example, that individuals value the psycho-social support this form of development offers. We also know that the vast majority of *effective* career discussions tend to take place *outside* any formal HR process, in semi-formal or informal settings (Kidd et al., 2001). And from studies of actual career progression and promotion, the importance of informal processes (like securing 'sponsors', impression management, networking practices and achieving visibility and high-profile assignments) continues to be underlined. Yet for all the benefits of informal and personalized development, a critical *diversity discourse* points to attendant and often hidden 'costs' (Box 10.3).

> ### Box 10.3   Hidden costs of informal and personalized development
>
> A biographical story-telling study of managers in a retail environment revealed that female managers were less likely than their male counterparts to use informal processes to advance their careers, either due to unequal access to such processes or due to a personal reluctance to engage in what they described as 'game playing' behaviours (Broadbridge, 2004). Such inequalities are compounded for those working part-time or reduced hours, often for family reasons, where the opportunity for networking, social relationships and taking opportunities for professional development are all severely curtailed, often leading to isolation from the informal information exchange of the workplace (McDermid et al., 2001).

Closely connected to informality is the issue of selectivity. The attention to developmental space appears to promote choice and self-determination in the arena of management development. For example, Arnaud (2004: 1135) points to the value of coaching interventions for providing a symbolic locus and space for potentially counter-cultural 'individual utterances' and the expression of 'otherness' inside organizations. But, too often, organizations have a way of making their developmental spaces open to some at the expense of others. This bifurcation of management cadres is revealed in a major survey of career management among 700 UK employers (CIPD, 2003). While most (79 per cent) agreed that career development should be available to all, rather than concentrated on an elite, only 26 per cent claimed to have a comprehensive career strategy for all staff, and only a quarter offered additional support for part-time staff, women-returners, those returning from a career break and older workers. While these observations apply to all employees and not just managers, a two-tier approach to managerial career development is commonplace in Europe, with 56 per cent of companies in the UK, France, Germany, Spain, Denmark, Norway and Romania using fast-track management development (Mabey and Ramirez, 2004). This is despite long-standing criticism that such a system can be elitist, difficult to manage, creates unrealistic expectations, discriminates against those taking career breaks (usually women) and encourages conformist behaviour and attitudes. So whether we are discussing networking, participant observation, executive coaching, mentoring or career development (all of which exemplify a switch of focus to processes, rather than programmes, of learning), account needs to be taken of both the structural and informal inequalities built into what otherwise appear to be empowering developmental experiences.

Why is there so little in the way of serious attempts to evaluate management development?

The functionalist answer to this question would point to the technical difficulties involved at various stages of the evaluation process. First, there is the issue of how to translate the frequently nebulous goals of management development into measurable yardsticks of success (see Table 3.1). An organization may say, for example, that it expects management development to translate into increased managerial or leadership 'capability'. It may even seek to calibrate that in terms of graduated capability or competency statements, for example expressed at levels of baseline, developing, experienced or mastery (Finch-Lees et al., 2005a). Progress through the levels can then be evaluated via periodic appraisal. But to what extent can this be attributed directly back to formal development interventions? Without a control group of identical individuals who have not participated in the intervention, there is no reliable way of doing so. But even if such a control group were to exist, how do we then tie this increased capability back to bottom-line profit impact? Despite the difficulties, there is no shortage of help available for those wishing to attempt this kind of functionalist evaluation (e.g. Bee and Bee, 2000). Some may reasonably claim that even an imperfect evaluation is better than no evaluation.

The constructivist answer to the question would draw our attention to the multiple nature of the criteria against which any programme might be evaluated. Sponsors and participants alike may each have their own ideas on this and their views may differ widely. Sponsors, for example, may seek to formally evaluate against the explicit or stated goals of the programme, all through the kind of functionalist lens set out above. Each participant may have other views as to the real motives for the programme, and will consciously or otherwise be evaluating against these. A participant may, for example, ask what an international secondment has done for them in terms of their profile and status within the organization. Another may see a diversity programme as a form of tokenism, spuriously designed to bolster company image both internally and externally. These less explicit and participant-driven forms of evaluation may be going on at a number of different levels, ranging from the 'happy sheet' at the end of a programme to informal conversations by the drinks machine. They may even be taking place almost subconsciously within the heads of individual participants. Going back to the original question, then, from the perspective of constructivist Discourse, evaluation is not necessarily a rare occurrence at all, except when it comes to the formal, functionalist and objectives-driven variety. On the contrary, evaluation is an ongoing and almost inevitable social process and an inherent part of individual and collective sense-making.

The dialogic would share this view but would also add some other ideas. For the dialogic, evaluation in any form is just another exercise in the social construction of knowledge and truth. What is more, according to Townley (1996: 576), 'the greater the obstacles and resistances "truth" has to overcome, the more "truthful" is the knowledge'. This dialogical (and Foucauldian) insight provides clues as to why functionalist forms of evaluation actually *need* to be difficult and hence rare (and be seen to be so). Viewed from a dialogic perspective, the very notion of 'difficulty' is crucial to the functionalist Discourse of evaluation and plays a key role in the dynamics of identity construction: those within the organization who champion and take responsibility for evaluation are constructing themselves as the rigorous, dogged and rational few. It is they and they alone who can save the organization from its pre-enlightenment acts of irrational faith.

For the critical Discourse, evaluation is a form of power. Those who call for, sponsor and implement evaluation, at least in its functionalist form, appropriate the power to dictate what gets evaluated and what gets shielded from view. And so, for the critically minded, efforts to evaluate the bottom-line impact of a pro-gramme provide a means to distract from the ways in which the same programme might, for example, be promoting inequality and exclusion, or preserving the status quo in terms of historically vested interests. Returning to our original question, the critical Discourse may see the rarity of other, more democratic and stakeholder-driven forms of evaluation as residing not so much in their technical difficulty but more in their lack of social desirability within a closed system of capitalist patronage:

> ...the actual process and content of management education is consciously shielded from crit-ical attention. Managers who have been selected to attend a training course are highly unlikely to openly criticize it. Similarly, participants in the immediate flush of enthusiasm at the end of the course will not tend to reflect on its potential weaknesses. (Ackers and Preston, 1997: 687)

Why does so much management development stress the importance of collective collaboration, yet employ methods that focus uniquely on the individual?

In various chapters throughout the book we have drawn attention to how the management development cycle will typically commence with some kind of diagnosis of individual strengths and weaknesses. This may take any number of forms, including assessment in a development centre, a battery of psychometric tests, 360-degree feedback, interviews with a trained psychologist, an appraisal meeting with the boss, or formal or informal career discussions with maybe a coach or mentor. All these are activities that have become rapidly subsumed within, and been lent gravitas by, best-practice discourse. In all cases, the focus will be on the individual and how that individual measures up to externally prescribed standards regarding their attitudes, values, behaviour, performance, etc. Our above discussion of competency is just one case in point.

From the functionalist perspective, all of this is eminently rational since the indi-vidual is the starting point for a whole host of organizational dynamics. Although, as the institutionalist discourse reminds us, the individual is enmeshed in a web of socio-cultural, meso-level factors which variously shape and constrain individual agency. As we mentioned in Chapter 1, functionalism's dualist epistemology leads this Discourse to consider causal relationships as unidirectional. It also considers that with appropriate research tools, these relationships can be faithfully determined. So whereas functionalism does not discount the possibility of the organizational and social context having an impact on the individual, it sees the individual as bearing primary responsibility for his/her own destiny. This includes the ability to improve the organizational environment, with an inability to do so being considered a fail-ure of individual capability. What functionalism certainly does not embrace is the duality of dialogic/constructivist epistemology, where the individual and the social context are mutually constitutive, discursive products of each other. Such dynamics transcend any kind of predictable causality as there are no variables as such that can be ontologically separated out.

It is, however, the critical Discourse that brings a political perspective to bear on such discussions. From the critical perspective, individualizing forms of management development are to be expected, precisely because they obscure the structural conditions of inequity about which each individual acting alone can do very little. Take our discussions of diversity training in Chapter 9, for example. Recall how various forms of women-only management development were critiqued for following a deficit model of difference. This is a model according to which women are implicitly or otherwise encouraged to adopt stereotypically male characteristics in order to 'get on'. This is a prime example of such an individualist approach in action. The critical perspective would see this type of initiative as a developmental dead end in as much as it does precisely nothing to impact or even raise awareness of patriarchal structures within society. These are structures that perpetuate masculine hegemony, extending to dominant forms of capitalism itself. Furthermore, critical Discourse may draw upon post-colonial theorizing in considering the individualist tendencies of management development to be symptomatic of its Western colonialist heritage.

Why does there continue to be so much investment in management development when its promise remains so often unfulfilled?

And so we return to the conundrum with which we began the book. The 'promise' of which the question speaks would, according to functionalism, be couched in terms of its explicitly stated objectives. These may often be qualitative in nature, linked perhaps to conceptions of managerial capability that range from the rather vague to the highly specific and reductionist. But, for the functionalist, these would ultimately need to be linked to enhanced organizational effectiveness. Typically this is operationalized in terms of hard numbers, such as return on investment or bottom-line growth. To be fair, however, rather than anticipating a direct and somewhat simplistic causal relationship between management development and organizational performance, an intermediate link is increasingly being recognized by functionalist researchers. This focuses on the psychological impact of training and development upon individual managers. So, for instance, studies demonstrate that consistent HRD policies will, over time, build motivation among employees which collectively improves the way the organization competes (e.g. Guest, 2001; Purcell et al., 2003). This will be partly due to the quality of its products and services (because motivated managers will be inventive and want to please customers), partly due to its ability to attract and retain essential staff (because the firm will gain a reputation as being progressive and caring for its staff) and partly due to the quality of its internal relations (because, over time, mutual trust will develop) (Figure 3.1). While the predicted intermediate outcomes of management development are not exclusively financial, the underlying functionalist assumption remains. To invest in management development without being able to demonstrate an adequate return, remains an irrational act of faith (Kamoche, 2000) and is therefore incomprehensible. In simple terms, therefore, functionalism offers no real answer to the question.

In stark contrast to this, constructivism offers potentially as many answers as there are stakeholders in management development. This is because such answers lie within people's subjective sense-making of the activity as opposed to any external, objective reality. Having said this, constructivism will normally focus on *shared* sense-making, thus reducing the scope of analysis to relatively consensual explanations, at least within the confines of identifiable stakeholder groupings. Thus, as best-practice discourse exemplifies, for programme sponsors (e.g. senior executives), management development may have far more to do with a need for them and their company to be seen as progressive, reputable and enlightened than with any desire to directly impact the bottom line. Of course it is highly unlikely that they will publicly admit this given the need to maintain an image of calculating, functionalist rationality *vis-à-vis* employees and the providers of capital. Similarly, managers themselves may individually and/or collectively read a certain ritualism into their participation in management development. For example, management development can, for its participants, come to symbolize their very value to the organization and serve as a means of signalling such value to significant others. Under these circumstances, even the minutest of details can take on meaning for participants. For example, is the location on or off-site? Are the facilities rather basic or are they luxurious? Does the programme end with some kind of celebratory ceremony of recognition, or do participants merely slope back off to their desks without further ado? All such factors and many more besides may contribute to the sense-making of participants and influence whether the programme is seen as a prestigious reward, a remedial sanction or indeed, any number of things. In turn, the symbolic outcomes of the programme may become equally if not more significant to participants as the more obvious functionalist benefits such as enhanced capability. As such, the 'promise' of which our original question speaks may have, for the constructivist, as much (if not more) to do with the symbolic outcomes of the programme as it does with the functional outcomes.

The dialogic perspective is in some ways similar to the constructivist in eschewing any singular objective meaning to management development. But whereas constructivism regards management development as being *symbolic*, the dialogic sees it as being *constitutive*. The difference is subtle but important. For constructivism, if management development can symbolize the value of an employee, this does not preclude that same employee from also considering him/herself to possess an intrinsic value, irrespective of how it is symbolized. In contrast to this, the dialogic sees no distinction between the symbolism of an activity and the underlying reality to which it relates. Symbolism for the dialogic *is* reality and vice versa. The implications of this go far beyond issues of value but stretch to potentially any aspect of identity. And since, for the dialogic, identity is constantly being constituted and reconstituted, accomplished and reaccomplished, resisted and re-resisted, management development becomes just one of many vehicles via which such dynamics play out (see Box 10.4).

Box 10.4   Management development and managerial subjectivity

Consider a programme of management development that contains a requirement to complete an assault course under the guise of team building (yes, we have come across this in our experience and our research!). The dialogic would seek to understand what kind of managerial identities (or 'subjectivities', see Chapter 5) are being constituted, not just during the course of such activity but perhaps for years thereafter in the talk of participants. The dialogic may typically conclude that the assault course forms part of a discourse that constructs managerial identity as able-bodied, masculine, competitive, youthful and athletic. Irrespective of their physical attributes (even their biological sex), participants in the programme may find themselves either engaging with or resisting the identities made available by it.

And so, for the dialogic, the 'promise' of which the original question speaks lies much more in the identity-securing aspects of management development than in any apparent functional benefits. For the dialogic, participation in management development is part and parcel of what actually permits an individual to accomplish his/her identity as manager. And since identity for the dialogic is never fixed, never fully accomplished and always subject to social negotiation, then management development becomes one of many practices which serve such purposes, albeit an important one.

But in addition to this, the dialogic would seek to deconstruct the entire question, perhaps even refusing to engage with it at all. At the very least, it would seek to uncover and perhaps overturn the implicit assumptions and dualisms within it. Take, for example, the way in which the question alludes to management development as an 'investment', indicating an inherent need for consequent 'returns'. The dialogic would take this as a manifestation of how accounting discourse has come to dominate corporate language and, as a result, how managerial identity comes to be all too frequently constructed in entrepreneurial terms. Managers come to be seen as mini-enterprises or clones of the overall corporate entity, to be invested in by the corporation in exchange for maximum returns (Covaleski et al., 1998; Fournier, 1998). Following on from this, the dialogic would perhaps seek to ironize, as just another manifestation of accounting discourse, the much touted slogan that an organization's people are its greatest 'assets'. The dialogic would not seek to impose any alternative view but would question why management development cannot be seen in terms that might include but go beyond those of accountancy. Why, it might ask, in our everyday talk and the metaphors we use, can we not speak in terms of management development taking place for reasons other than economic or instrumental 'returns'?

The accounting tenor of the question would also be significant from the perspective of critical Discourse, where the 'promise' of which the question speaks may well be one of control. As such, the critically minded may turn the question on its head by asking why there is so *little* expenditure on management development when it offers such *ample scope* for regulating and controlling the management ranks. The critical Discourse's view of management development may be to see it as frequently not allowing people to really develop at all. On the contrary, much of what happens in the name of development may actually keep managers (and indeed non-managers) from becoming too aware of their real situation, that is as pawns in a capitalist system that relies upon their inability to extract the just fruits of their own labour. And so, perversely, even if management development doesn't directly feed through into financial returns as a result of increased capability, it may do so in other ways. It may do so, for example, by instilling entrepreneurially careerist values that ensure that managers become psychologically if not physically chained to their desks. When was the last time you saw a part-time or job-sharing manager selected for some high-profile development activity? All in all, much management development, according to critical Discourse, serves the interests of maintaining the status quo when it comes to politics, power and control. And this may be far more important to the ruling elite than short-term financial gains. It may not be inconsistent with such concerns in any event.

Concluding comments

This brings us to the end of the journey we embarked upon in Chapter 1. With the help of four Grand Discourses and three meso-discourses, we hope to have provided some compass points for readers to become more critically reflexive of their engagement with management development. Our own position is that there are no inherently 'right' or 'wrong' answers in terms of what 'should be done' within the realm of management development, nor as to how it should be done. To make such recommendations would be to inevitably fall into the kind of mono-discourse thinking that this book has tried to transcend. Each Discourse or discourse will present its own view as to what 'should be done' and each individual will be drawn towards whichever one(s) appear appropriate for them at any one point in time. We fully acknowledge that those reading the book will be faced with regular decisions on the 'best' way to proceed, whether as sponsor, practitioner or participant in management development. In a bizarre kind of way, we are comforted by the knowledge that there is no shortage of prescriptive material on the shelves, much of it of the functionalist 'best-practice' variety. It is very easy for a critically reflexive, multi-Discourse approach, such as ours, to come across as overly dismissive of such prescription. This has certainly not been our intention. Rather, we hope that you will come to see the various prescriptive publications in a new light, not to dismiss them out of hand, but to critically scrutinize them as (potentially useful, potentially damaging) Discourses/discourses in their own right.

References

Acker, J. (1990) Hierarchies, jobs, bodies: a theory of gendered organizations. *Gender and Society*, 4(2): 139–58.

Ackers, P. and Preston, D. (1997) Born again? The ethics and efficacy of the conversion experience in contemporary management development. *Journal of Management Studies*, 34(5): 677–701.

Acosta, A.S. (2004) A diversity perspective on organizational learning and a learning perspective on organizational diversity. Paper presented to the Academy of Management conference, New Orleans, 6–11 August.

Adler, N. (1991) *International Dimensions of Organizational Behaviour.* Boston: Kent Publishers.

Agger, B. (1991) Critical theory, poststructuralism, postmodernism: their sociological relevance. *Annual Review of Sociology*, 17: 105–31.

Alimo-Metcalfe, B. (1998) 360 degree feedback and leadership development. *International Journal of Selection and Assessment*, 6(1): 35–44.

Alimo-Metcalfe, B. and Alban-Metcalfe, J. (2004) Leadership in public sector organizations. In J. Storey (ed.), *Leadership in Organizations: Current Issues and Key Trends.* London: Routledge, pp. 173–202.

Alvesson, M. (1990) On the popularity of organizational culture. *Acta Sociologica*, 33: 31–49.

Alvesson, M. and Deetz, S. (2000) *Doing Critical Management Research.* London: SAGE.

Alvesson, M. and Due Billing, Y. (2000) Beyond body-counting: a discussion of the social construction of gender at work, with the Scandinavian public sector as an example. Working paper series. Copenhagen: Institute of Economic Research.

Alvesson, M. and Kärreman, D. (2000) Varieties of discourse: on the study of organizations through discourse analysis. *Human Relations*, 53(9): 1125–49.

Alvesson, M. and Willmott, H. (2002) Identity regulation as organizational control: producing the appropriate individual. *Journal of Management Studies*, 39(5): 619–44.

Anderson, V. (2004) Women managers: does positive action training make a difference? A case study. *Journal of Management Development*, 23(8): 729–40.

Anderson-Gough, F., Grey, C. and Robson, K. (2005) 'Helping them to forget': the organizational embedding of gender relations in public audit firms. *Accounting, Organizations and Society*, 30: 469–90.

Antonacopoulou, E. (2000) Employee development through self-development in three retail banks. *Personnel Review*, 29(4): 491–508.

Arcimoles, C.-H. (1997) Human resource policies and company performance: a quantitative approach using longitudinal data. *Organization Studies*, 18(5): 857–74.

Argyris, C. (1992) *On Organizational Learning.* Oxford: Blackwell.

Arnaud, G. (2004) A coach or a couch? A Lacanian perspective on executive coaching and consulting, *Human Relations*, 56(9): 1131–54.

Ashford, E. (2005) To what extent does culture impact Turkish employees' perception of feedback and performance management systems within multinational organisations?

Unpublished MSc Dissertation, Department of Organizational Behaviour, Birkbeck College, London.

Athey, T. and Orth, M. (1999) Emerging competency methods for the future. *Human Resource Management*, 38(3): 215–26.

Aycan, Z. (2005) The interplay between cultural and institutional/structural contingencies in human resource management practices. *International Journal of Human Resource Management*, 16(7): 1083–119.

Aycan, Z., Kanungo, R., Mendonca, M., Yu, K., Deller, J., Stahl, G. and Kurshid, A. (2000) Impact of culture on human resource management practices: a 10-country comparison. *Applied Psychology*, 49(1): 192–222.

Bailey, C. and Fletcher, C. (2002) The impact of multi-source feedback on management development: findings from a longitudinal study. *Journal of Organizational Behaviour*, 23(7): 853–67.

Bakhtin, M. (1981) *The Dialogic Imagination: Four Essays*. Austin and London: University of Texas Press.

Baldwin, T. and Padgett, M. (1993) Management development: a review and commentary. In C. Cooper and I. Robertson (eds), *International Review of Industrial and Organizational Psychology* New York: Wiley, pp. 35–86.

Bartlett, C. and Ghoshal, S. (1989) *Managing Across Borders*. London: Hutchinson.

Bartlett, C. and Ghoshal, S. (1997) The myth of the generic manager: new personal competencies for new management roles. *California Management Review*, 40(1): 92–104.

Bartram, S. (2005) What is wrong with current approaches to management development in relation to women in management roles? *Women in Management Review*, 20(2): 107–16.

Baruch, Y. and Altman, Y. (2002) Expatriation and repatriation in MNC: a taxonomy. *Human Resource Management*, 41(2): 239–59.

Baruel, J. (1996) Spain in the contest of European human resource management. In T. Clarke (ed.), *European Human Resource Management*. Oxford: Blackwell, pp. 93–117.

Bass, B., Avolio, B. and Atwater, L. (1996) The transformational and transactional leadership of men and women. *Applied Psychology: An International Review*, 45(1): 5–34.

Bate, P. (1995) *Strategies for Cultural Change*. Oxford: Butterworth-Heinemann.

Bate, P. (2000) Changing the culture of a hospital: from hierarchy to networked community. *Public Administration*, 78(3): 485–512.

Becker, B. and Gerhart, B. (1996) The impact of human resource management on organizational performance: progress and prospects. *Academy of Management Journal*, 39: 779–801.

Becker, B. and Huselid, M. (1998) High performance work systems and firm performance: a synthesis of research and managerial implications. In G. Ferris (ed.), *Research in Personnel and Human Resource Management* (Vol. 16). Greenwich, CT: JAI Press 53–101.

Bee, F. and Bee, R. (2000) *The Complete Learning Evaluation Toolkit*. London: Chartered Institute of Personnel and Development.

Beeby, M. and Jones, W. (1997) Business schools and corporate management development. *The Journal of Management Development*, 16(7/8): 484–93.

Bell, E. and Taylor, S. (2004) 'From outward bound to inward bound': the prophetic voices and discursive practices of spiritual management development. *Human Relations*, 57(4): 439–66.

Bell, E., Taylor, S. and Thorpe, R. (2002a) Organizational differentiation through badging: Investors in People and the value of the sign. *Journal of Management Studies*, 39(8): 1071–85.

Bell, E., Taylor, S. and Thorpe, R. (2002b) Investors in People and the standardization of professional knowledge in personnel management. *Management Learning*, 32(2): 201–19.

Bennett, R. (1997) *European Business*. London: Pitman.

Berger, L. and Luckmann, T. (1966) *The Social Construction of Reality*. Harmondsworth: Penguin.

Bergquist, W. (1992) *The Four Cultures of the Academy: Insights and Strategies for Improving Leadership in Collegiate Organizations*. San Francisco: Jossey-Bass.

Berrell, M., Wright, P. and Tran Thi Van Hoa (1999) The influence of culture on managerial behaviour. *Journal of Management Development*, 18(7): 578–89.

Betters-Reed, B.L. and Moore, L.L. (1995) Shifting the management development paradigm for women. *Journal of Management Development*, 14(2): 24–38.

Birnbaum, R. (1992) *How Academy Leadership Works: Understanding Success and Failure in the College Presidency*. San Francisco: Jossey-Bass.

Bloom, N. and Van Reenen, J. (2007) Measuring and explaining management practices across firms and countries. *Oxford Review of Economic Policy*. Oxford: Oxford University Press.

Bolman, L. and Deal, T. (1997) *Reframing Organizations*. San Francisco: Jossey-Bass.

Bond, M. (1988) Finding universal dimensions of individual variation in multicultural studies of values: the Rokeach and Chinese value surveys, *Journal of Personality and Social Psychology*, 55(6): 1009–15.

Borgonjne, J. and Vanhonacker, W.R. (1992) Modernizing China's managers. *The China Business Review*, September/October: 12–15.

Boudreau, J. and Ramstad, P. (1997) Measuring intellectual capital: learning from financial history. *Human Resource Management*, 36(3): 343–56.

Bournois, F., Chauchat, J.-C. and Rousillon, S. (1994) Training and management development in Europe. In C. Brewster and A. Hegewisch (eds), *Policy and Practice in European HRM*. London: Routledge, pp. 122–38.

Bowen, D. and Lawler, E. (1995) Empowering service employees. *Sloan Management Review*, Summer: 73–84

Boxall, P. (1996) The strategic HRM debate and the resource-based view of the firm. *Human Resource Management Journal*, 6(5): 5–17.

Boyatzis, R., Leonard, D., Rhee, K. and Wheeler, J. (1996) Competencies can be developed but not in the way we thought. *Capability*, 2(2): 25–41.

Boyer, R. (1990) *The Regulation School: A Critical Introduction*. New York: Columbia University Press.

Boyett, I. and Currie, G. (2001) The failure of competence-based management education the public sector: a problem of generic transfer or implementation? *Personnel Review*, 30(1): 42–60.

Branine, M. (1996) Observations on training and management development in the People's Republic of China. *Personnel Review*, 25(1): 25–34.

Branine, M. (2005) Cross-cultural training of managers. *Journal of Management Development*, 24(5/6): 459–72.

Braverman, H. (1974) *Labor and Monopoly Capital*. New York: Monthly Review Press.

Brett, J. and Okumura, T. (1998) Inter- and intracultural negotiations: US and Japanese negotiators. *Academy of Management Journal*, 41: 495–510.

Brewis, J. (1996) The making of the competent manager: competency development, personal effectiveness and Foucault. *Management Learning*, 27(1): 65–86.

Brewster, C. (1995) Towards a European model of human resource management. *Journal of International Business Studies*, 26(1): 1–21.

Brewster, C. and Hegewisch, A. (eds) (1994) *Policy and Practice in European HRM*. London: Routledge.

Brewster, C., Mayrhofer, W. and Morley, M. (2004) *Human Resource Management in Europe: Evidence of Convergence?* London: Butterworth-Heinemann.

Broadbridge, A. (2004) It's not what you know, it's who you know. *Journal of Management Development*, 23(6): 551–62.

Brookfield, S. (2001) Repositioning ideology critique in a critical theory of adult learning. *Adult Education Quarterly*, 52(1): 7–22.

Brookfield, S. (1994) Tales from the dark side: a phenomenography of adult critical reflection. *International Journal of Lifelong Education*, 13(3): 203–16.

Brown, R. (2000) Personal and professional development programmes for women: paradigm and paradox. *The International Journal for Academic Development*, 5(1): 68–75.

Brown, W. (1972) A consideration of 'custom and practice'. *British Journal of Industrial Relations*, X (1): 42–61.

Brunsson, N. and Olsen, J. (1998) Reform as routine. In C. Mabey, G. Salaman and J. Storey (eds), *Strategic Human Resource Management: A Reader*. London: SAGE, pp. 297–309.

Bryans, P. and Mavin, S. (2003) Women learning to become managers: learning to fit in or to play a different game? *Management Learning*, 34(1): 111–34.

Budhwar, P. and Sparrow, P. (1998) National factors determining Indian and British HRM practices: an empirical study. *Management International Review*, 38(2): 105–21.

Budhwar, P. and Sparrow, P. (2002) An integrative framework for understanding cross-national human resource management. *Human Resource Management Review*, 10(7): 1–28.

Burawoy, M. (1979) *Manufacturing Consent: Changes in the Labor Process under Monopoly Capitalism*. Chicago: University of Chicago Press.

Burgoyne, J. (1988) Management development for the individual and the organization. *Personnel Management*, June: 20–4.

Burgoyne, J. and Jackson, B. (1997) The arena thesis: management development as a pluralistic meeting point. In J. Burgoyne and M. Reynolds (eds), *Management Learning: Integrating Perspectives in Theory and Practice*. London: SAGE, pp. 54–70.

Burgoyne, J., Hirsch, W. and Williams, S. (2004) The development of management and leadership capability and its contribution to performance: the evidence, the prospects and the research need. Department for Education and Skills, Sheffield, Research Report RR560.

Burrell, G. (1998) Modernism, postmodernism and organizational analysis: the contribution of Michel Foucault. In A. McKinlay and K. Starkey (eds), *Foucault, Management and Organization Theory*. London: SAGE, pp. 14–28.

Burrell, G. and Morgan, G. (1979) *Sociological Paradigms and Organizational Analysis*. London: Heinemann.

Butcher, D. and Clarke, M. (2002) Organizational politics: the cornerstone for organizational democracy. *Organizational Dynamics*, 31(1): 35–46.

Cabinet Office (2005) *Tomorrow's Leaders Group: A Strategic Review of Leadership Development*, July 2005 (Internal government presentation).

Calas, M. and Smircich, L. (1990) Thrusting toward more of the same with the Porter-McKibbin report. *Academy of Management Review*, 15(4): 698–705.

Calas, M. and Smircich, L. (1991) Voicing seduction to silence leadership. *Organization Studies*, 12(4): 567–602.

Calas, M. and Smircich, L. (1993) Dangerous liaisons: the 'feminine-in-management' meets 'globalization'. *Business Horizons*, March–April: 71–81.

Campbell, M. (2002) *Learn to Succeed*. Bristol: The Policy Press.

Carr, A. (2000) Critical theory and the management of change in organizations. *Journal of Organizational Change Management*, 13(3): 208–20.

Case, P. and Selvester, K. (2002) Watch your back: reflections on trust and mistrust in management education. *Management Learning*, 33(2): 231–47.

Cassell, C. and Walsh, S. (2004) Repertory grids. In C. Cassell and G. Symon (eds), *Essential Guide to Qualitative Methods in Organizational Research*. London: SAGE, pp. 61–72.

Cassis, Y. (1997) *Big Business: The European Experience in the Twentieth Century*. Oxford: Oxford University Press.

Cavanaugh, J.M. (2000) Head games: introducing tomorrow's business elites to institutionalized inequality. *Management Learning*, 31(4): 427–56.

Caven, V. (2006) Choice, diversity and 'false consciousness' in women's careers. *International Journal of Training and Development*, 10(1): 41–54.

CEML (2002) *Managers and Leaders: Raising Our Game*. London: Council for Excellence in Management and Leadership.

Chabon, M. (2006) *The Final Solution*. London: Harper Collins.

Chandler, A. and Hikino, T. (1997) The large industrial enterprise and the dynamics of modern economic growth. In A. Chandler, F. Amatori and T. Hakino (eds), *Big Business and the Wealth of Nations*. Cambridge: Cambridge University Press, Chapter 2.

Charlesworth, K., Cook, P. and Crozier, G. (2003) *Leading Change in the Public Sector: Making the Difference*. London: Chartered Institute of Management.

CIPD (2002) *Developing Managers for Effective Performance*. London: Chartered Institute of Personnel and Development.

CIPD (2003) *Managing Employee Careers: Issues, Trends and Prospects*. London: Chartered Institute of People Development.

Clarke, M. (1999) Management development as a game of meaningless outcomes. *Human Resource Management Journal*, 9(2): 38–49.

Clark, T. (1998) Experiencing HRM: the importance of the inside story. In C. Mabey, T. Clark and D. Skinner (eds), *Experiencing Human Resource Management*. London: SAGE.

Clark, T. and Salaman, G. (1996) The management guru as organizational witchdoctor. *Organization*, 31(1): 85–107.

Clark, T. and Salaman, G. (1998) Telling tales: management gurus' narratives and the construction of managerial identity. *Journal of Management Studies*, 32(2): 137–61.

Collinson, D. and Hearn, J. (1994) Naming men as men: implications for work, organization and management. *Gender, Work and Organization*, 1(1): 2–22.

Colquitt, J., LePine, J. and Noe, R. (2000) Toward an integrative theory of training motivation: a meta-analytic path of 20 years of research. *Journal of Applied Psychology*, 85: 678–707.

Contu, A., Grey, C. and Örtenbled, A. (2003) Against Learning. *Human Relations*, 56(8): 931–52.

Contu, A. and Willmott, H. (2003) Re-embedding situatedness: the importance of power relations in learning theory. *Organization Science*, 14(3): 283–96.

Cooke, B. (2003) The denial of slavery in management studies. *Journal of Management Studies*, 40(8): 1895–918.

Coopey, J. (1996) Crucial gaps in 'the learning organisation': power, politics and ideology. In E. Starkey (ed.), *How Organisations Learn*. London: Thomson Business Press, pp. 348–67.

Coopey, J. and Burgoyne, J. (2000) Politics and organizational learning. *Journal of Applied Management Studies*, 37(6): 869–85.

Covaleski, M., Dirsmith, M., Heian, J. and Samuel, S. (1998) The calculated and the avowed: techniques of discipline and struggles over identity in big six public accounting firms. *Administrative Science Quarterly*, 43: 293–327.

Cseh, M. (1999) The impact of globalisation on managerial learning: the case of Romania. *Advances in Developing Human Resources*, 4: 55–68.

Cunliffe, A.L. (2003) Reflexive enquiry in organizational research: questions and possibilities. *Human Relations*, 56(8): 983–1003.

Curran, J., Blackburn, R., Kitching, J. and North, J. (1998) Establishing small firms' training practices, needs, difficulties and use of industry training organisations. *DfEE Research Studies*. Sheffield: HMSO.

Currie, G. (1999) Resistance around a management development programme: negotiated order in a hospital trust. *Management Learning*, 30(1): 43–61.

CVTS (1994/1997) *Continuing Training in Enterprises: Facts and Figures*. Centre for Training Policy Studies, University of Sheffield, Sheffield.

Dale, M. (1993) *Developing Management Skills*. London: Kogan Page.

Dass, P. and Parker, B. (1999) Strategies for managing human resource diversity: from resistance to learning. *Academy of Management Executive*, 13(2): 68–80.

Day, D. (2001) Leadership development: a review in context, *Leadership Quarterly*, 11(4): 581–613.

De Cieri, H. and Dowling, P. (1999) Strategic HRM in multinational enterprises: theoretical and empirical developments. *Research in Personnel and HRM*, Supplement 4. JAI Press Inc.

Deci, E., Connell, J. and Ryan, R. (1989) Self-determination in work organization. *Journal of Applied Psychology*, 74: 580–90.

Deetz, S. (1985) Critical-cultural research: new sensibilities and old realities. *Journal of Management*, 11(2): 121–36.

Deetz, S. (1996) Describing differences in approaches to organization science: rethinking Burrell and Morgan and their legacy. *Organization Science*, 7(2): 191–207.

De Fillippi, R. and Arthur, M. (1998) Paradox in project-based enterprise: the case of film-making. *California Management Review*, 40(2): 125–39.

Delamare, F., Dutech, A., Klarsfeld, A., Lafoucriere, C. and Winterton, J. (2003) *Final Report on Management Training and Development in France*, Leonardo da Vinci Manager Training Database Programme, December.

Delaney, J. and Huselid, M. (1996) The impact of human resource management practices on perceptions of organizational performance. *Academy of Management Journal*, 39(4): 949–69.

Delbridge, R. (2006) Extended review: The vitality of labour process analysis. *Organization Studies*, 27(8): 1209–19.

Delery, J. and Doty, D. (1996) Modes of theorising in strategic human resource management: tests of universalistic, contingency and configurational performance predictions. *Academy of Management Journal*, 39(4): 802–35.

Denzin, N. and Lincoln, Y. (eds) (1994) *Handbook of Qualitative Research*. London: SAGE.

Derr, C.B. (1987) Managing high potential in Europe: some cross-cultural findings. *European Management Journal*, 5(2): 72–9.

Derr, C.B. and Laurent, A. (1989) The internal and external career: a theoretical and cross-cultural perspective. In M. Arthur, A. Laurence and D. Hall (eds), *The Handbook of Career Theory*. Cambridge: Cambridge University Press, pp. 454–71.

DfEE (1998) *The Learning Age*. London: Department for Education and Employment.

DfES/DTI (2002) The Government response to the Report of CEML (Centre for Excellence in Management and Leadership): London.

Diamond, I. and Quinby, L. (eds) (1988) *Feminism and Foucault: Reflections on Resistance*. Boston: Northeastern University Press.

Dick, P. and Cassell, C. (2002) Barriers to managing diversity in a UK constabulary: the role of discourse. *Journal of Management Studies*, 39(7): 953–76.

DiMaggio, P. and Powell, W. (1983) The iron cage revisited: institutional isomorphism and collective rationality in organizational fields. *American Sociological Review*, 35: 147–60.

Dore, R. (1986) *Flexible Rigidities: Industrial Policy and Structural Adjustment in the Japanese Economy 1970–80*. London: Athlone.

Drost, E., Frayne, C., Lowe, K. and Geringer, J. (2002) Benchmarking training and development practices: a multi-country analysis. *Human Resource Management*, 41(1): 67–86.

du Gay, P. (1996) *Consumption and Identity at Work*. London: SAGE.

du Gay, P. and Salaman, G. (1996) *Making up Managers: Contemporary Managerial Discourse and the Constitution of the 'Competent' Manager*. London: Economic and Social Research Council.

du Gay, P., Salaman, G. and Rees, B. (1996) The conduct of management and the management of conduct: contemporary managerial discourse and the constitution of the 'competent' manager. *Journal of Management Studies*, 33(3): 263–82.

Easterby-Smith, M. and Thorpe, R. (1997) Research traditions in management learning. In J. Burgoyne and M. Reynolds (eds), *Management Learning*. London: SAGE, pp. 38–53.

Edith Cowan University (1996) Gender issues in management. *Enterprising Nation: Renewing Australia's Managers to Meet the Challenges of the Asia Pacific Century*. Canberra: AGPS.

Edmondson, A. (1999) Psychological safety and learning behavior in work teams. *Administrative Science Quarterly*, 44: 350–83.

Ely, R.J. and Thomas, D.A. (2001) Cultural diversity at work: the effects of diversity perspectives on work group processes and outcomes. *Administrative Science Quarterly*, 46: 229–73.

EOC (2005) *Sex and Power: Who Runs Britain?* London: Equal Opportunities Commission.

EOC (2006) *Facts about Women and Men in Great Britain*. London: Equal Opportunities Commission.

Eriksson-Zetterquist, U. (2002) Construction of gender in corporations. In B. Czarniawska and H. Hopfl (eds), *Casting the Other: The Production and Maintenance of Inequality in Organizations*. London: Routledge, pp. 89–103.

Estevez-Abe, M., Iversen, T. and Soskice, D. (2001) Social protection and the forma-
    tion of skills: a reinterpretation of the welfare state. In P.A. Hall and D. Soskice (eds),
    Varieties of Capitalism: The Institutional Foundations of Comparative Advantage. Oxford:
    Oxford University Press, pp. 145–83.
ETF (1997) *Evaluation of Activities in the Field of Management Training in the NIS, Final
    Report*. Turin: The EU Tacis Programme and the European Training Foundation.
European Commission (2000) *The Quality of Vocational Training: Proposal for Action*.
    Brussels: Directorate General for Education and Training.
European Commission (2002a) *Business Demography in Europe*. Luxembourg:
    European Commission.
European Commission (2002b) *SMEs in Europe, including a First Glance at EU Candidate
    Countries*. Brussels: European Commission.
European Commission (2003) *Competence Development in SMEs*. Luxembourg: European
    Commission.
Evans, M. (2001) Understanding the dialectics in policy network analysis. *Political
    Studies*, 49: 542–50.
Evans, P., Lank, E. and Farquhar, A. (1989) Managing human resources in the inter-
    national firm. In P. Evans, Y. Doz and A. Laurent (eds), *Human Resource Management
    in International Firms*. London: Macmillan, pp. 113–43.
Evans, P., Pucik, V. and Barsoux, J.-L. (2002) *The Global Challenge: Frameworks for
    International Human Resource Management*. Chicago: McGraw-Hill/Irwin.
Eyraud, F., Marsden, D. and Silvestre, J. (1990) Internal and occupational labour
    markets in Britain and France. *International Labour Review*, 129(4): 501–17.
Ezzamel, M., Lilley, S., Wilkinson, A. and Willmott, H. (1996) Practices and practicali-
    ties in human resource management. *Human Resource Management*, 6(1): 63–80.
Fairclough, N. (1992) *Discourse and Social Change*. Cambridge: Polity Press.
Fairclough, N. (2003) *Analysing Discourse: Textual Analysis for Social Research*. London:
    Routledge.
Fairclough, N. (2005) Discourse analysis in organizational studies: the case for critical
    realism. *Organization Studies*, 26(6): 915–39.
Fairclough, N. and Hardy, G. (1997) Management learning as discourse. In J. Burgoyne
    and M. Reynolds (eds), *Management Learning: Integrating Perspectives in Theory and
    Practice*. London: SAGE, pp. 144–160.
Fenwick, T. (2004) Toward a critical HRD in theory and practice. *Adult Education
    Quarterly*, 54(3): 193–209.
Fenwick, T. (2005) Ethical dilemmas of critical management education within class-
    rooms and beyond. *Management Learning*, 36(1): 31–48.
Ferdinand, J. (2004) Power, politics and state intervention in organizational learning.
    Management Learning, 35(4): 435–50.
Fernandes, E. and Cabral-Cardoso, C. (2003) Gender asymmetries and the manager
    stereotype among management students. *2003*, 18(1/2): 77–87.
Fiedler, F. (1996) Research on leadership selection and training: one view of the
    future. *Administrative Science Quarterly*, 41: 241–50.
Finch-Lees, T., Mabey, C. and Liefooghe, A. (2005a) 'In the name of capability': a
    critical discursive evaluation of competency-based management development.
    Human Relations, 58(9): 1185–222.
Finch-Lees, T., Mabey, C. and Liefooghe, A. (2005b) Management development as a
    gendered order of discourse. Paper presented to the Academy of Management
    Conference. Honolulu, 5–10 August.

Fletcher, C. and Baldry, C. (1999) Multi-source feedback systems a research perspective. In C. Cooper and I. Robertson (eds) *Informational Review of Industrial and Organizational Psychology*. Vol. 14. Chichester: Wiley.

Fonda, N. (1988) Management development: the missing link in sustained business performance. *Personnel Management*, December: 50–3.

Fondas, N. (1997) Feminization unveiled: management qualities in contemporary writings. *Academy of Management Review*, 22(1): 257–82.

Foucault, M. (1977) *Discipline and Punish: The Birth of the Prison*. London: Allen Lane.

Foucault, M. (1980) *Power/Knowledge: Selected Interviews and Other Writings by Michel Foucault, 1972–7*. Ed. C. Gordon. Brighton: Harvester.

Foucault, M. (1983) The subject and power. In H.L. Dreyfus and P. Rabinow (eds), *Michel Foucault: Beyond Structuralism and Hermeneutics*. Chicago: University of Chicago Press, pp. 208–26.

Foucault, M. (1984) The order of discourse. In M. Shapiro (ed.), *Language and Politics*. Oxford: Basil Blackwell, pp. 108–38.

Foucault, M. (1988) Technologies of the self. In L. Martin, H. Gutman and P.H. Hutton (eds), *Technologies of the Self*. London: Tavistock, pp. 16–49.

Fournier, V. (1998) Stories of development and exploitation: militant voices in enterprise culture. *Organization*, 5(1): 55–80.

Fournier, V. (2006) Breaking from the weight of the eternal present: teaching organizational difference. *Management Learning*, 37(3): 295–311.

Fournier, V. and Grey, C. (2000) At the critical moment: conditions and prospects for critical management studies. *Human Relations*, 53(1): 7–32.

Fox, S. (1997) From management education and development to the study of management learning. In J. Burgoyne and M. Reynolds (eds), *Management Learning*. London: SAGE, pp. 21–37.

Fox, S. and McLeay, S. (1991) An approach to researching managerial labour markets: HRM, corporate strategy and financial performance in UK manufacturing. *The International Journal of Human Resources*, 3(3): 523-54

Francis, J. (2001) Training across cultures. In M. Albrecht (ed.), *International HRM: Managing Diversity in the Workplace*. Malden, MA: Blackwell, pp. 190–5.

Frayne, A. and Geringer, J. (2000) Self-management training for improving job performance: a field experiment involving sales people. *Journal of Applied Psychology*, 85: 361–72.

Frenkel, M. and Shenhav, Y. (2003) From Americanization to colonization: binarism to hybridity: the diffusion of productivity models revisited. *Organization Studies*, 24(9): 1537–61.

Frenkel, M. and Shenhav, Y. (2006) From binarism back to hybridity: a postcolonial reading of management and organization studies. *Organization Studies*, 27(6): 855–76.

Frost, P. (1987) Power, politics and influence. In F. Jablin, K. Putnam and L. Porter (eds), *Handbook of Organizational Communication*. Newbury Park, CA: SAGE.

Fu, P. and Tsui, A. (2003) Utilizing printed media to understand desired leadership attributes in the People's Republic of China. *Asia Pacific Journal of Management*, 20: 423–46.

Gabriel, Y. (2000) *Storytelling in Organizations*. Oxford: Oxford University Press.

Garavan, T., Costine, P. and Heraty, N. (1995) *Training and development in Ireland: context, policy and practice*. Dublin: Oak Tree.

Garavan, T., Heraty, N. and Morley, M. (1998) Actors in the HRD process. *International Studies of Management and Organization*, 28(1): 114–35.

Gardner, J. (1968) *No Easy Victories*. New York: Harper.

Garrick, J. and Clegg, S. (2001) Stressed-out knowledge workers in performative times: a postmodern take on project-based learning. *Management Learning*, 32(1): 119–34.

Garrick, J. and Rhodes, C. (1998) Deconstruction, research and organisational learning. Paper presented to the Association for Active Educational Researchers (AARE) Conference, Adelaide, December.

Geppert, M., Matten, D. and Williams, K. (2002) *Challenges for European Management in a Global Context: Experiences from Britain and Germany*. Basingstoke: Palgrave Macmillan.

Gertsen, M.C. (1990) Intercultural competence and expatriates. *International Journal of Human Resource Management*, 1(3): 341–62.

Gioia, D. and Pitre, E. (1990) Multiparadigm perspectives on theory building. *Academy of Management Review*, 15(4): 528–602.

Gold, J. and Smith, V. (2003) Advances towards a learning movement: translations at work. *Human Resource Development International*, 6(2): 139–52.

Goldstein, I. (1993) *Training in Organizations*. Pacific Grove, CA: Brooks Cole.

Gomez-Meija, L. (1988) The role of human resource strategy in export performance: a longitudinal study. *Strategic Management*, 9: 493–505.

Gooderham, P. (2006) Knowledge-transfer in multi-national corporations. In R. Lines, I. Stensasker and A. Langley (eds), *New Perspectives on Organizational Change and Learning*. Bergen: Fagbokforlat, pp. 35–53.

Gooderham, P. and Brewster, C. (2003) Convergence, stasis or divergence? Personnel management in Europe. *International Management of Human Resources, Beta Scandinavian Journal of Business Research*, special issue, 1(17): 6-18

Gooderham, P., Morley, M., Mayrhofer, W. and Brewster, C. (2004) HRM: a universal concept? In C. Brewster, W. Mayrhofer and M. Morley (eds) *European HRM: Convergence or Divergence?* London: Butterworth Heinemann, pp. 1–26.

Gooderham, P. and Nordhaug, O. (2002) The decline of cultural differences in Europe. *European Business Focus*, 8 (Winter): 48–53.

Gooderham, P.N., Nordhaug, O. and Ringdal, K. (1999) Institutional and rational determinants of organizational practices: human resource management in European firms. *Administrative Science Quarterly*, 44(3): 507–31.

Graen, G. and Uhl-Bien, M. (1995) Relationship-based approach to leadership: development of leader–member exchange (LMX) theory of leadership over 25 years. *Leadership Quarterly*, 6(2): 218–47.

Graham, R., Donoghue, K., Gray, C. and Mabey, C. (2000) *Management Development in the Republic of Ireland: Patterns and Trends*. A Report for Forfas and Price WaterhouseCoopers. Dublin: Open University Business School.

Gramsci, A. (1995) *Further Selections from the Prison Notebooks: Antonio Gramsci.* (ed. D. Boothman). Minneapolis: University of Minnesota Press.

Grant, A.M. (2003) Keeping up with the cheese! Research as a foundation for professional coaching of the future. In I.F. Stein (ed.) (2004), *Proceedings of the First ICF Coaching Research Symposium*. Mooresville, NC: International Coach Federation.

Gratton, L. (1996) Implementing a strategic vision: key factors for success. *Long Range Planning*, 29(3): 290–303.

Gratton, L., Hope-Hailey, V., Stiles, P. and Truss, C. (1999) *Strategic Human Resource Management*. Oxford: Oxford University Press.

Gray, C. and Mabey, C. (2005) Management development: key differences between small and large business in Europe. *International Small Business Journal*, 23(5): 467–83.

Grey, C. (1994) Career as a project of the self and labour process discipline. *Sociology*, 28(2): 479–97.

Grey, C. (1999) 'We are all managers now', 'We always were': on the development and demise of management. *Journal of Management Studies*, 36(5): 561–85.

Grey, C. (2004) Reinventing business schools: the contribution of critical management education. *Academy of Management Learning and Education*, 3(2): 178–86.

Grugulis, I. (2000) The Management NVQ: a critique of the myth of relevance. *Journal of Vocational Education and Training*, 52(1): 79–99.

Grugulis, I. (2002) Nothing serious? Candidates' use of humour in management training. *Human Relations*, 55(4): 387–406.

Grugulis, I. and Stoyanova, D. (2006) *Skills and Performance*, SKOPE Issue Paper 9. Swindon: Economic and Social Research Council.

Grugulis, I. and Wilkinson, A. (2002) Managing culture and British Airways: hype, hope and reality. *Long Range Planning*, 35:

Gudic, M. (2001) Assessing management training needs in Central and Eastern Europe: a cross-country survey. Turin: European Training Foundation/CEEMAN.

Guest, D. (1999) Human resource management: the workers' verdict. *Human Resource Management Journal*, 9(3): 5–25.

Guest, D. (2001) Human resource management: when research confronts theory. *International Journal of Human Resource Management*, November: 1092–106.

Guest, D., Michie, J., Conway, N. and Sheehan, M. (2003) Human resource management and corporate performance in the UK. *British Journal of Industrial Relations*, 41(2): 291–314.

Guthrie, J. (2001) High-involvement work practices, turnover and productivity: evidence from New Zealand. *Academy of Management Journal*, 44(1): 180–90.

Gupta, A.K. and Govindarajan, V. (2000) Knowledge flows within multinational corporations. *Strategic Management Journal*, 21(4): 473–96.

Haines, V. and Saba, T. (1999) International mobility policies and practices: are there gender differences in importance ratings? *Career Development International*, 4(4): 206–12.

Halford, S., Savage, M. and Witz, A. (1997) *Gender, Careers and Organisations*. Basingstoke: Macmillan.

Hall, P. and Soskice, D. (2001) *Varieties of Capitalism: The Institutional Foundations of Comparative Advantage*. Oxford: Oxford University Press.

Hall-Taylor, B. (1997) The construction of women's management skills and the marginalization of women in senior management. *Women in Management Review*, 12(7): 255–63.

Hardy, C. and Clegg, S. (1997) Relativity without relativism: reflexivity in post-paradigm organizational studies. *British Journal of Management* (special issue), 8: S5–S17.

Harris, H. (2002) Think international manager, think male: why are women not selected for international management assignments? *Thunderbird International Business Review*, 44(2): 175–203.

Harris, H. and Brewster, C. (1999) The coffee-machine system: how international selection really works. *International Journal of Human Resource Management*, 10(3): 488–502.

Harzing, A.-W. and Ruysseveldt, J. (1995) *International Human Resource Management*. London: SAGE.

Hassard, J. (1991) Multiple paradigms and organizational analysis: a case study. *Organization Studies*, 12(2): 275–99.

Hatcher, C. (2003) Refashioning a passionate manager: gender at work. *Gender, Work and Organization*, 10(4): 391–412.

Hayes, J. and Allison, C. (1998) Cognitive style and the theory and practice of individual and collective learning in organizations. *Human Relations*, 51: 847–71.

Hazucha, J., Hezlett, S. and Schneider, R. (1993) The impact of 360 degree feedback on management skills development. *Human Resource Management*, 32(2–3): 325–51.

Hearn, J. (2000) On the complexity of feminist intervention in organizations. *Organization*, 7(4): 609–24.

Hirsch, W. and Carter, A. (2002) *New Directions in Management Development* (Report No. 387). Brighton: Institute of Employment Studies.

Hofstede, G. (1980) *Culture's Consequences: International Differences in Work-related Values*. Newbury Park, CA: SAGE.

Hofstede, G. (2002) The author's reply. *European Business Focus*, 8(Winter): 53.

Hofstede, G. and Bond, M. (1988) Confucius and economic growth: new trends in culture's consequences. *Organizational Dynamics*, 16: 4–21.

Holland,G. (1986) Management Education policy. Paper presented at the British Institute of Management Conference on Management Education and Training, London.

Holton, E. (2002) Theoretical assumptions underlying the performance paradigm of human resource development. *Human Resource Development International*, 5(2): 199–216.

Hopfl, H. and Dawes, F. (1995) 'A whole can of worms!' The contested frontiers of management development and learning. *Personnel Review*, 24(6): 19–28.

Hoque, K., Taylor, S., Westwood, A. and Bell, E. (2002) *Some of the People, Some of the Time: Ten Years of Investors in People*. Current Affairs Series No. 3. London: The Work Foundation.

House, R., Javidan, M., Hanges, P. and Dorman, P. (2002) Understanding cultures and implicit leadership theories across the globe: an introduction to Project Globe. *Journal of World Business*, 37(1): 3–10.

Huff, A.S. (1990) Wives of the organization. Paper presented to the Women and Work Conference, Arlington,TX, 11 May.

Hunt, B. (2000) The new battleground for capitalism. *Financial Times*, Mastering Management Supplement, 9 October.

Huselid, M. (1995) The impact of human resource management and practices on turnover, productivity and financial performance. *Academy of Management Journal*, 38(3): 635–72.

Huselid, M., Jackson, S. and Schuler, R. (1997) Technical and strategic human resource management effectiveness as determinants of firm performance. *Academy of Management Journal* 40: 171–88.

Iles, P. (1993) Achieving strategic coherence in HRD through competence-based management and organizational development. *Personnel Review*, 22(6): 63–80.

Iles, P. and Yolles, M. (2003) International HRD alliances in viable knowledge migration and development: the Czech Academic Link Project. *Human Resource Development International*, 6(3): 301–24.

Jackson, L. (2005) The counter-cultural consequences of executive coaching for senior civil servants: an exploratory study inside a government department. Unpublished

MSc research dissertation, Department of Organizational Behaviour, Birkbeck College, University of London.

Jackson, N. and Carter, P. (1998) Labour as dressage. In A. McKinlay and K. Starkey (eds), *Foucault, Management and Organization Theory*. London: SAGE, pp. 49–64.

Jackson, S. and Schuler, R. (1995) Understanding Human Resource Management in the context of organizations and their environments. *Annual Review of Psychology*, 46: 237–64.

James, P. (2001) The double edge of competency training: contradictory discourses and lived experience. *Journal of Vocational Education and Training*, 53(2): 301–24.

Janssens, M. and Steyaert, C. (2003) *Theories of diversity within organisation studies: debates and future trajectories*. Milan: Fondazione Eni Enrico Mattei.

Jaros, S.J. (2005) Marxian critiques of Thompson's (1990) 'core' labour process theory: an evaluation and extension. *Ephemera*, 5(1): 5–25.

Johnson, P. and Duberley, J. (2000) *Understanding Management Research*. London: SAGE.

Johnston, W. and Packer, A. (1987) *Workforce 2000: Work and Workers for the 21st Century*. Indianapolis: Hudson Institute.

Kamoche, K. (1994) A critique and a proposed reformulation of strategic human resource management. *Human Resource Management Journal*, 4(4): 29–41.

Kamoche, K. (1996) Human resources as a strategic asset: an evolutionary resource based theory. *Journal of Management Studies*, 33(6): 757–85.

Kamoche, K. (2000) Developing managers: the functional, the symbolic, the sacred and the profane. *Organization Studies*, 21(4): 747–74.

Kamoche, K. and Mueller, F. (1995) Human Resources and competitive advantage: an appropriatability – learning perspective. Working Paper RP512, Aston University Business School: UK.

Kampa-Kokesch, S. and Anderson, M.Z. (2001) Executive coaching: a comprehensive review of the literature. *Consulting Psychology Journal: Practice and Research*, 53(4): 205–28.

Kanungo, R. and Aycan, Z. (1997) Organizational cultures and human resource practices from a cross-cultural perspective. Paper presented at a symposium conducted at the Canadian Psychological Association Annual Conference, Toronto.

Katz, D. and Kahn, R. (1978) *The Social Psychology of Organizations*. New York: John Wiley.

Kay, J. (2003) *The Truth About Markets*. London: Allen Lane.

Keenoy, T. and Anthony, P. (1992) HRM: metaphor, meaning and morality. In T. Blyton and P. Turnbull (eds), *Reassessing Human Resource Management*. London: SAGE, pp. 233–60.

Kellerman, B. (2004) Leadership warts and all. *Harvard Business Review*, January: 40–5.

Kerfoot, D. and Knights, D. (1998) Managing masculinity in contemporary organizational life: a managerial project. *Organization*, 5(1): 7–26.

Kersten, A. (2000) Diversity management: dialogue, dialectics and diversion. *Journal of Organizational Change Management*, 13(3): 235–48.

Khurana, R. (2002) *Searching for the Corporate Saviour,* Princeton, NJ: Princeton University Press.

Kidd, J., Jackson, C. and Hirsch, W. (2001) *The Outcomes of Effective Career Discussions at Work*. Management and Organizational Psychology Working paper Series OP296. London: Birkbeck College, University of London.

Kilduff, M. and Mehra, A. (1997) Postmodernism and organization as research, *Academy of Management Review*, 22: 453–81.

Kirkpatrick, D. (1958) Techniques for evaluating training programmes, *Journal for American Society of Training Directors*, 13 November.

Kirkpatrick, S. and Locke, E. (1991) Leadership: do traits matter? *Academy of Management Executive*, 5(2).

Klarsfeld, A. and Mabey, C. (2004) Management development in Europe: do national models persist? *European Management Journal*, 22(6): 649–58.

Knights, D. and McCabe, D. (1998) When 'life is but a dream': Obliterating politics through business process re-engineering. *Human Relations*, 51(6): 761–98.

Knights, D. and Willmott, H. (1985) Power and identity in theory and practice. *Sociological Review*, 33: 22–46.

Koch, M. and McGrath, R. (1996) Improving labor productivity – human resource policies do matter. *Strategic Management Journal*, 17(5): 335–54.

Kogut, B. and Zander, U. (1996) What do firms do?: coordination, identity and learning. *Organization Science*, 7(5): 502–18.

Kolb, D. (1984) *Experiential Learning*. Englewood Cliffs, NJ: Prentice-Hall.

Kotter, J. (1990) What leaders really do. *Harvard Business Review*, 68(3): 103–11, reprinted in *Harvard Business Review*, December 2001: 85–96.

Kozlowski, S. and Salas, E. (1994) A multilevel organizational systems approach for the implementation and transfer of training. In J.K. Ford and Associates (ed.), *Improving Training Interventions at Work*. Hillsdale, NJ: Lawrence Erlbaum Associates.

Kristeva, J. (1986) Word, dialogue and novel. In T. Moi (ed.), *The Kristeva Reader*. Oxford: Basil Blackwell, pp. 24–33.

Kyriakidou, O. (2005) Operational aspects of international human resource management. In M. Özbilgin (ed.), *International Human Resource Management: Theory and Practice*. Basingstoke: Palgrave Macmillan.

Lafer, G. (1999) Sleight of hand: the political success and economic failure of job training policy in the United States. *International Journal of Manpower*, 20(34): 139–50.

Laird, D. (1985) *Approaches to Training and Development*. New York: John Wiley.

Lam, A. (1994) The utilisation of human resources: a comparative study of British and Japanese engineers in electronics industries. *Human Resource Management Journal*, 4(3): 22–40.

Lane, C. (1989) *Management and Labour in Europe*. London: Edward Elgar.

Larkin, E. (2005) *Secret Histories: Finding George Orwell in a Burmese Teashop*. London: John Murray.

Larsen, H. (1994) *Key issues in training and development*. In C. Brewster and A. Hegewisch (eds), *Policy and Practice in European Human Resource Management*. London: Routledge, pp. 107–21.

Larsen, H. (2004) Experiential learning as management development: theoretical perspectives and empirical illustrations. *Advances in Developing Human Resources*, 6(4): 486–503.

Latham, G. and Seijts, G. (1998) Management development. In P. Drenth, H. Thierry and C. Wolff (eds), *Handbook of Work and Organization Psychology* (2nd edn). Psychology Press, pp. 257–72.

Latour, B. (1987) *Science in Action*. Cambridge, MA: Harvard Business Press.

Laurent, A. (1986) The cross-cultural puzzle of human resource management. *Human Resource Management*, 25(1): 91–102.

Lave, J. and Wenger, E. (1991) *Situated Learning: Legitimate Peripheral Participation*. New York: Cambridge University Press.

Lawrence, P. (1993) Management development in Europe: a study in cultural contrast. *Human Resource Management Journal*, 3(1): 11–23.

Lees, S. (1992) Ten faces of management development. *Management Education and Development*, 23(2): 89–105.

Legge, K. (1996) *Human Resource Management*. Basingstoke: Macmillan Business Press.

Lewin, K. (1951) *Field Research in Social Sciences*. New York: Harper Collins.

London, M. and Smither, J. (1999) Empowered self-development and continuous learning. *Human Resource Management*, 38(1): 3–15.

Liff, S. and Wajcman, J. (1996) 'Sameness' and 'difference' revisited: which way forward for equal opportunities initiatives. *Journal of Management Studies*, 33(1): 79–94.

Linnehan, F. and Konrad, A. (1999) Diluting diversity: implications for intergroup inequality in organizations. *Journal of Management Inquiry*, 8(4): 399–414.

Litvin, D. (1997) The discourse of diversity: from biology to management. *Organization*, 4(2): 187–209.

Litvin, D. (2002) The business case for diversity and the 'Iron Cage'. In B. Czarniawska and H. Hopfl (eds), *Casting the Other: The Production and Maintenance of Inequality in Organizations*. London: Routledge, pp. 160–84.

London, M. and Smithers, J. (1995) Can multi-source feedback change self evaluations, skills development and performance? *Personnel Psychology*, 48: 803–39.

Lorbiecki, A. (2001) Changing views on diversity management: the rise of the learning perspective and the need to recognize social and political contradictions. *Management Learning*, 32(3): 345–61.

Louart, P. (2003) L'impact des systèmes éducatifs sur la gestion des compétences, une comparaison internationale. In A. Klarsfeld and E. Oiry (eds) *Gérer les compétences: des instruments aux processus*. Paris: Vuibert, pp.33–58.

Mabey, C. (2001) Closing the circle: participant views of a 360 degree feedback programme. *Journal of Human Resource Management*, 11(1): 41–53.

Mabey, C. (2002) Mapping management development. *Journal of Management Studies*, 39(8): 1139–60.

Mabey, C. (2003) Reframing human resource development. *Human Resource Development Review*, 2(4): 430–52.

Mabey, C. (2005) *Management Development Works: The Evidence*. Achieving Management Excellence Research Series 1996–2005. London: Chartered Management Institute.

Mabey, C. and Gooderham, P. (2005) The impact of management development on the organizational performance of European firms. *European Management Review*, 2 (2): 131–42.

Mabey, C. and Ramirez, M. (2004) *Developing Managers: A European Perspective*. London: Chartered Management Institute.

Mabey, C. and Ramirez, M. (2005) Does management development ignore organizational productivity? A six-country analysis of European firms: *International Journal of Human Resource Management*, 16(7): 1067–82.

Mabey, C., Salaman, G. and Storey, J. (1998) *Human Resource Management: A Strategic Introduction*. Oxford: Blackwell.

Mama, A. (1995) *Beyond the Masks: Gender, Race and Subjectivity*. London: Routledge.

Mangham, I. (2004) Leadership and integrity. In J. Storey (ed.), *Leadership in Organizations*. London: Routledge, pp. 41–57.

Mant, A. (1977) *The Rise and Fall of the British Manager*. London: Macmillan.

Marchington, M. and Grugulis, I. (2000) 'Best practice' human resource management: perfect opportunity or dangerous illusion? *International Journal of Human Resource Management*, 11(4): 1104–24.

Margerison, C. (1990) *Making Management Development Work*. London: McGraw-Hill.

Marsick, V., Volpe, M. and Watkins, K. (1999) Theory and practice of informal learning in the knowledge era. *Advances in Developing Human Resources*, 3: 80–95.

Marsick, V.J. and Watkins, K. (1997) Lessons from informal and incidental learning. In J. Burgoyne and M. Reynolds (eds), *Management Learning: Integrating Perspectives in Theory and Practice*. Thousand Oaks, CA: SAGE, pp. 295–311.

Martin, J. (1990) Deconstructing organizational taboos: the suppression of gender conflict in organizations. *Organization Science*, 1(4): 339–59.

Martin, G., Pate, J. and McGoldrick, J. (1999) Do HRD investment strategies pay? Exploring the relationship between life-long learning and psychological contracts. *International Journal of Training and Development*, 3(3): 200–14.

Martocchio, J. and Baldwin, T. (1997) The evolution of strategic organizational training. *Research in Personnel and Human Resources Management*, 15: 1–46.

Maurer, T. and Tarulli, B. (1996) Acceptance of peer/upward appraisal systems: role of work context factors and beliefs about managers' development capability. *Human Resource Management*, 35(2): 217–41.

Maurer, T., Mitchell, D. and Barbeite, F. (2002) Predictors of attitudes toward a 360 degree feedback system and involvement in post-feedback management development activity. *Journal of Occupational and Organizational Psychology*, 75(1): 87–107.

Maurice, M., Sellier, F. and Silvestre, J.-J. (1986) *The Social Foundations of Industrial Power*. Cambridge: Cambridge University Press.

Mavin, S., Bryans, P. and Waring, T. (2004) Gender on the agenda 2: unlearning gender blindness in management education. *Women in Management Review*, 19(6): 293–303.

Mayrhofer, W. and Brewster, C. (2005) European human resource management: researching developments over time. *Management Revue*, 16(1): 36–62.

McCall Smith, A. (2004) *In the Company of Cheerful Ladies*. London: Abacus.

McCauley, C., Ruderman, M., Ohlott, P. and Morrow, J. (1994) Assessing the developmental components of managerial jobs. *Journal of Applied Psychology*, 79(4): 544–60.

McCauley, C. and Van Elsor, E. (eds) (2004) *Handbook of Leadership Development*. Center for Creative Leadership. San Francisco: Jossey-Bass.

McDermid, S., Lee, M., Buck, M. and Williams, M. (2001) Alternative work arrangements among professionals and managers. *Journal of Management Development*, 20(4): 305–17.

McDowall, A. (2005) A framework for employee development: a quantitative and qualitative study of individual differences and development outcomes. Unpublished PhD, City University, London.

McEvoy, G. and Beatty, R. (1989) Assessment centres and subordinate appraisal of managers: a seven-year longitudinal examination of predictive validity. *Personnel Psychology*, 42(1): 37–52.

McGregor, D. (1967) *The Professional Man*. New York: McGraw-Hill.

McKinlay, A. (2002) 'Dead selves': the birth of the modern career. *Organization*, 9(4): 595–614.

McLagan, P. (1989) Models for HRD practice. *Training and Development Journal*, September: 49–59.

McSweeney, B. (2002) Hofstede's model of national cultural differences and their consequences: a triumph of faith – a failure of analysis. *Human Relations*, 55(1): 89–118.

Meyerson, D. and Fletcher, J. (2000) A modest manifesto for shattering the glass ceiling. *Harvard Business Review*, Jan.-Feb.: 127–36.

Meyerson, D. and Kolb, D. (2000) Moving out of the 'armchair': developing a framework to bridge the gap between feminist theory and practice. *Organization,* 7(4): 553–71.

Michie, J. and Sheehan-Quinn, M. (2001) Labour market flexibility, human resource management and corporate performance. *British Journal of Management*, 12(4): 287–306.

Miles, M. and Huberman, A. (1994) *Qualitative Data Analysis: An Expanded Sourcebook*, (2nd ed). Thousand Oaks, CA: SAGE.

Mintzberg, H. (1975) The manager's job: folklore and fact. *Harvard Business Review*, July/August: 49–61.

Mole, G. (1996) The management training industry in the UK: an HRD director's critique. *Human Resource Management Journal*, 6(1): 19–26.

Mole, G. (2000) *Managing Management Development.* Buckingham: Open University Press.

Mole, G. (2004) Can leadership be taught? In J. Storey (ed.), *Leadership in Organizations: Current Issues and Key Trends*. London: Routledge, pp. 125–37.

Morgan, G. (1990) Paradigm diversity in organizational research. In J. Hassard and D. Pym (eds), *The Theory and Philosophy of Organizations: Critical Issues and New Perspectives*. London: Routledge, pp. 13–29.

Morgan, P. (2000) Paradigms lost and paradigms regained? Recent developments and new directions for HRM/OB in the UK and USA. *International Journal of Human Resource Management*, 11(4): 853–66.

Mueller, F. (1996) Human Resources as strategic assets: an evolutionary resource-based view. *Journal of Management Studies*, 33: 757–85.

Mumford, A. (1997) *Management Development: Strategies for Action* (3rd edn). London: Institute for Personnel and Development.

Nahapiet, J. and Ghoshal, S. (1998) Social capital, intellectual capital and the organizational advantage. *Academy of Management Review*, 23(2): 242–66.

Newell, S., Swan, J. and Kautz, K. (2001) The role of funding bodies in the creation and diffusion of management fads and fashions. *Organization*, 8(1): 97–120.

Newman, J. (2000) The New Public Management, modernization and institutional change: disruptions, disjunctures and dilemmas. In K. McLaughlin, S.P. Osborne and Nicholson, N. (eds), *Executive Instinct: Managing the Human Animal in the Information Age*. New York: Crown Publications.

Nickell, S. and Van Reenen, J. (2002) The United Kingdom. In B. Steil, D. Victor and R. Nelson (eds), *Technological Innovation and Economic Performance*. Princeton, NJ: Princeton University Press, Chapter 7.

Nkomo, S. (1992) The emperor has no clothes: rewriting 'race in organizations'. *Academy of Management Review*, 17(3): 487–513.

Noble, C. (1997) The management of training in multinational corporations: comparative case studies. *Journal of European Industrial Training*, 21(Feb./Mar.): 102–10.

Nonaka, I. and Takeuchi, H. (1995) *The Knowledge Creating Company*. Oxford: Oxford University Press.

Nyhan, B. (1998) Promoting a European Vocational Educational and Research Tradition: the role of the survey and analysis measure of the LEONARDO da Vinci programme. In A. Dietzen and M. Kuhn (eds), *Building a European Co-operative Research Tradition in Vocational Education and Training*. Berlin: BMB+F.

O'Doherty, D. and Willmott, H. (2001) Debating labour process theory: the issue of subjectivity and the relevance of poststructuralism. *Sociology*, 35(2): 457–76.

O'Donnell, D., Mcguire, D. and Cross, C. (2006) Critically challenging some assumptions in HRD. *International Journal of Training and Development*, 10(1): 4–16.

O'Dwyer, M. and Ryan, E. (2000) Management development issues for owners/managers of micro-enterprises. *Journal of European Industrial Training*, 24(6): 345–50.

OECD (2003) *Managment Training in SMEs: Synthesis Report*. Paris: Organization for Economic Cooperation and Development.

Ogbonna, E. and Harris, L. (1998) Managing organizational culture: compliance or genuine change? *British Journal of Management*, 9: 273–88.

O'Mahoney, M. and de Boer, W. (2002) Britain's relative productivity performance: updates from 1999. London: National Institute of Economic and Social Research.

O'Mahoney, M. and Van Ark, B. (eds) (2004) *EU Productivity and Competitiveness: An Industry Perspective: Can Europe Resume the Catching Up Process?* Luxembourg: European Commission.

Olsson, S. (2002) Gendered heroes: male and female self-representations of executive identity. *Women in Management Review*, 17(3/4): 142–50.

Ortenblad, A. (2002) Organizational learning: a radical perspective. *International Journal of Management Reviews*, 4(1): 87–100.

Osman-Gani, A. and Tan, W.-L. (2000) International training briefing: training and development in Singapore. *International Journal of Training and Development*, 4(4): 305–23.

Ostroff, C., Atwater, L. and Feinberg, B. (2004) Understanding self–other agreement: a look at rater and rate characteristics, context and outcomes. *Personnel Psychology*, 57: 333–75.

Oswick, C., Anthony, P., Keenoy, T., Mangham, I. and Grant, D. (2000) A dialogic analysis of organizational learning. *Journal of Management Studies*, 376(6): 887–902.

Oswick, C. and Grant, D. (1996) *Organization Development: Metaphorical Explorations*. London: Pitman.

Paauwe, J. and Williams, R. (2001) Seven key issues for management development. *Journal of Management Development*, 20(2): 90–102.

Palmer, I. and Dunford, R. (1996) Interrogating reframing: evaluating metaphor-based analysis of organizations. In S. Clegg and G. Palmer (eds), *The Politics of Management Knowledge*. London: SAGE, pp. 141–54.

Paradella, M., Saez, F., Sanroma, E. and Torres, C. (2002) *La Formazion Continua en las Empresas Espanolas y el Papel de las Universidades*. Madrid: Civitas.

Parker, M. (1999) Capitalism, subjectivity and ethics: debating labour process analysis. *Organization Studies*, 20(1): 25–45.

Parker, M. (2000) 'The less important sideshow': the limits of epistemology in organizational analysis. *Organization*, 7(3): 519–23.

Parker, M. (2002a) *Against Management*. Cambridge: Polity Press.

Parker, M. (2002b) Queering management and organization. *Gender, Work and Organization*, 9(2): 147–66.

Paton, R., Taylor, S. and Storey, J. (2004) Corporate universities and leadership development. In J. Storey (ed.), *Leadership in Organizations*. London: Routledge, pp. 81–102.

Pattison, S. (1997) *The Faith of the Managers: When Management Becomes Religion*. London: Cassell.

Patton, D. and Marlow, S. (2002) The determinants of management training within smaller firms in the UK: what role does strategy play? *Journal of Small Business and Enterprise Development*, 9(3): 260–70.

Penrose, E.T. (1959) *The Theory of the Growth of the Firm*. New York: Wiley.

Pfeiffer, J. and Jones, J. (1983) *Reference Guide to Handbooks and Annuals*. San Diego, CA: University Associates.

Pfeffer, J. (1993) *Competitive Advantage through People: Unleashing the Power of the Workforce*. Boston, MA: Harvard Business School Press.

Pfeffer, J. (1998) Seven Practices of Successful Organizations. *California Management Review*, 40(2): 96–123.

Platt, L. (2006) *Pay Gaps: The Position of Ethnic Minority Women and Men*. London: Equal Opportunities Commission.

Porter, M. (2003) Building the microeconomic foundations of prosperity. In *Global Competitiveness Report*, 2002–3, World Economic Forum.

Prasad, P. (1997) The protestant ethic and the myth of the frontier: cultural imprints, organizational structuring, and workplace diversity. In A. Prasad, A.J. Mills, M. Elmes and P. Prasad (eds) *Managing the Organizational Melting Pot: Dilemmas of Workplace Diversity*. Thousand Oaks, CA: SAGE, pp. 127–47.

Prasad, A. and Mills, A.J. (1997) From showcase to shadow: understanding the dilemmas of managing workplace diversity. In A. Prasad, A.J. Mills, M. Elmes and P. Prasad (eds), *Managing the Organizational Melting Pot: Dilemmas of Workplace Diversity*. Thousand Oaks, CA: SAGE, pp. 3–27.

Preston, D. and Hart, C. (1997) A trail of clues for graduate employees. In C. Mabey, T. Clark and D. Skinner (eds), *Experiencing Human Resource Management*. London: SAGE, pp. 205–17.

Purcell, J., Kinnie, N., Hutchinson, S., Rayton, B. and Swart, J. (2003) *Understanding the People and Performance Link: Unlocking the Black Box*. London: Chartered Institute of People Development.

Raelin, J. (1997) A model of work-based learning. *Organization Science*, 8(6): 563–78.

Raelin, J. (2000) *Work-Based Learning: The New Frontier of Management Development*. Englewood Cliffs, NJ: Prentice-Hall.

Raelin, J. (2001) Public reflection as the basis of learning. *Management Learning*, 32(1): 11–30.

Raelin, J. (2004) Don't bother putting leadership into people. *Academy of Management Executive*, 18(3): 131–5.

Ralston, D., Pounder, J., Lo, C., Wong, Y.-Y., Egri, C. and Stauffer, J. (2006) Stability and change in managerial work values: a longitudinal study of China, Hong Kong and the US. *Management and Organization Review*, 2(1): 67–94.

Ramirez, M. (2004) Comparing European approaches to management education, training and development. *Advances in Developing Human Resources*, 6(4): 428–50.

Rankin, N. (2001) Benchmarking survey of the 8th Competency Survey: raising performance through people, competency and emotional intelligence, 2000/2001. Benchmarking Report. London: IRS Eclipse Group Ltd.

Raven, J. (2003) CPD – what should we be doing? *The Psychologist*, 16(7): 360–2.

Ray, T., Clegg, S. and Gordon, R. (2004) A new look at dispersed leadership: power, knowledge and context. In J. Storey (ed.), *Leadership in Organizations*. London: Routledge, pp. 319–36.

Reed, M. (1997) In praise of duality and dualism: rethinking agency and structure in organizational analysis. *Organization Studies*, 18(1): 21–42.

Reed, M. and Anthony, P. (1992) Professionalizing management and managing professionalization: British management in the 1980s. *Journal of Management Studies*, 29(5): 591–613.

Rees, B. and Garnsey, E. (2003) Analysing competence: gender and identity at work. *Gender, Work and Organization*, 10(5): 551–78.

Rees, D. (2004) *Women in the Boardroom: A Bird's Eye View*. London: Chartered Institute of Personnel and Development.

Revans, R. (1965) *Science and the Manager*. London: Macdonald.

Revans, R.W. (1987) *International Perspectives on Action Learning*. Manchester Training Handbooks. Manchester: IDPM Publications.

Reynolds, M. (1999) Grasping the nettle: possibilities and pitfalls of a critical management pedagogy. *British Journal of Management*, 9: 171–84.

Richard, O. and Johnson, N. (2001) Strategic human resource management effectiveness and firm performance. *International Journal of Human Resource Management*, 12(2): 299–310.

Richards, S. and Rodrigues, J. (1993) Strategies for management in the Civil Service: change of direction. *Public Money and Management*, April–June: 33–8.

Robinson, N. (2004) Is there a gender difference in self-ratings of effectiveness against different dimensions of leadership behaviours valued by organisations? Unpublished MSc Research Project, Department of Organization Psychology, Birkbeck College, University of London.

Rogers, A. (1986) *Teaching Adults*, Milton Keynes: Open University Press.

Ronen, S. (1986) *Comparative and Multinational Management*. New York: John Wiley & Sons.

Rouiller, J. and Goldstein, I. (1993) The relationship between organization transfer climate and positive transfer of learning. *Human Resource Development Quarterly*, 4: 377–90.

Rousseau, D. (1995) *Psychological Contracts in Organizations: Understanding Written and Unwritten Agreements*. Thousand Oaks, CA: SAGE.

Rousseau, D.M. and House, R.J. (1994) Meso organizational behaviour: avoiding three fundamental biases. In C.L. Cooper and D.M. Rousseau (eds), *Trends in Organizational Behaviour* (Vol. 1). New York: John Wiley, pp. 13–30.

Rubery, J. and Grimshaw, D. (2003) *The Organization of Employment: An Institutional Perspective*. Basingstoke: Palgrave Macmillan.

Rusaw, C.A. (2000) Uncovering training resistance. *Journal of Organizational Change Management*, 13(3): 249–63.

Ruth, D. (2003) Management development in New Zealand: towards a conceptual basis for enquiry. Paper presented to 17th ANZAM conference, Fremantle, Western Australia, December.

Sadler, P. (1988) *Managerial Leadership in the Post-Industrial Society*. Aldershot: Gower.

Said, E. (1978) *Orientalism*. London: Routledge and Kegan Paul.

Salaman, G. (2004) Competences of managers, competences of leaders. In J. Storey (ed.), *Leadership in Organizations*. London: Routledge, pp. 58–78.

Salaman, G. and Butler, J. (1990) Why managers won't learn. *Management Education and Development*, 21(3): 183–91.

Sandberg, J. (2000) Understanding human competence at work: an interpretative approach. *Academy of Management Journal*, 43(1): 9–25.

Savage, M. (1998) Discipline, surveillance and the 'career': employment on the Great Western Railway 1833–1914. In A. McKinlay and K. Starkey (eds), *Foucault, Management and Organization Theory*. London: SAGE, pp. 65–92.

Scarborough, H., Swan, J., Laurent, S., Bresnen, M., Edelman, L. and Newell, S. (2004) Project-based learning and the role of learning boundaries. *Organization Studies*, 25(9): 1579–600.

Schofield, J. (2002) The old ways are the best? The durability and usefulness of bureaucracy in public sector management. *Organization*, 8(1): 77–96.

Schön, D. (1983) *The Reflective Practitioner.* New York: Basic Books.

Schuler, R., Budwhar, P. and Florkowski, G. (2002) International human resource management: review and critique. *International Journal of Management Reviews*, 4(1): 41–70.

Schultz, M. and Hatch, M. (1996) Living with multiple paradigms: the case of paradigm interplay in organizational culture studies. *Academy of Management Review*, 21(2): 529–57.

Schultze, U. and Stabell, C. (2004) Knowing what you don't know: discourses and contradictions in knowledge management research. *Journal of Management Studies*, 41(4): 549–73.

Scullion, H. and Starkey, K. (2000) In search of the changing role of the corporate human resource function in the international firm. *International Journal of Human Resource Management*, 11(6): 1061–81.

Segalla, M., Jacobs-Belschak, G. and Muller, H. (2001a) Cultural influences on employee termination decisions: firing the good, average or the old. *European Management Journal*, 19(1): 58–71.

Segalla, M., Sauquet, A. and Turati, B. (2001b) Symbolic vs functional recruitment: cultural influences on employee recruitment policy. *European Management Journal*, 19(1): 32–41.

Shenkar, O., Ronen, S., Shefty, E. and Chow, I. (1998) The role structure of Chinese managers. *Human Relations*, 51(1): 51–72.

Shenton, G. (1996) Management education model in Europe: diversity and integration. In M. Lee, H. Letiche and R. Crawshaw (eds) *Management Education in the New Europe*. London: International Thomson, pp. 32–47.

Shipper, F., Hoffman, I. and Rotondo, D. (2004) Does the 360 degree feedback process create actionable knowledge equally across cultures? Paper presented to the Academy of Management Annual Conference, New Orleans, August.

Siebert, K. and Hall, D. (1995) Staffing policy as a strategic response: a typology of career systems. *Academy of Management Review*, 13(4): 568–600.

Siefert, C., Yukl, G. and McDonald, R. (2001) A field experiment to evaluate the effects of multi-score feedback on managerial behaviour. Paper presented to the 10th European Congress of Work and Organization Psychology, Prague, May.

Simpson, R. (2000) Winners and losers: who benefits most from the MBA. *Management Learning*, 31: 331–51.

Sinclair, A. (2000) Teaching managers about masculinities: are you kidding? *Management Learning*, 31(1): 81–101.

Singh, V. and Vinnicombe, S. (2005) *The female FTSE Index 2005.* Cranfield: Cranfield School of Management.

Sinha, J. (1997) A cultural perspective on organizational behaviour in India. In P. Earley and M. Erez (eds), *New Perspectives on International Industrial/Organizational Psychology*. San Francisco: The New Lexington Press, pp. 53–75.

Sitkin, S., Sutcliffe, S. and Schroeder, R. (1994) Distinguishing control from learning in total quality management: a contingency perspective. *Academy of Management Review*, 19(3): 537–64.

Smithson, J. and Stokoe, E.H. (2005) Discourse of work–life balance: negotiating 'genderblind' terms in organizations. *Gender, Work and Organization*, 12(2): 147–68.

Sparrow, P. (1996) Careers and the psychological contract: understanding the European context. *European Journal of Work and Organizational Psychology*, 5(4): 479–500.

Sparrow, J. and Arnott, J. (2004) *The Coaching Study 2004: Coaching works but it could get better*. Presentation of research findings given to the Academy of Executive Coaching, London, February.

Sparrow, P. and Bognanno, M. (1993) Competency requirement forecasting: issues for selection and assessment. *International Journal of Selection and Assessment*, 1(1): 50–8.

Sparrow, P., Brewster, C. and Harris, H. (2004) *Globalising Human Resource Management*, London: Routledge.

Sparrow, P. and Daniels, K. (1999) Human resource management and the virtual organization: mapping the future research issues. In C. Cooper and D. Rousseau (eds), *Trends in Organizational Behaviour*. London: John Wiley, pp. 45–61.

Spencer, L. (1986) *Calculating Human Resource Costs and Benefits: Cutting Costs and Improving Productivity*. New York: Wiley.

Starkey, K. (ed.) 1996 *How Organizations Learn*. London: International Thomson Business Press.

Starkey, K. and McKinlay, A. (1998) Afterword: deconstructing organization – discipline and desire. In A. McKinlay and K. Starkey (eds), *Foucault, Management and Organization Theory*. London: SAGE, pp. 230–41.

Stewart, T. (1997) *Intellectual Capital: The New Wealth of Organizations*. New York: Doubleday.

Stiles, P., Gratton, L., Truss, C., Hope-Hailey, V. and McGovern, P. (1997) Performance management and the psychological contract. *Human Resource Management Journal*, 7(1): 57–66.

Storey, J., Edwards, P. and Sisson, K. (1997) *Managers in the Making: Careers, Development and Control in Corporate Britain and Japan*. London: SAGE.

Storey, J. and Tate, W. (2000) Management development. In S. Bach and K. Sisson (eds), *Personnel Management* (3rd edn). Oxford: Blackwell, pp. 185–217.

Streeck, W. (1993) National diversity, regime competition and institutional deadlock: problems in forming a European industrial relations system. *Journal of Public Policy*, 12: 301–30.

Swanson, R. (2001) *Assessing the Financial Benefits of Human Resource Development*. Cambridge, MA: Perseus.

Symon, G. and Cassell, C. (2006) Neglected perspectives in work and organizational psychology. *Journal of Occupational and Organizational Psychology*, 79(3): 307–14.

Tamkin, P. and Hillage, J. (1998) *Management Development in the UK: A Framework of Indicators*. Brighton: Institute for Employment Studies.

Tamkin, P., Mabey, C. and Beech, D. (2006) *The Comparative Capability of UK Managers*. Skills for Business Research Report 17. Brighton: Institute of Employment Studies.

Tannenbaum, S. and Yukl, G. (1991) Training and development in work organizations. *Annual Review of Psychology*, 74: 599–621.

Tayeb, M. (2000) Conducting research across cultures: drawbacks and obstacles. Paper presented to the British Academy of Management Annual Conference, Edinburgh, 13–15 September.

Taylor, S. (2007) Deconstruction. In R. Holt and R. Thorpe (eds), *SAGE Dictionary of Qualitative Management Research*. London: SAGE, pp. 71–2.

Teigland, R. (2000) Communities of practice. In J. Birkinshaw and P. Hagström (eds), *The Flexible Firm*. Oxford: Oxford University Press.

Thomas, D.A. and Ely, R.J. (1996) Making differences matter: a new paradigm for managing diversity. *Harvard Business Review*, Sept.–Oct.: 79–90.

Thomson, M. (2000) *Changing Management Capabilities in UK Aerospace*. London: The Society of British Aerospace Companies.

Thomson, A., Mabey, C., Storey, J., Gray, C. and Iles, P. (2001) *Changing Patterns of Management Development*. Oxford: Blackwell.

Townley, B. (1993) Foucault, power/knowledge and its relevance for HRM. *Academy of Management Review*, 18(3): 518–45.

Townley, B. (1994) *Reframing Human Resource Management: Power, Ethics and the Subject at Work*. London: SAGE.

Townley, B. (1996) Accounting in detail: accounting for individual performance. *Critical Perspectives on Accounting*, 7: 565–84.

Townley, B. (1998) Beyond good and evil: depth and division in the management of human resources. In A. McKinley and K. Starkey (eds), *Foucault, Management and Organization Theory*. London: SAGE, pp. 191–210.

Townley, B. (1999) Nietsche, competencies and *ubermensch*: reflections on human and inhuman resource management. *Organization*, 6(2): 285–305.

Townley, B. (2002) Managing with modernity. *Organization*, 9(4): 549–73.

Tracey, J. and Hinkin, J. (2001) The influence of individual characteristics and the work environment on varying levels of training outcomes. *Human Resource Development Quarterly*, 12(1): 5–23.

Tregaskis, O. (1997) The role of national context and HR strategy in shaping training and development practice in French and UK organizations. *Organization Studies*, 18(5): 839–56.

Tregaskis, O. (2001) HRD in multinationals: the global/local mix. *Human Resource Management Journal*, 11(2): 34–56.

Triandis, H., Leung, K., Villarreal, M. and Chack, F. (1985) Allocentric versus idiocentric tendencies: convergent and discriminant validation. *Journal of Research in Personality*, 19: 395–415.

Trice, H.M. and Beyer, J.M. (1993) *The Culture of Work Organizations*. Englewood Cliffs, NJ: Prentice-Hall.

Trompenaars, F. (1993) *Riding the Wave of Culture: Understanding Diversity in Global Business*. London: Economist Books.

Trompenaars, F. and Hampden-Turner, C. (1998) *Riding the Waves of Culture: Understanding Cultural Diversity in Global Business* (2nd edn). New York: McGraw-Hill.

Truss, C. (2001) Complexities and controversies in linking HRM with organizational performance. *Journal of Management Studies*, 38(8): 1121–48.

Tsang, E. (1994) Human resource management problems in Sino-foreign joint ventures. *International Journal of Manpower*, 15(9): 139–49.

Tsang, E.W.K. (2001) Managerial learning in foreign-invested enterprises of China. *Management International Review*, 41(1): 29–51.

Tsui-Auch, L. and Lee, Y-L. (2003) The state matters: management models of Singaporean Chinese and Korean groups. *Organization Studies*, 24(4): 507–23.

Tsui, A., Schoonhoven, C., Meyer, M., Lau, C. and Milkovich, G. (2004) Organization and management in the midst of societal transformation: the People's Republic of China. *Organizational Science*, 15(2): 133–44.

Turnbull, S. (2001a) Corporate ideology: meanings and contradictions for middle managers. *British Journal of Management*, 12: 231–42.

Turnbull, S. (2001b) Quasi-religious experiences in a corporate change programme: the roles of conversion and the confessional in corporate evangelism. Paper presented to the Critical Management Studies Conference. Manchester, 11–13 July.

Turnbull, S. (2002) *Bricolage* as an alternative approach to HRD theory building. *Human Resource Development Review*, 1(1): 111–28.

Valentin, C. (2006) Researching human resource development: emergence of a critical approach to HRD enquiry. *International Journal of Training and Development*, 10(1): 17–29.

van der Boon, M. (2003) Women in international management: an international perspective on women's ways of leadership. *Women in Management Review*, 18(3): 132–46.

Vieira Da Cunha, J. and Pina e Cunha, M. (2002) Reading between the lines: unveiling masculinity in feminine management practices. *Women in Management Review*, 17(1): 5–11.

Vinnicombe, S. and Singh, V. (2002) Sex role stereotyping and requisites of successful top managers. *Women in Management Review*, 17(3/4): 120–30.

Visvanathan, S. (2001) The grand sociology of Manuel Castells. In J. Muller, N. Cloete and S. Badat (eds), *Challenges of Globalization: South African debates with Manuel Castells*. Maskew Miller Longman: Pinelands.

Von Glinow, M., Huo, Y. and Lowe, K. (1999) Leadership across the Pacific Ocean: a tri-national comparison. *International Business Review*, 8(1): 1–15.

Walder, A. (1989) Factory and manager in an era of reform. *The China Quarterly*, 118: 242–64.

Wang, Z. (1999) Current models and innovative strategies in management education in China. *Education & Training*, 41(6/7): 312–18.

Wang, J. and Wang, G. (2006) Exploring human resource development: a case of China management development in a transitioning context. *Human Resource Development Review*, 5(2): 176–201.

Warner, M. (1992) *How Chinese Managers Learn*. London: Macmillan.

Warr, P. (2002) Learning and training. In P. Warr (ed.), *Psychology at Work*. London: Penguin.

Watson, T. (1994) *In Search of Management*. London: Routledge.

Watson, T. (2001) The emergent manager and processes of management pre-learning. *Management Learning*, 32(2): 221–35.

Watson, T. (2005) Review essay: The organization and disorganization of organization studies. *Journal of Management Studies*, 43(2): 367–82.

Watson Wyatt (2002) *Linking Human Capital and Shareholder Value: Human Capital Index*. Fourth European Survey Report. London: Watson Wyatt Worldwide.

Wehrle, A. (1982) Review article: *The Dialogic Imagination*. Four essays by M.M. Bakhtin. *The Slavic and East European Journal*, 26(1): 106–7.

Weick, K. (1995) *Sensemaking in Organizations*. London: SAGE.

Weinstein, K. (1995) *Action Learning: A Journey in Discovery and Development*. London: Harper Collins.

West, M., Borrill, C., Dawson, J., Scully, J., Carter, M., Anelay, S. and Patterson, M. (2002) The link between the management of employees and patient mortality in hospitals. *International Journal of Human Resource Management*, 13(8): 1299–310.

Westenholz, A. (1993) Paradoxical thinking and change in the frames of reference. *Organization Studies*, 14(4): 37–58.

Whitley, R. (1992) *European Business Systems: Firms and Markets in their National Contexts*. London: SAGE.

Wicks, A. and Freeman, R. (1998) Organization studies and the new pragmatism: positivism, anti-positivism and the search for ethics. *Organization Science*, 9(2): 123–40.

Wilkins, S. (2001) International briefing 9: Training and development in the United Arab Emirates. *International Journal of Human Resource Management*, 5(2): 153–65.

Wille, E. (1990) *People Development and Improved Business Performance*. Berkhampsted: Ashridge Management Research Group, Ashridge Management College.

Willig, C. (2001) *Qualitative Research in Psychology: A Practical Guide to Theory and Method*. Buckingham: Open University Press.

Willmott, H. (1993a) Strength is ignorance; slavery is freedom: managing culture in modern organizations. *Journal of Management Studies*, 30(4): 515–52.

Willmott, H. (1993b) Breaking the paradigm mentality. *Organization Studies*, 14(5): 681–719.

Willmott, H. (1994a) Business process re-engineering and human resource management. *Personnel Review*, 23(3): 34–46.

Willmott, H. (1994b) Management education: provocations to a debate. *Management Learning*, 25(1): 105–36.

Willmott, H. (1997) Critical management learning. In J. Burgoyne and M. Reynolds (eds), *Management Learning: Integrating Perspectives in Theory and Practice*. London: SAGE, pp. 161–76.

Wilson, D. (2005) 'Comrades in Adversity': work-based learning in a knowledge intensive organisation: the learner's perspective. Unpublished MSc Dissertation, Department of Organization Psychology, Birkbeck College, University of London.

Winterton, J. and Winterton, R. (1997) Does management development matter? *British Journal of Management*, Special issue, 8: S65–S76.

Winterton, J. and Winterton, R. (1999) *Developing Managerial Competence*, London: Routledge.

Withers, P. (2001) Bigger and Better, *BC Business*, 29(4): 50–6.

Wong, C., Marshall, J., Alderman, N. and Thwaites, A. (1997) Management thinking in small and medium-sized enterprises: methodological and conceptual issues, *International Journal of Human Resource Management*, 8(1): 44–65.

Wong, C., Hui, C., Wong, W.-T. and Law, K. (2001) The significant role of Chinese employees' organizational commitment: implications for managing employees in Chinese societies. *Journal of World Business*, 26(3): 326–41.

Wood, S. (1999) Human resource management and performance. *International Journal of Management Reviews*, 1: 367–413.

Wood, S. and de Menezes, L. (1998) High commitment management in the UK: evidence from the Workplace Industrial Relations Survey and the Employers' Manpower and Skills Practices Survey. *Human Relations*, 51(4): 485–513.

Woodall, J. and Winstanley, D. (1998) *Management Development: Strategy and Practice*. Oxford: Blackwell.

Woodruffe, C. (1993) *Assessment Centres: Identifying and Developing Competence*. London: Institute of Personnel Management.

Wootton, B. (1955) *The Social Foundations of Wage Policy: A Study of Contemporary British Wage and Salary Structure*. London: Allen & Unwin.

Wright, P. and Snell, S. (1998) Toward a unifying framework for exploring fit and flexibility in strategic human resource management. *Academy of Management Review*, 23: 756–72.

Wright, P., Szeto, W. and Cheng, L. (2002) Guanxi and professional conduct in China: a management development perspective. *Human Resource Management*, 13(1): 156–82.

Yanow, D. (2000) Seeing organizational learning: a 'cultural' view. *Organization*, 7(2): 247–68.

Yeung, A. and Berman, B. (1997) Adding value through human resource measurement to drive business performance. *Human Resource Management Journal*, 36(3): 321–35.

Yukl, G. (1998) *Leadership in Organizations* (4th edn). Englewood Cliffs, NJ: Prentice-Hall.

Zaleznik, A. (1977) Managers and leaders: are they different? *Harvard Business Review*, 55(3): 67–78.

Index